WORMWOOD STAR:

THE MAGICKAL LIFE OF MARJORIE CAMERON

New Updated Edition

SPENCER KANSA

© Spencer Kansa 2025

Fourth Edition.

All rights reserved. No part of this work may be reproduced, stored in a retrieval system, or transmitted in any form or by any means, electronic, mechanical, photocopying, recording or otherwise without the prior permission of the publisher.

DISCLAIMER:

Unfortunately, permission was not granted to reproduce some of Cameron's artworks; however, most of those mentioned in this book can be viewed online using Google Images.

Contents

Praise for earlier editions of
  Wormwood Star 4
Acknowledgements 6
Dedications 10
1 - American Gothic 11
2 - Ghost in the Machine 29
3 - Belarion Antichrist 39
4 - Occam's Razor 72
5 - The Children 107
6 - Welcome to the Pleasure Dome 127
7 - Sherry 145
8 - The Wormwood Star 165
9 - ERONBU 185
10 - Night Tide 201
11 - Black Pilgrimage 211
12 - Exorcising Ghosts 239
13 - Thumbsuck 265
14 - Seasons of the Witch 276
1984-1995 286
15 - Epilogue 313
 - Appendix 321
 - Author Interview 338
 - Index 347

Praise for earlier editions of *Wormwood Star*

"After reading *Wormwood Star*, I was left very impressed with Spencer Kansa's treatment of Cameron. To have gone to all the effort he did to provide the public with a compassionate yet balanced, and not gushingly fannish, portrayal of such a complicated figure. He walked the fine line of keeping his head out of la-la land and grounded in facts, providing the necessary perspective for the reader, making Cameron's legendary status undeniable and understandable. This story really did need to be told once and for all, so hats off to him for doing it."
- **Zeena Schreck**, co-author *Demons of the Flesh: The Complete Guide to Left Hand Path Sex Magic*.

"*Wormwood Star* is a fascinating and very, very well-researched look into Cameron's perplexingly strange life. Criss-crossing the country and tracking down all of the various characters the author spoke to must have been quite a chore and, as a reader and long-time admirer of Cameron's work, I'm grateful for the attention Spencer Kansa paid to detail." - **Richard Metzger**, *Dangerous Minds.com*

"*Wormwood Star* describes a magickal woman and artist, not as a tragedy as is all too tritely easy to do to those who have been allotted the role of a magickal partner, but as a true Babalon. A woman and creative being in her own right who, rather than change to the dictates of an oppressive society, became a defining part of a changing one. Fabulous!"
- **Charlotte Rodgers**, author *The Bloody Sacrifice*.

"*Wormwood Star* is a superb effort on every level, incorporating impeccable research and very well-observed viewpoints with a flair for explaining abstruse concepts and ideas in a concise and succinct way. More to the point, it brought Cameron alive for me. This very well-written,

entertaining and exciting work deserves to be widely regarded as one of the best books of 2011!"
- **Stephen Sennitt**, author *The Infernal Texts: Nox and Liber Koth*.

"Spencer Kansa brings to life the countless cabals and social occasions that Cameron enjoyed to the hilt. He might as well have been there when it all happened too, so authoritative is his knowledge and feel for the sometimes penniless world of the practising magician."
- **Joe Ambrose**, *Outside Left.com*

"A groundbreaking biography... that signals a big step towards Cameron's long overdue recognition." - **Marc Olmsted**, *The Beat Review*.

"*Wormwood Star* is a little gem. I respect the author for stepping way beyond the mainstream to go in search of Cameron."
- **Nina Antonia**, author *Johnny Thunders - In Cold Blood*.

"An essential read for anyone interested in Magik or the cult world. Kansa did a good job in research and the book is totally readable and super interesting. Get it before it disappears!"
- **Tosh Berman**, author *Tosh: Growing Up in Wallace Berman's World*.

Wormwood Star is essential and fascinating reading for anyone with an interest in Cameron's life and work. (A) caring but warts-and-all biography (that) is invaluable in preserving memories of a remarkable but often troubled woman." - **David V Barrett**, *Fortean Times*.

"*Wormwood Star* is a pulsating account of a vibrant individual. Someone who lived her life in a magickal way and whose legendary position in occult annals has been skillfully captured and shared in this well-researched bio." - ***Spirituality Today***.

Acknowledgements

This book has been a labour of love, but it would simply not have been possible to complete without the help and generosity of so many people. To that end, I am deeply indebted to the following:

To my publisher Mogg Morgan, and O.T.O. scholars Martin P. Starr and William Breeze, who all initially helped launch this project off the ground and shared their in-depth knowledge. Furthermore, I'm grateful to Bill for his counsel, the representations he made on my behalf, and for allowing me access to the O.T.O. Archives.

I'm indebted to Judy Schlesselman at the *Belle Plaine Union* newspaper, for laying such incredible groundwork for me in Belle Plaine. I also owe her and her husband, Jack, a debt of gratitude for coming to the rescue of a somewhat befuddled traveller and setting him safely on his way.

To my other angel of mercy Betty Rusk (R.I.P.), without whose help I would still be stranded in a hotel in the wilds of Iowa. A gracious guide with whom I shared a magical day together. We met as strangers and parted as old friends.

To Cameron's other Belle Plaine peers who kindly shared their memories of her: Dorothy Miller, Jack Miller, Ruth Swalm Mikita, Carol Froning and Ray Foley.

To the following people, who were all friends of Cameron over a span of five decades, who all generously collaborated with me: David Meltzer (R.I.P.) and Aya (R.I.P.), who opened up their lives, homes, hearts and histories to me. Adios amigos.

Shirley Berman (R.I.P.), for all the incredible memories she shared, the kind hospitality she showered on the "Christmas orphans," and for granting permission, together with Tosh Berman, for us to use the image of Cameron from the cover of *Semina 1*.

Joan Whitney Copeland (R.I.P.), Joan (Martin) Mackay, and Charles Brittin (R.I.P.), who not only shared their personal memories of Cameron but also their private photographs. Dean Stockwell (R.I.P.), Linda Lawson (R.I.P.), Pat Quinn, Russ Tamblyn and John Gilmore (R.I.P.), all took a much-appreciated walk down memory lane for me.

The following people also kindly shared their personal memories of Cameron: Donald Morand, Allen Midgette (R.I.P.), George Frey, Buddy Anderson (R.I.P.), Charmian (R.I.P.), Tosh Berman, John Carruthers (R.I.P.), Chick Strand (R.I.P.), Darryl Copeland, Herb Cohen (R.I.P.), Ira Odessky, Ned Wynn, Ledru Shoopman Baker III (R.I.P.), Exene Cervenka, Sal Ganci (R.I.P.), Judy Macdonald, Alex Macdonald II, Andrew Haley Jr., John Fles, Mike Getz, Christopher Tree, Christopher Harris, Jack Larson (R.I.P.), Rick and Andee Nathanson, John Chamberlain (R.I.P.), Judy Chester (R.I.P.), Bobby Beausoleil, Robert Aiken, Loreon Vigne (R.I.P), Sallie Ann Glassman, Dr. Bill Bailey, Dr. Strawberry Gatts (R.I.P.), Marshall Berle, Peter Adams, Lynne McGinnis, Marsha Getzler (R.I.P.), Sandra Starr, Margaret Percy, Wendy Hyland, Hal Glicksman, Michael Greene, Robert Mundy and Duncan Chamberlain.

Towards the end of my research for the original version of *Wormwood Star*, I managed to track down the master copy of Ed Silverstone Taylor's film short, *Street Fair San Francisco*, to the Berkeley Art Museum and Pacific Film Archive. I spoke with Jon Shibata, the film archivist there, and impressed upon him what a valuable document the film was of Cameron's life, and he readily agreed, and through his sterling efforts the necessary funds were obtained to have the film digitally transferred by the California Audiovisual Preservation Project (CAVPP). The film was recently uploaded onto the Berkeley Art Museum and Pacific Film Archive website, and can be viewed here: http://archive.org/details/cbpf_000048

I owe a special debt of gratitude to Kristine McKenna, who opened so many doors for me. And Jack Parsons' biographer, George Pendle, generously shared some of his thoughts, ideas and research with me.

I must also thank Linda Macfarlane, for sharing her Cameron memories and granting me permission to include her stunning portrait of Cameron. You can view more of Linda's amazing artwork at www.lindamacfarlaneart.com Carla Weber kindly shared some of her wonderful photographs: You can view more of Carla's work at www.carlaweber.com

My good pal, Joe Ambrose (R.I.P), a veteran biographer, was always on hand to dispense sound advice and encouragement. Gone too soon. And my old mucker, Bari Glew, who was a huge help again with his technical wizardry.

A big thank you to Dorothy, Krista and Loretta at the Belle Plaine Library for all their kind help, as well as Bev Winkie at the Belle Plaine Historical Society, and Stacey Tomlin at Belle Plaine High School.

Jill Kraye was a great source of help at the Warburg Institute, as was Ian Jones in the photographic department. I'm thankful to Anthony Iannotti for all his kind help at the O.T.O. Archives, and to Lisa Janssen for casting a fresh, knowledgeable eye over everything. Thanks also to Anuja Navare at the Pasadena Museum of History.

The following people all generously helped with information and contacts: Schuyler Van Johnson, Raymond Foye, Adam Gorightly, Cargill Hall, Russell Castonguay, Bette Kelinson, Graham Tayar, George Clayton Johnson (R.I.P.), Jonathan B. Crane, John Yorke, Hayley Yeeles, Paul Green, Jonathan Sellers (R.I.P.), Conrad M. Cummings, Anne Bassett, Jack Herer (R.I.P.), Colum Hayward, Timotha Bialy, Barbara Beausoleil (R.I.P.), Bill Wudrum, David Hollander, Mary Kerr, Jon Shibata, Linda Zuborg, Paul Waters, Craig Baldwin, Scott Mcinnis, Mary Freeman at the Department for Veterans Affairs, and Lisa Falk at the L.A. Central Library.

To Steve and the boys at the De Brier house – you guys always treat me so well. And a very special thanks to the Cameron family: Crystal, Lola and Loren (R.I.P.).

Author's note: The latest 2025 version of this book contains valuable new information and images regarding Cameron's life that I've amassed over the past five years. I'd particularly like to thank Katerina Stefanescu for coming through for me big time, as well as Stephanie Magnuson and the John Chamberlain Estate for permission to use the shots from *Thumbsuck*. I'd also like to extend my appreciation to LunamGrove and Chris Sheridan for the helpful tip-offs they shared with me.

Dedications

This book is dedicated to my darling grandparents George Crowhurst (1917-2006) and Norah Crowhurst (1920-2007), who always looked out for me.

To Curtis Harrington (1928-2007). A wonderful filmmaker and a proper old-fashioned gentleman, who was an invaluable help to this project.

To my dear friend Juliet Anderson (1938-2010). Triple X-rated Goddess of the Golden Age.

To Dennis Hopper (1936-2010). A maverick spirit throughout the arts and an all-time, cool-ass mamajama.

And to Babs and Debs, for sustaining me throughout this project.

1 - American Gothic

"From childhood's hour, I have not been as others were; I have not seen as others saw, I could not bring my passions from a common spring."
Edgar Allan Poe, 'Alone.'

In 1882, after a lifetime of travels and crusading, the Czech poet, philosopher and freethinker, František Matouš Klácel, died in Belle Plaine, a railroad town in the wilds of Iowa. Though he had trained as a Catholic priest in his native country, this prime product of bohemia renounced his monastic calling "to emancipate my mind from the shackles of slavery," and began to pursue a life dedicated to rationalism and freedom of religious thought.

Settling in America in 1869, he hoped to realize his dream of a free society and published his thoughts on such matters to a small but loyal audience. Despite his high-minded status, his later years were marred by poverty, and by 1881, the venerable but destitute scholar was forced to accept shelter from a patron in Belle Plaine, where he lived out the remaining two years of his life. Though he died a pauper's death, his followers chipped together enough money to erect a statue of their man, which stands nobly in the local cemetery to this day.

In the same town, some forty years later, another extraordinary free spirit, possessed of equally adventurous and bohemian ways, entered the earthly plane at precisely 6:57 pm, on April 23rd, 1922. Marjorie Elizabeth Cameron was the firstborn child to Hill Leslie Cameron and his wife Carrie, a young couple in their early twenties.

The Camerons, who originally hailed from County Antrim in the north of Ireland, immigrated to America in the late 19th century as part of the Scots-Irish diaspora. Headed by Donald and Joan Cameron, the family landed in Chicago, Illinois, and out of the three brothers and sisters that made the trip over, two sisters stayed on in the Windy City, while another moved west to raise a family in Nebraska. Of the brothers, one journeyed forth to Canada to start a new life, while Alexander Russell Cameron moved to neighbouring Iowa, taking his deaf and dumb younger brother, William, with him.

Having first moved to Hawarden, in the northwest part of the state, by the turn of the century they'd settled in Belle Plaine where, despite his disabilities, William found employment as a cobbler and Alexander worked on the railroad and as a farmer. After losing his first wife Maria to consumption early on in their marriage, Alexander remarried, to another woman named Maria, but despite fathering two daughters, the by then ageing patriarch began seeking a son to carry on the family name.

Born a Wilson in Chicago in 1902, Hill Cameron was orphaned as a toddler when his mother died and his father abandoned him following her death. He was given a new start in life when he was adopted by Alexander Cameron and his wife and taken to live in Belle Plaine. With its Anglo-Scot derivation, Wilson was a common name in County Antrim, and it's conceivable the Camerons may have known the Wilson family back in Chicago, and perhaps even had links with them dating back to the old country.

Tragedy befell the family in May 1917, when 66-year-old William Cameron was struck by a steam train as he walked along the railway bridge while out on one of his long Sunday afternoon walks. Due to his impairment, he was unable to hear the train's warning whistle or observe the oncoming locomotive until it was too late, probably because he was studying the wooden ties beneath the tracks so as not to fall. When he did eventually look up, William attempted to crouch down to the stringer of the bridge but was hit and thrown twenty feet to the ground below, where members of the freight crew found him fatally injured, having sustained a fractured skull and a broken neck. Described as "a man of good habits and generally respected," his obituary concluded with the heartbreaking note: "Owing to his afflictions, however, he found it difficult to make many friends."

Hill Cameron was in his late teens when the tragic accident occurred and had developed into a wiry young man, who worked as a machinist at the Roundhouse where the trains were repaired, crews were changed, and the big steam engines shunted around. His betrothed, Carrie, was a homely-looking woman, daughter to one of Belle Plaine's founding families, the Ridenours, who were of Dutch extraction. Her grandfather, on her mother's side, one Thomas Brentlinger, had been a well-liked pioneer in the community, who worked as the town's beekeeper, dispensing his honey door-to-door from his horse and cart. Her father, Cyrus Ridenour, also worked as a machinist for the railroad company, before rising to become the foreman at the Roundhouse.

The birth of the young couple's first child was a truly agonizing affair, with Carrie forced to deliver "dry" when her waters failed to break. Despite her desire to name her newborn Gail, she was overruled by her controlling older sister Nell, a catholic convert, who insisted the child be christened Marjorie Elizabeth, which she translated as meaning "Pearl of God." Nell was suffering from tuberculosis by then, and perhaps in deference, or as a final request to her dying sister, Carrie relented and baptised her daughter with a name she would grow up to despise.

Nell had correctly predicted that Carrie's firstborn would be a female child with red hair and blue eyes, and she now prayed that her second dream would also come true: that the infant would grow up to become a nun and take the veil as a bride of Christ. It would be something she would never live to see, for within a year she was dead from her disease aged just 25. Yet Nell's ghostly presence would live on and become a bête noire for the young girl she'd christened, for when Marjorie was forced to sleep in her dead aunt's bedroom, she was plagued by terrible nightmares and could palpably sense the traces of death that still permeated the air. Such morbid experiences aroused a macabre sensibility within her.

The Cameron family grew rapidly through the 1920s. A year after her birth, Marjorie was joined by a brother, James Russell Cameron, and a younger sister, Mary Lou, was born in 1927.[1] Two years later, the family heralded the arrival of another son, Robert.

The railroad town of Belle Plaine was first established as a division terminus during the decade between 1862 and 1872 when the Chicago and North Western Railroad Company redeveloped the wild prairie to accommodate the expansion of routes throughout the Midwest. The railway traditionally provided the bulk of jobs for the townsfolk, including the Camerons. With its handsome clapboard houses and leafy, tree-lined avenues, it developed into a prototypical heartland town. Bordered by outlying farm areas, where windmills and corn silos still punctuate the overarching skyline, its pastoral scenery remains relatively unchanged today.

Although an outsider would be hard put to notice any difference, the town was historically divided in two, between those who lived in the more expensive homes above the railway tracks, and those more impoverished townspeople who lived below them. Looks could be deceiving though, as Betty Rusk, who grew up below the tracks, and attended the same school as Marjorie, points out: "People above the tracks didn't always have the money they seemed, but they had credit in Cedar Rapids and paid for things whether they could afford it or not."

Hill Cameron's respectable income meant his family could afford to live above the tracks, and Marjorie grew up in a pleasant clapboard house on 3rd Avenue, in the west part of town. On the surface, they were a quintessential, hardworking middle-class family. Lady Grey, Marjorie's pet dog, completed the family unit and accompanied them on trips to Sheboygan Bay in the northernmost part of Wisconsin. The loneliness of the lakes and forests there left its mark on her, and she was haunted by the local legend of an Indian maiden stranded on a lonely isle, calling out to her far-flung lover.

Back home there were nights when the young girl was assailed by queer visions, like the phantom procession of four white horses floating by her bedroom window, and she became convinced that a well in her maternal grandparents' back garden was an infernal "hole to Hell." It gradually became evident that such an acute sensitivity and creative imagination were attributes that derived from her being a natural-born artist.

After attending Whittier Elementary School, Marjorie progressed to Belle Plaine High, staying on until the 11th grade. Academically she was an average student at best, failing in algebra, civic lessons and Latin, but though she never made the honor roll, she did make an impact in the more creative classes, which would all have major bearings on her later life.

Dorothy Miller shared an English class with Marjorie and remembers, in particular, her descriptive prowess: "She was very good at writing and had very descriptive phrases. I remember her once describing a basement, saying how it had a 'musty purple smell' – which is incredibly descriptive." Their teacher encouraged Marjorie's literary interest and introduced her to the work of the New England poets, Emily Dickinson and Edna St. Vincent Millay, which inspired her to compile her own first book of poetry.

Miller and others also talk impressively of Marjorie's performance in the school play, *The Purple Masquerade*, where she got her first taste for dramatic roleplaying by portraying one of a pair of red-haired twins. Another schoolmate, Ruth Swalm Mikita, recalls how Marjorie was selected to be the vocalist for the school's newly organised swing band, while her other extracurricular activities included girls' athletics, mixed chorus and glee club.

In home economics class, Marjorie was taught how to sew and quickly became a first-class seamstress, a talent she would rely on throughout the rest of her life, especially when she was low on funds and had to stitch together her own outfits using her trusty Singer sewing machine. "Most of us girls made our own clothes, including Marjorie," explains Dorothy Miller. "In the Depression years, our skirts were mid-calf, and by the time we were sophomores they altered and the skirts got shorter, which went with being a bobbysoxer."

But it was Marjorie's skill as an artist that really made her stand out to her peers. Former next-door neighbour Jack Miller recalls: "Marjorie really was a terrific artist; she could really paint. She was the best one by far in art class, but she was quite eccentric. She was not particularly popular with boys, and though she associated with girls, she was more of a loner."

Dorothy Miller confirms that Marjorie was cut from a different cloth too, but emphasises how she remained popular despite her otherness: "People were friendly with her; she was likeable and full of fun, but she had a bit of oddness about her. She was just a little bit different. She thought differently to a lot of us."

Betty Rusk was in the local Girl Scout troop with Marjorie and a photo of them, taken on a trip to Palisades-Kepler State Park, back in the late 30s, symbolises for her, Marjorie's aloofness from the other girls. "The picture shows her sat off to the side from the rest of us. Marjorie was not a rebel, she just thought and talked differently to the rest of us. Like the way some people have higher IQs; she was considered smarter than everyone else. She was like a genius."

Betty's late husband, Bill, grew up with the Camerons, and in later life spoke of how highly he thought of Marjorie's natural talent. For years he kept some of the earliest pictures she gifted him. Betty also remembers that when the roads were about to be tarred over, Marjorie would draw in the sand and gravel banks by the side of them, using her fingers or a stick; and there's a lingering folk memory about the time a section of road was blocked off by Belle Plaine officials so that the townspeople could go and view her artwork.

Because of her well-known artistic flair, the teachers kept Marjorie busy and put her creative prowess to good use. In her junior year, she was put in charge of the decorating committee that turned the school gym into The Blue Moon Club for the senior prom, as another student, Carol Froning, remembers: "Anything we had to have done, Marjorie did it. She was so talented and such a neat person, very attractive, and a beautiful artist."

Marjorie grew up living her formative years through the Great Depression. With a small populace and an abundance of home-grown local produce, the town was spared the hardships that afflicted big cities in other parts of the country, where soup kitchens were set up to feed the long, pitiful breadlines. One upshot of the Depression was that it gave people a feeling for the underdog and a sense that everyone was in it together. With its strong community spirit, Belle Plaine was no exception, and people rallied around to help each other.

"Those of us who grew up in the Depression had the best time to live in," Dorothy Miller recollects, perhaps surprisingly. "We didn't have the responsibility our parents did. There were few people of wealth. Most of us were average, so everyone was in the same boat."

Sometimes acts of generosity had unexpected results: "They did pass out free food. The Barr family had broken windows, not even stuffed with cardboard, and the butcher's shop gave them free liver. We had a health check in school and the Barr kid came in and it turned out he had a high haemoglobin level because he'd eaten so much liver!"

To get by, people had to scrimp and save and use their initiative, and Marjorie and her brothers were often sent out to scavenge coal from the sides of the railway tracks to bring home for the fire. Although the railway managed to run through the Depression, some of the men were laid off, and others had to move to Mason City in order to get work. In the poignant, Depression-era lament, 'Brother Can You Spare a Dime,' Bing Crosby sang a song that struck a powerful chord with the nation's wounded psyche, and one verse, in particular, resonated very close to home:

> "*Once I built a railroad, made it run, made it race against time.*
> *Once I built a railroad, now it's done. Brother, can you spare a dime?*" 2

Prohibition may have killed off many repositories for fun and entertainment, but there was always one source that could be relied upon to provide some much-needed escapism: the local movie house, which in Belle Plaine meant the King Theatre on Main Street. There, at least, folks could lose themselves for a couple of hours in the latest Hollywood spectacular.

"Cedar Rapids got the big movies first," Dorothy Miller stresses. "*Gone with the Wind* didn't come to Belle Plaine for ages; we were all still in high school at the time."

As a self-confessed child of the movies, Marjorie idolised the headstrong actresses of the era, revering them as goddesses of a new religion upon whom you could project your own unconscious desires. She would later testify: "Joan Crawford taught us how to walk into a room and Bette Davis showed us how to cry."[3] But her major heroine was the beautiful dancer and choreographer Tilly Losch, who ate up the screen with her sensuous and magical ballet performances.[4]

A future friend of Marjorie's, the photographer Charles Brittin, grew up in nearby Cedar Rapids during the same period, and is keen to emphasize that Iowa was not the cultural backwater some might think: "You'd get the Jose Limon Dance Company which toured the local college, and Cedar Rapids was only a 45-minute drive to Iowa City. The University of Iowa was very rich culturally, even then."

One enduring image of Iowa from that time would grow to become a renowned work of Americana: Grant Wood's painting *American Gothic*. The artwork, depicting a dour-looking farmer with his shrewish spinster daughter, was part of the new "regionalism" movement of American artists, who turned away from Europe and looked to their own backyard for inspiration. When it was first exhibited in 1930, Grant weathered a critical backlash from some Iowans, who were offended at what they saw as their portrayal as sour-faced Puritans. However, as the Depression dealt out its bad hand, the painting became a symbol of fortitude and steadfastness and, as time went on, the "Gothic" in the title became not only a reference to the architectural style of the frame house pictured but to the somewhat unsettling nature of the composition. Today, in contemporary popular culture, it has come to symbolise the macabre lurking behind the everyday veneer.

Marjorie's childhood left its mark on her in another important way, too. Growing up during a repressive era, where shame-laden attitudes towards sex were common, she was stuck in an emotionally crippled, sexually stunted household, where any carnal curiosity was forbidden. When she was caught pleasuring herself at the age of nine, she was punished with a beating from her father and sent to bed without food by her mother. Such backward attempts to clamp down on their daughter's natural, sexual urges only helped to conceal her libidinous activities, and, unbeknownst to her parents and peers, by the time she was 14, Marjorie was living a clandestine life, sneaking out at night for illicit liaisons. Her sexual antics only came out into the open when she fell pregnant at 15. In a panic, she confessed all to her mother, and to spare the family's shame – not to mention save her daughter from another strapping – Carrie performed a home abortion. Such a traumatic experience not only helped shape Marjorie's attitude towards sex but kindled that macabre side of her personality: a dark, romantic perversity that took on gothic dimensions when she began making nocturnal visits to the town's Oak Hill Cemetery.

That same year, Marjorie joined the local branch of the International Order of the Rainbow Girls, a then-popular Masonic youth organisation, with chapters dotted across the country, which sought to promote community service and good citizenship. Every Rainbow Girl was designated a colour representing a particular virtue to which they should concern themselves; for Cameron, it was yellow, denoting nature as her special area of interest.

During this period, she developed what appears to have been an unnaturally close friendship with a fellow Rainbow Girl named Jeanne Spalding. Spalding was a deeply troubled girl, who'd been given up for adoption by her birth parents when she was two years old. She lived locally with her foster parents but was prone to suicide attempts and, on July 1st, 1937, she was found unconscious in her clothes closet by them, with her head on a pillow, having ingested Anytal sleeping powder and other patent medicines. She never awoke. Reportedly, she'd been acting strangely for quite some time, and her parents had sought help for her at the psychopathic hospital in Iowa City. It was said that she'd recently been brooding over the lack of communication from a female classmate at her school, but varying versions surrounding the real cause of this tragic event have resounded down the years, with claims that her suicide was sparked by a breakup or death of a boyfriend, and the accompanying inference that Marjorie was so distraught over her death, she attempted to take her own life as well. What *is* known is that she formed part of the Rainbow Girl team of pallbearers at Spalding's swiftly arranged funeral, just two days later.

As befits a small town, the local newspaper, the *Belle Plaine Union*, often ran coverage of its citizenry that might strike contemporary minds as quaint, such as the time they shared the news on how thirteen-year-old Marjorie had recently had her tonsils removed, or how she's been part of the Ridenour family reunion picnic, or helped organise a Halloween party for her Girl Scout troop. In fact, throughout her girlhood, the paper provided a series of snapshots of her life: from the Easter, Valentine's Day and Thanksgiving pictures she created in 6th grade, to her portrayal of Jenie, the female lead in a one-act school play entitled *Elmer*. And, in the February 3rd, 1938, edition – which also conveyed how she'd appeared in a short play teaching the correct etiquette to use at a dance, and had auditioned for the glee club – they actually profiled her, shining a light on this "feminine artist" in their community.

Although Marjorie wasn't quoted directly, her thoughts and aspirations were shared with the readership, and she revealed her first artistic inspiration derived from a charcoal drawing, titled *The French Woman Weeping*, that she'd seen during a visit to the Art Institute of Chicago.[5] With the image still fresh in her head, she made a copy of it as soon as she returned home. Using charcoal and pencil, she was fond of sketching nudes and "profiles of movie actors and historical figures." Though paints proved too costly, she liked to use watercolours "to paint people of different races, like Chinese and Negroes." And her ambition was "to one day attend the Art Institute of Chicago, but she has not yet decided whether she would like to take commercial art or portrait painting."

The December 22nd, 1938, edition of the paper revealed how she had recited the poem 'In Bethlehem' during a Christmas service at the First Congregational Church, and then held "patrons spellbound with her blues singing," at a social event that same evening. And, the following month, she made their gossip column for her Brilliant Suggestion of the Week, which was that "her high school should be equipped with lounges, a ballroom, and a cocktail bar!"

On more than one occasion the paper billed her as "Marge," yet the plainness of her name seemed at odds with how prepossessing she now was. This, as well as her Titian locks, did not go unnoticed and, that August, she was chosen as the town's representative for the 'Queen of the Iowa Redheads' beauty contest held at the Iowa State Fair. She was vying against 199 other girls for the state title and the chance to win a trip to Hollywood to make a motion picture screen test. The competition was judged, on the day, by redheaded movie starlet Susan Hayward, but, surprisingly, Marjorie didn't even place amongst the finalists. Still, her striking looks would serve her well in the coming years, and the small-town girl would imprint her own unique stamp on celluloid without ever having to audition at all.

In 1940, Hill Cameron secured a new job at the Rock Island Arsenal, a weapons and munitions factory located on the Illinois state border, which was expanding its workforce in the build-up to war. The facility looked out on the Upper Mississippi River and across into the neighbouring Iowan town of Davenport, which was where he relocated his family, setting up home at 1213 College Avenue.

Marjorie enrolled at Davenport High School for her final year and was featured in the local newspaper, *The Democrat and Leader*, in an article on students who'd enrolled for Saturday morning art classes at the Davenport Municipal Art Gallery. Although she graduated in the class of 1940, she did not pose for her high school yearbook (one of nine students deemed "camera shy"), and her sole yearbook entry described her as "dramatically inclined."

Following graduation, Marjorie found employment working as an office manager at Becker Roofing Company and as a display artist in the Petersen Harned Von Maur department store in downtown Davenport. Her time as a Rainbow Girl may have expired when she turned twenty, but her service to the community continued unabated and she helped organise a dance to raise funds to buy uniforms and equipment for the local Red Wings baseball team.

She also experienced her first significant love affair in the shape of Sam Kelinson, a ladies' man, sixteen years her senior, from a Jewish family that had relocated, first to Davenport and then to Rock Island, from Woodbine, New Jersey. According to his niece-in-law, Bette Kelinson: "Sam was a bit of a roué, a smooth operator. He was good-looking, tall with a medium complexion and brown hair. He was a hotel manager first and then he got involved in real estate, mostly resort property." Sam was particularly close with Bette Kelinson's husband Norman: "They were buddies and when the draft was expanded they both enlisted in the Army."

The drumbeat of war was growing louder for Marjorie too, and though it spelt the end of her love affair with Sam, it also offered the new horizons she was looking for. And so, in February 1943, she quit her job and enlisted in the newly established U.S. Navy for women.

The Cameron family home: 1404 3rd Avenue, Belle Plaine.
(Photograph taken by the author.)

Belle Plaine High School as it appears today. (Photograph taken by the author.)

Alexander Cameron's home in Belle Plaine, where Marjorie's father, Hill, grew up. (Photograph taken by the author.)

Marjorie sat opposite Betty Rusk (second from left) and her fellow girl scouts during a trip to Palisades-Kepler State Park. Late 1930s. (Courtesy of Betty Rusk.)

The Oak Hill Cemetery in Belle Plaine that Marjorie used to haunt as a girl. (Photograph taken by the author.)

The Cameron family home in Davenport, Iowa.
(Photo by Cusack's Digital Arts, Davenport, Iowa.)

High School, Davenport, Iowa.

Marjorie featured twice on the front page of the *Davenport Democrat and Leader* with fellow art class students.

2 - Ghost in the Machine

> *"WAVES of the Navy, there's a ship sailing down the bay. And she won't slip into port again until that Victory Day. Carry on for that gallant ship and for every hero brave. Who will find ashore, his man-sized chore was done by a Navy WAVE."*
> –'WAVES of the Navy' anthem.[1]

Having held strong for three years, America's non-interventionist stance was finally shattered in December 1941, following the sneak attack on its naval base at Pearl Harbor, Hawaii, by the Imperial Japanese Army Air Force. As the Nazi Wehrmacht continued to monopolise mainland Europe, America declared war on Germany and joined forces with her British and Soviet allies in their struggle against the Axis Powers.

With American troops committed to fighting on two fronts, women were recruited to take up the slack and fulfil non-combatant roles in the armed forces. At the behest of First Lady Eleanor Roosevelt, the WAVES (Women Accepted for Volunteer Emergency Service) were inaugurated in August of 1942, the first female division of the American Navy.

Four months later, following a successful physical examination, Marjorie enlisted and was sent to boot camp at the Iowa State Teachers College in Cedar Falls. And, in the wake of her call-up, she was made an honorary member of the Glenn Youngkin Navy Mothers' Club, a charitable support group for servicemen/women and their families, where her mother served as a trustee.

Now in her early twenties, she'd blossomed into an uncommonly beautiful young woman. With her upswept auburn hair, sharp cheekbones and fair, freckled skin, she was reminiscent of Katharine Hepburn. Her Celtic colourings seemed to bear out the theory that the Wilson family were also of Scotch-Irish stock, though her slant eyes lent her an exotic air of mystery. Her slender frame made her look taller than her five foot five ½ inches, and her prominent mouth, now often smeared in scarlet lipstick, gave her an obscenely sensuous pout.

In stark contrast to the other wide-eyed, fresh-faced recruits, she looked like a beguiling femme fatale who'd stepped straight out of a film noir movie. The dramatic difference was never more evident than in her naval ID, which captured her steely gaze and suggested an inner confidence that belied her tender years. Marjorie gave a display of such moxie during a layover in Chicago, en route to her posting in Washington, D.C. When her fellow ratings voiced how they wanted to see the sights of Chicago, she gathered them up into a platoon and marched them through the middle of traffic, giving the general public their first glimpse of what a woman in naval uniform looked like.

The leadership qualities instilled in her during her time as a Rainbow Girl, as well as her captivating continence, caught the eye of the military brass in Washington, and she landed a job with the Joint Chiefs of Staff, working first as a cartographer drafting military maps, the only female in an office full of men. After a three-month stint there, she was taken off desk duties and deployed in a cloak-and-dagger mission that, to this day, raises more questions than it answers.

Details remain sketchy, but while working for the Joint Chiefs of Staff, Marjorie claimed that she was used as bait in a shadowy honeytrap. The sting involved a man who was suspected of operating as the paymaster for the German American Bund, a domestic pressure group established in 1936 to promote Nazi Party propaganda in America. A plan was hatched to lure this man to a hotel in Washington, where Marjorie materialised like a Midwestern Mata Hari to sexually seduce him and elicit information. There, unfortunately, the intrigue ends, but the undercover thrills were only a curtain-raiser for further excitements awaiting her in a city that was currently at the centre of world affairs.

As a prerequisite of her position, Marjorie was privy to some memorable moments in history. In May 1943, she was part of the receiving line of staffers that were presented to Winston Churchill during his visit to the capital and was also present in the line-up that greeted General De Gaulle when he visited in July the following year. By then, Marjorie's duties had shifted to the Naval Photographic Laboratory in Anacostia, where she worked as a make-up artist and wardrobe mistress on propaganda films.

Graced by such movie star talents as Gene Kelly and Van Johnson, the production unit quickly became known as the "Hollywood Navy."[2] Assisting the famous hoofers were staff made up of strong union people who began to educate Marjorie about the military and the wider political ramifications of what was going on during the war. Away from work, Marjorie enjoyed Washington's social whirl in the company of her work colleagues, which included her roommate Jean Selby and a photographer named Arthur Napoleon with whom she began a romantic affair.[3] Six feet tall, swarthy in appearance, with a sturdy build and heavy features, Nap, as he was known, brought her some much-needed light relief from the many stresses inherent in her job, especially the heated exchanges with her superior officer Commander Thorne Donnelley, whom she regarded as an "out and out pig."[4]

Their combative rapport began early on when the two of them came to verbal blows arguing over the merits of German culture, which, Donnelley contended, had contributed nothing for the last 100 years. As a Wagner enthusiast, Marjorie begged to differ, and it's a testament to her chutzpah that she would even challenge someone with whom she was meant to be subordinate. Their association only worsened over time, and Marjorie believed Donnelley remained suspicious of her because of her background working as a spook for the Joint Chiefs of Staff.

One of Marjorie's grimmer duties as wardrobe mistress was to recycle the often bloodied fatigues that had been stripped from the corpses of dead servicemen abroad so that they could be reused as wardrobe in the documentary films. The terrible toll of war was brought home to her when she'd invariably find a battered photograph of a sweetheart, or a letter from a loved one, buried deep in some young G.I.'s pocket.

The fate of one conscript, in particular, began to dominate her thoughts, when word reached her that her brother James – who'd won his wings and become a tail gunner – had been wounded in battle. When she was refused compassionate leave to return home to Iowa and visit him, Marjorie went AWOL. Arriving unannounced, she white lied to her parents that she'd been granted permission to visit her brother in the hospital, unaware that her superiors had already notified them of her illegal absence.

She was ordered back to base forthwith and, on her return, she was court-martialed for desertion. As punishment, Marjorie was transferred from her lodgings at 509 Oakwood Street to the naval barracks in West Potomac Park, where she was persecuted by a female superior officer who was jealous of her easy way with men. The woman made her life such a misery Marjorie even contemplated killing the "impossible monster,"[5] and, by that point, the entire experience of the military machine had turned her into a conscientious objector.

Some respite came when she was granted a special pass to visit her folks, who'd recently relocated to Pasadena, California, where her father had landed a job in the Jet Propulsion Laboratory at the California Institute of Technology. Marjorie knew the town well. Two of her mother's sisters had resettled there decades ago and, throughout her childhood, she and her siblings had spent their summer holidays there, staying with their aunts.

But the entire trip was a jarring experience. First, she was robbed of her money and ID, and then she fell sick and had to be treated at the local Pasadena station hospital for a severe bout of hay fever, brought on by allergies that made her hypersensitive to house dust, feathers and certain foods and cosmetics. She then endured a disturbing return journey back to Washington, when, for four days and four nights, she travelled on a packed troop train full of shell-shocked survivors from the Guadalcanal campaign. In their dank, shade-drawn cabins, the servicemen sat like zombies in silence, unable to bring themselves to even look at her, even though she was the only woman amongst them.

It was a brutal chapter amongst many, as the Second World War marked a new low in orchestrated inhumanity. A paradigm that was reflected in the art and culture that did and did not follow in its wake. Words seemed useless in the face of the full, concentrated horror of the holocaust, leading the German philosopher Theodor W. Adorno to remark: "... to write a poem after Auschwitz is barbaric." While in the visual arts, the darkest imaginings and primordial desires of the Surrealists, which had provoked so much shock and awe during the pre-war period, withered when faced with the atrocity exhibitions of the death camps, gulags, and massacred civilian populations, not to mention the Godforsaken battlefields upon which so many million lives were extinguished.

Furthermore, an unsettling notion arose suggesting the civilian population of Hiroshima and Nagasaki were not just physically exterminated but spiritually, too. If the make-up of the human soul is akin to an electromagnetic forcefield, as some spiritually-minded people believe it is, and the blast of an atomic bomb can wipe out an electromagnetic forcefield, then the discharging of J. Robert Oppenheimer's "Little Boy" from the Enola Gay meant a new soul-killer had been born. Reacting to that portentous moment in history, the author William Burroughs would later write: "Scientists always said there was no such thing as a soul. Now they are in a position to prove it."

The war shifted people's political perceptions also and, in Britain, the Blitz-worn working classes, who had sacrificed and lost so much during the hostilities, were not about to return to live under the same social subjugation that existed before the war began. As a result, the 1945 general election saw Churchill, the great Tory war leader and national hero, unceremoniously dumped out of office, just months after the Allied victory, by a country craving a New Jerusalem. While the battle-scarred British contemplated a grim future of austerity measures and rationing and clung on to socialist promises of "jam tomorrow," America continued to bask in its wartime economic boom.

Demobbed in November 1945, Marjorie was surprised to find that, despite being court-martialed, she'd received an honourable discharge, and suspected that someone high up in the Navy Lab had pulled strings and expunged the conviction from her record, perhaps as recompense for her covert derring-do. After visiting her family in California, she planned to return to the East Coast to rejoin Napoleon in New York, where using the contacts they'd made in the photo lab, they'd pursue job opportunities that had been offered them at CBS Television and on Broadway, where Marjorie was offered a chance to work on a revue with the actor Melvyn Douglas.[6] However, in California, she would meet a man who would blow all those plans out of the water.

Margaret Cameron To Report for Duty With WAVES Feb. 25

Miss Margaret Cameron, daughter of Mr and Mrs H. L. Cameron, 1213 College avenue, has received her orders to report for preliminary training in the WAVES at Cedar Falls Feb. 25.

Miss Cameron took her physical examination and was sworn into the service in Chicago on Dec. 9 and has been home waiting for orders to report for training. She is employed in the advertising department of Petersen's.

A brother, James Cameron, has been in the navy for several months.

Despite a misspell, Marjorie's recruitment into the WAVES was gazetted by the local press.

Joins WAVES

MARJORIE CAMERON

Miss Marjorie Cameron, daughter of Mr and Mrs H. L. Cameron, 1213 College avenue, Davenport, will report Thursday at Cedar Falls, to begin training with the WAVES. She enlisted in the service on Dec. 9 and since that time has been awaiting call. Miss Cameron holds the rank of seaman first class.

She is a graduate of the Davenport high school and has recently been employed as a display artist for Petersen-Harned-Von Maur.

Miss Marjorie E. Cameron, second class seaman, daughter of Mr and Mrs H. L. Cameron, 1213 College avenue, was graduated Saturday from the WAVE basic training station at Cedar Falls. Mrs Cameron left Friday to attend the graduation. Miss Cameron left immediately for an assignment in the east as a commercial artist. She enlisted on March 23 and was sent directly to Cedar Falls.

Miss Cameron Is Honored at Party By Navy Mothers

The Glenn Youngkin Navy Mothers' club welcomed Mrs Vera Miller and Mrs Caroline Jordan as active members, and Miss Marjorie Cameron, who is joining the WAVES, as an honorary member at a party last evening in the Iowa-Illinois Gas & Electric Co. auditorium, given to honor Miss Cameron. She was presented with a gift. About 35 were present.

During the war, Marjorie's parents both fulfilled their patriotic duty: Hill Cameron became an auxiliary fireman for the Davenport Fire Department, plugging the gaps left by younger man who'd enlisted, while Carrie Cameron was a Red Cross volunteer, as well as a trustee and matron-at-arms for the Glenn Youngkin Naval Mothers' Club, which welcomed Marjorie as an honorary member in 1943. (*Davenport Daily Times*.)

GUNNER—James R. Cameron, son of Mr. and Mrs. Hill L. Cameron, 1213 College avenue, has completed a course in the aerial gunnery school of the AAF Training command at Harlingen army air field, Texas., and received a pair of aerial gunner's wings and a promotion in grade. Besides learning to fire every type weapon from camera guns to the deadly caliber .50 Brownings, he studied turret manipulation, aircraft identification and learned to tear down and assemble machine guns blindfolded. He climaxed the course by firing on towed targets from Texas training planes, medium bombers and Liberators.

CAMERON.

The military progress of Marjorie's oldest brother, James, was also charted by the local press.

Marjorie resplendent in her naval uniform. Washington, D.C., 1943.
(Courtesy of the Warburg Institute.)

Marjorie's wartime beau, Arthur "Nap" Napoleon.

"Looking like a femme fatale." Cameron's Naval ID.

3 - Belarion Antichrist

> "We must be willing to get rid of the life we've planned, so as to have the life that is waiting for us. The old skin has to be shed before the new one can come."
> – Joseph Campbell, *The Hero's Journey*.

While she waited for opportunities to open up in Manhattan, Marjorie kicked her heels at her parent's house at 1962 North Garfield Avenue in Pasadena and got back into the swing of civilian life. During a visit to the unemployment office to collect her discharge benefits,[1] she ran into a guy with whom she'd had a fractious relationship back at the photo lab in DC. This unnamed man was currently residing at the home belonging to a "mad scientist," in the ritzy part of Pasadena known locally as 'Millionaires Row.'

During a dinner with this gentleman and a woman who also lived at the house, Marjorie learned about the intriguing characters who boarded there, as well as some of the racy goings-on, like the fertility rites where naked women jumped through the flames of a fire set in the back garden. The stories piqued her interest, and when the man offered to take her over for a visit, Marjorie readily accepted. One day, in December, they pulled up outside the impressive Fleming mansion on 1003 South Orange Grove Boulevard. The American Craftsman-style residence was never known as the "Parsonage," but perhaps it should, for its leaseholder was a tall, dark, devilishly handsome man named John Whiteside Parsons.

On entering, Marjorie immediately spied the master of the house, talking on the telephone in the hallway, wearing a shorty robe. Their eyes locked on to each other and Parsons smiled, knowingly. Marjorie had brought some records along with her that she'd picked up in New York, including cast recordings of the musicals *On The Town* and *A Connecticut Yankee*.[2] She found a record player in an alcove room off the main entrance and proceeded to play them. Parsons then reappeared, fully dressed, smiled again and left abruptly, without saying a word, yet Marjorie intuitively knew that she was going to hear from him.

Early in the New Year, she ran into the same ex-colleague again, only this time he was in an agitated state: "Thank God I found you!" he exclaimed with relief. "They were going to kill me if I didn't."[3] On her second visit to 1003, on January 18th, Marjorie waited all afternoon until Parsons returned home at sundown. To his delight, the elemental he'd summoned had returned. Overwhelmed by their mutual sexual attraction, the two of them retired upstairs, where they spent the next fortnight in bed together. The small-town girl had hooked one helluva catch.

By day, Jack Parsons plied his trade as a rocket technician at JPL, the Jet Propulsion Laboratory, a company he'd co-founded. He was born eight years earlier than Marjorie and was raised as an only child by his doting mother Ruth and his wealthy maternal grandparents. His father, Marvel, who served in The Great War and rose to the rank of Major, had been thrown out on his ear for his philandering ways whilst Parsons was still a bairn, and this lack of a father figure seemed to breed in him a desperate longing for an older male role model in his life, as well as a willingness to challenge authority.[4] Although he was originally christened Marvel, after his father, his mother scrubbed his first name following their acrimonious divorce and renamed him John, though, as is custom, he was more often addressed as Jack.

Though he possessed only an autodidactic knowledge of chemistry, Jack managed to parlay his boyhood obsession with rocketry and science fantasy magazines into a cutting-edge career. In 1942, under the auspices of Theodore von Kármán, the director of the Guggenheim Aeronautical Laboratory at the Californian Institute of Technology, he co-founded the Aerojet Engineering Corporation and, accompanied by his high school buddy Ed Forman and Caltech undergraduate Frank Malina, he began experimenting with solid rocket fuels and JATO (Jet Assisted Take-Off) rocket motors in the scrubland of Pasadena's Arroyo Seco. Due to the hazardous nature of their work, they were pithily dubbed "The Suicide Squad." But off the back of their technological breakthroughs, Jack helped establish JPL as a militarily important research laboratory.

At night, however, Jack was often engaged in alchemy of a quite different kind, administering his role as the recently appointed Master of the Agape Lodge, the only functioning fraternity dedicated to the teachings of one of the most controversial and fascinating figures to emerge out of the Machine Age... Aleister Crowley.

Described by the literary critic Cyril Connolly as "the Picasso of the occult," and by the yellow press of Fleet Street as "The wickedest man in the world," Edward Alexander Crowley's storied life originated in the most conventional of circumstances. Born in 1875, in the English town of Royal Leamington Spa, Master Crowley was raised in a well-to-do family, who adhered to the Christian evangelism espoused by the Plymouth Brethren church.

After the death of his beloved father, the teenage Crowley began to rebel against the religious strictures of his upbringing and grew to despise his zealot of a mother, who anointed her wilful son, 'The Great Beast 666,' which was how Emperor Nero was characterised in the apocalyptic verses of the Book of Revelation. To needle his mother, Crowley turned the epithet on its head and wore it as a badge of honour, an early example of his mordant sense of humour.

A Cambridge education fostered Crowley's literary bent, grounding the aspiring poet in the classics (as well as homosexuality) and, once emancipated, his sizeable inheritance empowered him to luxuriate in a libertine life. In emulation of his intrepid boyhood hero, Sir Richard Burton, Crowley scoured the globe, exposing himself to a wide range of metaphysical experiences. By fusing his knowledge of Western esotericism with Eastern practices such as tantra, yoga and meditation, he synthesised a potent neo-pagan system of spirituality that he baptised Thelema.

The mid-late 19th-century period saw a flourishing of new spiritual movements that challenged the social, political and religious orthodoxy of the times and broadened the narrow definition of what constituted religious worship. American Transcendentalists like Margaret Fuller and Ralph Waldo Emerson believed the divine could be experienced through spiritual introspection and brotherhood, and in an appreciation of the beauty of the natural world, without the necessity of a church or priesthood. This theology informed their positions on such pressing issues as the abolition of slavery and women's rights and was enshrined in their essays and sermons, as well as the poetry of their committed confreres, Walt Whitman and Henry David Thoreau.

Spiritualism boomed during this period, too, its rank and file swelled by many vocal reformists, including radical Quakers. Although ostensibly a Christian organization, it flouted Biblical dogma, especially in its practice of mediumship, and séances became a popular pastime for Victorians anxious to make contact with their dear, departed ones on the other side. (This pastime peaked again at the end of the First World War, with so many families desperate to make contact with their fallen menfolk.)

The Transcendentalists incorporated tenants from the Hindu holy book *The Bhagavad Gita* into their teachings, and precepts and practices of Eastern mysticism were further disseminated by the Theravada Buddhist-based Theosophical Society, founded by Madame Helena Blavatsky in 1875. In her magnum opus *The Secret Doctrine*, Blavatsky described her inter-dimensional contact with Ascended Masters or Mahatmas, spiritually enlightened beings who imparted their wisdom to her from the astral plane. The authenticity of Blavatsky's revelations has long since been disputed, but the social activism of her successor, Annie Besant, has most certainly not, especially when it came to her controversial endorsement of birth control, which brought her in direct conflict with the Church of England.

For those coming from a quite different, irreligious perspective, most notably Dr. Sigmund Freud, psychoanalysis was seen as the key to discovering the self by pinpointing the cause of dysfunctional behavioural patterns and personal neuroses. In the wake of Friedrich Nietzsche's philosophical proclamation that "God is dead!" Freud's clinical work left many Western intellectuals ruminating that God may actually be *dad.*

As Crowley was formulating his own spiritual system, other representatives of London's intelligentsia were resurrecting earlier Adamite concepts drawn from renegade Christian sects who practised "ecstatic sex." In 1907, the Godfather of science fiction, H. G. Wells, promulgated free love at a meeting of the socialist Fabian Society, a notion that was soon taken up by other smart sets like the Bloomsbury Group, and bandied about by anarchists like Emma Goldman. Such shared human values and interconnected links between non-mainstream religious organizations and their literary and political contemporaries have latterly been hailed as a primary force in the establishment of modern social liberalism.

Crowley's own curiosity for an alternative belief system led him into The Hermetic Order Of The Golden Dawn, a magical order that schooled its students in the mysteries of Qabalah, astrology, the tarot and astral projection. Its ranks included some famous cultural figures of the time, such as the actress Florence Farr, Oscar Wilde's wife Constance, and the brilliant Irish poet William Butler Yeats, with whom Crowley shared a mutual disdain. Crowley quickly discovered that he had a natural aptitude for magick, as he'd later rechristen the practice to differentiate it from the popular stage illusionism of the time, and his rise through the grades was meteoric. But the order was riven by factional infighting, and when the group splintered, Crowley left and went his own way, exploring the spiritual path as a practising Buddhist.

Then, in 1904, while honeymooning in Egypt with his first wife Rose, Crowley transcribed a paranormal communiqué delivered to him by an alleged preterhuman entity named Aiwass, an emissary of the Egyptian God Horus, whose life, death and resurrection were recycled into the Biblical story of Jesus. Crowley described the apparition as being tall, dark and vaguely Persian in appearance with "The face of a savage king." Reflecting on this momentous encounter, in retrospect, Crowley came to regard the intelligence as his Holy Guardian Angel, while his acolyte, Israel Regardie, later argued that Aiwass was actually an unconscious projection of Crowley's own personality.

Whatever its source was, the epiphany imparted to Crowley was laid down in *Liber Al vel Legis* or *The Book of the Law*, an explosive manifesto that heralded the Twilight of the Gods and a new aeon of spiritual individualism and rebellion, symbolised by Horus, The Crowned and Conquering Child. The book's powerhouse verses tore up the dictates of monotheism and resurrected the religious ecstasies of a pre-Christian era, where sacred sexuality and the sacramental use of intoxicants were blessed paths to enlightenment. The book's most famous maxim: "Do what thou wilt shall be the whole of the law," was a Rabelaisian clarion call for individuals to actualize their divine self, free from the illusions of the ego, and to fulfil their true purpose in life, allowing others the freedom to do the same.

In 1912, Crowley was appointed National Grand Master General of the Ordo Templi Orientis (Order of the Temple of the East, or the Order of Oriental Templars) for Great Britain and Ireland, a quasi-Masonic order founded in Germany around the turn of the century. In his new capacity, Crowley streamlined O.T.O. rituals and incorporated Thelema and *The Book of the Law* as its central creed.

In one section of *The Secret Doctrine*, Madame Blavatsky envisioned the human race mutating into a species of superior, supernal beings, an evolutionary process that was predicted to begin in America. By the end of the 19th century, the Theosophical Society numbered over 100 lodges dotted all over the country, and California, in particular, was proving a haven for seekers interested in practising an alternative belief system and lifestyle.

During the twenties alone this lotusland was home to Mount Helios, a free love communist compound in Glassell Park, ministered by Edith Maida Lessing, as well as the infamous Blackburn Cult, led by the mother/daughter duo, May Otis Blackburn and Ruth Wieland, who claimed to receive revelations from the archangel Gabriel, and were, subsequently, accused of animal sacrifice and murder.

In November 1915, Crowley breezed through Hollywood, himself, surveying its "cinema crowd of cocaine-crazed sexual lunatics" with bemusement. You could be forgiven for thinking that this enclave of sensualists might have proved a rich recruitment ground for his doctrine, but things didn't quite work out that way, and, in the intervening years, his Californian coterie remained modest.

In 1927, Annie Besant established an educational foundation in the pristine Ojai Valley, northwest of Los Angeles, where she nurtured her spiritual protégé, Jiddu Krishnamurti, to become a "World Teacher." Although Jack Parsons and his wife, Helen, had attended some Theosophical Society meetings, they found many of their principles not to their liking. Crowley's red-blooded, pagan philosophy, on the other hand, helped assuage the guilt Jack felt over his marital infidelities, and he and Helen became eager converts.[5]

In 1942, as a mark of his largesse, Parsons turned his mansion on South Orange Grove into the Agape Lodge's swanky new headquarters. At this juncture, the lodge was presided over by Wilfred Talbot Smith, an expatriate Englishman who'd been initiated into the O.T.O. by

Crowley's magical heir Charles Stansfeld Jones, the Grand Master at the now-defunct Agape Lodge No. 1 in British Columbia. Another senior member was Jane Wolfe, a retired silent movie actress, who was the only disciple to have personally studied with Crowley at his Abbey of Thelema in Cefalu, Sicily, back in the early 1920s.

To fill the remaining rooms in the house, Jack advertised in the local papers, voicing a preference for anarchists, atheists, and artist types and, with the Thelemites in attendance, this proto-commune quickly became a thrumming hive of offbeat activity that shook up the genteel neighbourhood. Its already amorous ambiance took on an incestuous tinge when Jack transferred his romantic affections from his wife Helen to her young, minxy half-sister Sara, known communally as Betty. In return, Helen hooked up with Wilfred Smith, who up until then had been an avuncular presence in Jack's life. The familial resentments and simmering sexual tensions caused by this switcheroo became so uncomfortable, it marked the beginning of the end for the intimate group.

As he was based across the pond in England, Crowley relied on reports filed by his disciples to keep him abreast of the lodge's activities. This was especially true of his loyal viceroy in America, Karl Germer, a man who'd endured much in life due, in no small part, to his association with Crowley. Germer had already translated several Crowley titles into his native German language, prior to meeting the man himself in 1925 and, consequently, he'd establish a book publishing house in Leipzig, dedicated to the author's works. Crowley, in turn, initiated Germer into Thelema and groomed him as an heir apparent.

After stints living in various European cities, Germer moved to America, until an expired visa forced him to return to Germany where, in 1935, he was arrested by the Gestapo for being an alleged high-grade freemason and a recruitment officer for To Mega Therion. Despite his background as a decorated intelligence officer for the German army during the First World War, Germer was sentenced and imprisoned in a Nazi concentration camp. His confinement lasted seven months and, though he was forbidden to leave Germany, he fled to Belgium, where he lived for several years working in the export business. This lasted until the now-conquered Belgian authorities turned him over to the Nazis again, who dispatched him to another concentration camp, this time in France.

His eight-month internment ended in February 1941, when his wealthy American wife, Cora, managed to procure an immigration visa for him to return to the States. There, he became a neutralised citizen and served as the Grand Treasurer of the O.T.O. Yet, even in his adopted homeland, he remained a scrutinised suspect of the secret police, only this time the surveillance was sanctioned by J. Edgar Hoover, the head of the FBI, who ordered his agents to investigate allegations that Germer was a Nazi sympathizer, in spite of his previous detentions. (At the Samuel Weiser occult bookshop in New York, Germer was overheard by an FBI informant expressing his belief that the Germans *were* a master race. This, however, ignored the nuanced point Germer was making, as a proud Prussian, in drawing a distinction between Germans and Nazis. Additionally, Germer's soon-to-be second wife, Sascha, was a Jewish émigré.) Like the Gestapo, Hoover was equally perturbed by Germer's representations on behalf of Crowley, who was described as a "notorious moral pervert" in one FBI report, and it all conspired to scupper Germer's plan of rescuing Crowley from the nightly aerial bombardment of London, to live as an exile in America.

When salacious tales of bed-hopping and partner swapping by lodge members filtered back to Crowley in England, he accused Smith of neglecting the Great Work of Thelema and using it as an excuse for his own self-gratification. This was a bit rich coming from Crowley, and the real reason behind his dissatisfaction had more to do with Smith's lack of leadership skills, particularly his recruitment failure, for the lodge's meagre membership now stalled at around 20 disciples. Crowley depended on the monthly dues from lodge members for his upkeep, as well as financing the printing costs of his books and so, as a consequence, he relieved Smith of his stewardship and sent him on a magical retirement to discover the hidden God within himself. He then placed Parsons in his stead, a man in whom he initially saw great promise.

Jack was also highly admired by the members of the Los Angeles Science Fantasy Society and served as an important conduit between those literary seers and the eggheads at Caltech and JPL. This fertile cross-pollination enabled fantasy writers to pick the brains of the savants behind the latest technological innovations and draw upon them for their own material. A case in point was the Jack-inspired Hugo Chantrelle character in Anthony Boucher's murder mystery *Rocket to the Morgue*.

One such scribe who supped from the fount of Jack's esoteric knowledge and contributed to the philosophically stimulating atmosphere at 1003 was Lafayette Ronald Hubbard. From the accounts of people who were around at the time, Hubbard's knack for storytelling, in real life as well as in the pages of his prodigiously produced pulp novels, split people into two camps: those who enjoyed him as an entertaining raconteur and those who regarded him as a fantasist of the highest order. However, unlike Jack, who could be snobbish and aloof if he didn't think someone was on his wavelength, Hubbard was garrulous and egalitarian in his outlook and willing to engage with people.

Jack was enamoured of Hubbard's science fiction sagas and became so personally convinced of his magical prowess that he wrote to Crowley, lauding his newly acquired accomplice in glowing terms as "a natural Thelemite." Jack's endorsement was partly self-serving, for he was itching to find a new magical partner to work with, as his former aide, Ed Forman, had quit in terror, haunted by the spectre of wailing banshees hovering outside his bedroom window following a previous ritual.

Collaborating with Hubbard, however, came at a cost. What L. Ron lacked in looks he more than made up with in charm, and his gift of the gab gave him a winning way with women. One female of the species who succumbed to his magnetism was Jack's inamorata Betty, who saw Hubbard as a potential husband and father of her children, a role that Jack made clear he had no interest in fulfilling. Crowley taught that sexual jealousy was ridiculous, and though evidently bruised by the loss of his lover, as a good Thelemite, Jack tried to rise above such petty emotions.

On the surface he did, and that February and March he continued to collaborate with Hubbard on a series of magical rites that became known as the Babalon Working. The first part of these rituals had already culminated in the successful conjuration of his new mate… Marjorie. The second part concentrated on the invocation of the Biblical Whore of Babylon (whom Crowley renamed Babalon for numerological reasons), who is described in Revelation as "The Mother of Harlots and abominations… drunken with the blood of the saints, and with the blood of the martyrs of Jesus." This blasphemous figure is regarded by Biblical scholars as symbolising the pagan wickedness of Rome, but in Crowley's cosmology, Babalon was transfigured from a Christian pariah into a sacred Goddess of sex magick.

Using the Enochian Calls, an arcane system of magic originated by the Elizabethan magus John Dee and his scrying sidekick Edward Kelley, Jack and Hubbard embarked on a series of magical invocations to the Goddess, with Jack inhabiting Dee's role as the principal magician and Hubbard acting as the seer, describing what was happening on the astral plane. Their aim: to unleash Babalon's licentious spirit on a populace tyrannised by Christianity's strangulating attitude to sexuality – seen by Jack as the underlying root cause of psychological torment and societal bigotry – and to set in motion Crowley's revolutionary new aeon.

It was an act of theurgy that fed into Jack's fantasy of women as sexually voracious beasts, an ideal that was depicted in one of his favourite novels, Jack Williamson's *Darker Than You Think*. Also, as he admitted to himself, it provided him with a psychological way of working through his own Oedipal complex. Furthermore, as a notorious womaniser, Jack was well aware of how the sexual mores of the country had been shaken up during the war. It wasn't just whoring serviceman abroad who were taking their pleasures where they could find them, but also the men-starved womenfolk back home. Jack was under no illusion that, given the right circumstances, even apparently straight-laced, God-fearing citizens were only too willing to indulge in illicit sexual activity, although it remained a dirty little secret as the country returned to peacetime conventionality.

One thing that did manifest from the magical operation was *Liber 49: The Book of Babalon*, a channelled revelation dictated to Jack in the Mojave Desert, which he regarded as the denouement to *The Book of the Law*. Jack's inspiration for the Babalon Working was drawn from the pages of *The Vision and The Voice*, Crowley's own astral journey through the Enochian Aires. Complete with its own alphabet and syntax, the guttural Enochian language had allegedly been communicated to Kelley and Dee by the archangel Uriel. Dee believed it was the ancient language Adam used to converse with God and his angels, which ultimately died out with the death of Enoch, Adam's great-grandson. The mischievous Uriel eventually destroyed Dee and Kelley's magical partnership, after she instructed them to swap wives and, having reprised the roles of their Elizabethan counterparts, Jack and Hubbard's relationship was now heading towards the same fate.

For the time being Marjorie was kept completely in the dark about the ongoing magical rites. It would be years before Jack revealed their real significance to her and, until then, the two were occupied with more prosaic concerns. Needing a change of clothes after their frisky fortnight of fun, Marjorie returned home and introduced her dashing new prince to her mother and father who, as a JPL employee, was no doubt aware of who Jack was. This exciting new development in her life left Marjorie in a quandary. Did she stay on with Jack in California or rejoin Napoleon in New York as planned? Ultimately, she decided that Jack was the future, but felt she owed Napoleon an explanation in person, so that March she drove to New York, accompanied by the mystery man who first introduced them. From the get-go, the trip was beset with problems. Even before she had to deal with the break-up with Napoleon, and try to figure out the best way of letting him down gently, Marjorie spent much of the journey spurning the overtures of her travel companion, just as she had during their navy days. On top of all this, once she made it to New York, she discovered she'd fallen pregnant, and although the pregnancy was short-lived, it provided an even greater incentive to return to California. Jack, meanwhile, couldn't understand why she even bothered going to all that trouble to bring her former relationship to an end. To him, their union had been magickally sanctioned. It was a *fait accompli*.

Jack was smitten with his elemental – a supernatural entity that can serve magicians during a magical rite – and praised his fiery new flame in a letter to Crowley. Jack was so blinded by her beauty, he initially mistook the colour of Marjorie's blue eyes for green. The discrepancy was explained by their ability to change tone, depending on the shade of clothing she wore, but for Jack, it only added to her unearthly allure.

While Marjorie was away, Jack and Hubbard set up *Allied Enterprises*, a business partnership in which they could consolidate the rewards from their respective endeavours. To kick-start this venture, Hubbard hatched a plan to travel down to Florida with Betty, where they would buy yachts and sail them back to California, via the Panama Canal, where they could sell them at a profit. It seemed a dubious proposition from the start, and many at 1003 were alarmed by Jack's blind trust in someone he'd barely known for a year. Regardless, Jack stumped up the lion's share of the investment, about $20k, a considerable sum at the time, and Hubbard left with Betty in tow. But Jack began to have second thoughts about the risky venture, and when it appeared that Hubbard was using the trip as an all-expenses-paid jolly for him and his bride-to-be, he cursed his foolhardiness and sprung into action.

Crowley was kept abreast of the unfolding drama, first by Germer, then by Jack himself, who had travelled down to Miami in pursuit of his quarry. When Hubbard and Betty learned that Jack was in town looking for his money, they set sail hoping to evade him. Unable to pursue them on the sea, Jack turned to conjury, and tracing a magic circle on the floor of his seafront hotel room, he performed an invocation to Bartzabel, the spirit of Mars, the malefic planet of war. "As above, so below," so the magic adage goes and, according to Jack, the ritual whipped up a sudden squall, forcing Hubbard's vessel back to shore.

When Jack initiated legal proceedings against his former business partner, Hubbard threatened to inform the authorities about Jack's sexual relationship with Betty, which began when she was 17. Hubbard then reconsidered, fearing Jack might reveal some unsavoury truths about him in return, such as his bigamist marriage to Betty that August, and the threat was rescinded. Still, in the subsequent judgement, Jack only recouped a fraction of his savings. When Marjorie returned from New York and discovered how her lover's faith had been repaid with treachery, she retaliated by painting a gory portrait of Betty with her legs cut off at the bloody knees. Hubbard's bad vibes seemed to permeate the residence, and when Jack and Marjorie consulted a Ouija board, it instructed them to clean out Hubbard's room and vacate the premises.

The directive from the spirit world neatly coincided with the redevelopment going on in the area. Several properties along Orange Grove, including the Fleming Mansion, were earmarked for demolition so that modern, new, compact condominiums could be built to help alleviate the post-war housing shortage; so, that summer, as the bulldozers honed in, Jack tendered his resignation as Master of the Agape Lodge and contemplated his next move with his prospective bride.

On the 19th October, 1946, four days after his divorce from Helen was finalised, Jack and Marjorie were married at the Santa Ana County courthouse in Orange County, officiated by Justice of the Peace, Marco Forster, in a civil ceremony witnessed by Ed Forman and his wife Jeanne. The nuptials heralded a new era for the newlyweds. Jack had already secured a position at North American Aviation in Culver City, prompting their relocation to Manhattan Beach, an upscale locale that was home to personnel in the defence and aerospace industries.

Strangely enough, around the time the prepubescent Marjorie was experiencing mystical visions and fixating on the hole to Hell in her grandparent's back garden, 13-year-old Jack was conjuring Satan and scaring himself silly when Old Scratch made a one-off appearance in his bedroom. Yet in spite of the infernal obsession they shared in childhood, Marjorie remained bemused by the magical side of Jack's life. It made for some comic incidents, like the day a windstorm swept up from the beach, blowing the French doors of the house wide open. While Marjorie scrambled to close the doors and windows, Jack ran upstairs and retrieved his magic dagger to quell the raging gales outside. Marjorie maintained an aversion to religion of any kind, be it organised or not; nevertheless, her husband divined something in her that she, herself, was presently unaware of: her innate supernatural being.

It all began with her name. Due to its homespun quality and religious derivation, Marjorie had always abhorred her first name, so she welcomed the new magical moniker Jack bestowed upon her: Candida, often shortened to Candy. She also began introducing herself to new friends simply as Cameron, a form of address she'd grown accustomed to while in the service. *Marjorie* was memory-holed.

While taking a walk along Manhattan Beach one day, Cameron met George Frey, an aeronautical engineer who worked at Boeing Aircraft. As he was in a similar line of work as her husband, Cameron brought him home and introduced him to Jack. To Frey, they seemed a perfect if unusual couple: "Jack had a nice personality and I noted the necklace he was wearing, which was a winged penis. Candy was something else. She thought about things and reasoned."

Shortly after they'd gotten to know each other, Frey asked Jack how he'd met his wife and was told a story that detoured significantly from Cameron's version of events: "Jack said he wanted to find a witch to be head of his new religion and to support him in his magical development. He had spoken to Wilfred Smith who'd told him to write to Crowley, who prescribed a mystical ceremony to produce her. Jack used L. Ron Hubbard as a familiar in the ceremony and said he was in the kitchen one day when there was a bolt of lightning outside, and then a knock at the front door and, when he answered, it was Candy, who was shaking, and said, 'I don't know who I am or where I came from.' She told Jack she'd been in an automobile accident in front of the house and Jack realised she was his witch and convinced her to move in."

Frey confirms that, at that juncture, Cameron still hadn't accepted the role Jack envisaged for her and recalls the day a group of kids called her a witch when her car pulled up at a set of traffic lights: "Candy was disturbed by that, but it only validated Jack's belief in her. She didn't buy into things Jack told her at first, she felt it was ridiculous. Candy refused to believe she was his witch, or that his magical aspirations had any validity. She only expressed to me negative feelings concerning Crowley and his philosophy. Jack told me this had disappointed him, but it didn't dissuade him from believing that she would eventually come around to realise her destined role in his life."

Through Jack, Frey met Wilfred and Helen Smith, and despite not being an O.T.O. member, he was invited to attend The Gnostic Mass, Crowley's ritualised celebration of sacred sexuality. "Jack didn't press anything on me or pressure me into joining the group," Frey points out. "I'd read The Bible, The Koran, The Book of Mormon, The Torah, The Bhagavad Gita, and he thought I had a lot of answers to things, different to mystical answers. They took me to most of the places they went. We spent a lot of time together. They were very compatible and used to laugh a lot when I was with them. There were no arguments but mental conversations and stimulations. Jack was not a fighter and Candy was easy to get on with. She was always calm. I never saw her get excited. She laughed a lot. Part of her humour was in her paintings, which I thought were kind of bizarre." Through Cameron, Frey began to discover a whole other side to Manhattan Beach, like the nest she took him to belonging to a sewing circle of middle-aged, pipe-smoking lesbians who hailed from New York.

Jack's love of Norse and Celtic myths and Arthurian legends was reflected in much of the poetry he wrote and influenced the naming of the German shepherd dog he got to keep Cameron company while he was at work: Freya. When he and Cameron went away on weekend trips to Catalina Island, they'd often leave the dog with Frey, digging the synchronicity between their two names.

Jack, meanwhile, kept in touch with his old science fiction cronies, including the author Robert Heinlein, a man who shared his social libertarian outlook. Thanks to Jack, he acquired a storyteller's curiosity for *The Book of the Law*, and later incorporated Thelemic themes into his own writings. Additionally, both men were mutually interested in organic living environments, and they spent time together brainstorming new design concepts for the home. One of Jack's ideas was a globe of light that appeared above a person's head when they wanted to read, which could then switch itself off once they finished. For a while, the two men and their wives made a formidable quartet, although Heinlein's ladies' man pretensions and Hollywood shuck didn't quite jive with Cameron's tastes. Having grown fond of Heinlein's wife Leslyn, who dabbled in white magic and was quite a radical thinker in her own right, Cameron was turned off when the author traded her in for a younger redhead named Virginia, seemingly to compete with Jack.

The Parsons also socialised with Jack's fellow directors at Aerojet, especially Andrew Haley and his wife Delphine, who threw wonderful parties at their home on South Orange Grove, just down the street from their former residence. Some delightful home movie footage from that time captures Jack and Cameron with the Haleys and their children, little Delphine and Andrew Jr., spilling out of the house and wandering into the red blossom-scented back garden, where Cameron and the kids take turns petting Freya.

As comfortable as it was, living the life of a lotus-eater on the beautiful beachfront of California, Cameron hankered to pursue an artistic life and, with Jack's approval, she made plans to travel to Paris, the gateway to the arts. Reasons for the trip to Europe were two-fold. Using the G.I. Bill, and a letter of recommendation from Larser Feitelson, who taught at the Art Center School in Pasadena, Cameron hoped to enrol at the Académie de la Grande Chaumière, one of the most prestigious art schools in Paris, which boasted Alberto Giacometti and Amedeo Modigliani amongst its previous alumni. She also planned to visit Crowley in England, to put Jack's side of the Hubbard debacle over to him in person, rather than have him base his views on the one-sided communications he'd received from fellow Agape Lodge members. Crowley was mystified by the missives Jack sent him regarding the Babalon Working and was left far from impressed with the financial fallout that followed. Aware that he had fallen in Crowley estimations, Jack hoped this might help repair his relationship with the man he once considered his beloved father; and in a letter he wrote to him prior to

Cameron's departure, Jack reassured him that he had rebuilt his life both financially and emotionally over the last year, and was now back on his feet.

By this stage, after a lifetime of exotic travels and wild exploration, Crowley had retired to the aptly named Netherwood guest house in Hastings on the south coast of England, where he was destined to live out his final days. Physically, he was a gaunt shadow of his former robust self, but as his letters proved, he was still remarkably agile of mind, in spite of the crotchetiness that comes with age, deteriorating health and the prolonged use of opiates administered to help ameliorate his asthma.

In late September 1947, Cameron enrolled at the International Berlitz Language School (at 213 Burlington Avenue), using the G.I. Bill, to learn some functioning French in preparation for her new adventure. And then, the following month, she left the sunny climes of Southern California, with Freya by her side, and journeyed to New York, where she boarded the SS *America* ocean liner, bound for chilly Europe. En route, she dined with the officers at the captain's table, as was custom for fragrant female passengers travelling alone, and met the *New York Times* Washington correspondent Arthur Krock. Perhaps due to a mixture of wartime paranoia and her overactive imagination, Cameron began to wonder if the Pulitzer Prize-winning bureau chief was tailing her for the government, suspicious of why the wife of an important rocket scientist was journeying alone to Europe. But baser motives were also on show, and when the 60-year-old goat made a play for her, she rebuffed his advances.

Arriving at Le Havre, Cameron travelled on to Paris by train, but The City of Light that greeted her that winter was, in her own words, "extreme and bleak."[6] The city was still coming to terms with the aftermath of the war and, on the streets, she witnessed the wretched sight of prostitutes whose heads had recently been shaved as punishment for fraternising with the Nazi occupiers. Cameron later claimed that, while in town, she befriended the then-unknown chanson singer, Juliette Greco. Although she was, at the time, little more than an attractive face on the scene, Greco would soon rise to become a darling of the bohemian Left Bank, appearing as one of the rebellious teens in Jean Cocteau's film *Orpheus*, dating the Dark Prince of jazz Miles Davis, and becoming something of a successor to Edith Piaf.

For whatever reason, Cameron's enrollment at the Académie de la Grande Chaumière did not pan out, and neither did her forthcoming visit to Crowley in Hastings. For although she'd written to him about her travel plans, she was informed by newsmen that the Great Beast 666 roared no more, having died on December 1st from a respiratory infection. Deirdre MacAlpine, who was mother to Crowley's young son, Aleister Ataturk, and was present at his bedside, recorded how his death was greeted with a peal of thunder by the Gods.

Despite the considerable charms of Ms. Greco, Cameron left Paris, seemingly on a caprice, and travelled to Switzerland, where she wound up in the small, scenic town of Lugano. She booked into a hotel next to the local convent overlooking the lake and spent most of her days out walking by herself, unable to parley with the locals. She was often relieved to escape the racket of the convent bells that struck every hour on the hour and shook the walls of her room. By the end of her three-week stay, the deafening din took its toll and, with recent events catching up with her, Cameron underwent something of a psychotic breakdown, bordering on lycanthropy. In her own words, she ended up in a dreadful state in her hotel room: "Naked, with my hair all dishevelled hanging over my eyes, growling at myself in the mirror."[7] In desperation, she contacted Jack, who wired her some money to get her back to Paris and eventually home. In the end, her entire European excursion cost him $2,500 in total (over $36k in today's money).

On the train journey from Lugano to Berne, Cameron found herself locked in a mental duel with a priest sat opposite her, and new espionage intrigue, either real or imagined, occurred later when a tall, blonde man in a trench coat appeared like a character out of a spy novel, whistling the tune 'Someone to Watch Over Me,' pointedly in her direction. Whether he was, as he claimed, returning to San Francisco from a six-month sojourn in Lapland, or selling a cover story, to Cameron's mind he was tailing her. More melodrama followed when the connecting train bound for Paris derailed, and its occupants were left stranded on a siding for 24 hours. The inconvenience caused some understandable consternation amongst the confined passengers, who now included a troupe of showgirls fresh from their performance at an army camp. When hunger came upon them, people broke out their own provisions and survived on a shared diet of wine and cookies. Initially, everyone bonded together, but the bonhomie began wearing thin, especially when every passing train showered their carriage with soot as it sped by. As the hours dragged on, tempers frayed and patience snapped as the stressed-out travellers started to turn on one another. When the sorry lot eventually arrived in Paris, they could barely stand to look at each other. The whole trip left a bad taste in Cameron's mouth, and it would be decades before the real significance behind the whole strange Lugano affair became fully understood by her.

In September 1948, in an effort to get a handle on the roots of her neuroses, Cameron enrolled at the University of Southern California, where she took a course in psychology. On December 30th, at her request, she was given a vocational and educational guidance test or analysis at the Veterans Guidance Centre at the University on 737 West Jefferson Boulevard. The analyst, James F. Craine, concluded: "(Subject) is nervous but has a good mental ability and possesses high interest patterns in common with successful artists, authors and social workers." While, in a separate analysis, he observed: "She is quite nervous and possibly has mental instability."

In 1947, the House of Un-American Activities Committee (HUAC) held hearings into the alleged influence of communism and pro-Soviet propaganda in the Motion Picture Industry. Though many movie stars and studio heads complied with the investigation, a small group of mostly screenwriters refused to testify and were convicted of contempt. As a result, they were blacklisted by the movie industry. This hollow victory emboldened the committee to widen its net and cast its eye over government employees, especially those entrusted with security clearances. Penalties were stiff, so when information came to light regarding Jack's alleged association with communist sympathisers at the Caltech campus dating back to the late 1930s, his employment at North American Aviation was suspended, and he was brought in for some routine questioning by federal agents.

In truth, Jack had attended some meetings there, and he'd also subscribed to *The People's Daily World*, the Communist Party's West Coast daily newspaper, his interest growing out of a shared alarm at the rise of Fascism across Europe, and the belief that the Soviets offered the only adequate bulwark against it. There was also a certain cachet at the time for men of means, like Jack, to sympathize with the working man's struggle and a general and daresay willful naiveté as to what was really happening under the Stalinist regime.

When Jack was initially questioned by the Feds, about his involvement with leftist individuals, he explained how he ultimately rejected the communist message and severed all connections with the group. Jack's membership in the "Church of Thelema" was also looked into at that time, to discover if the "religious cult who broadly hinted at free love," as investigators described it, was a hotbed of subversive activity. From their research, federal investigators dug up some old records and police complaints regarding some of the rum behaviour at the Fleming mansion,[8] but Jack asserted that his group was just a fraternal organization, dedicated to brotherhood, freedom and liberty of the individual, who were anti-communist and anti-fascist and totally behind the war effort. No action was taken following that original investigation, and Jack presently informed the federal agents that he was no longer part of that religious group, though he remained an individualist. The authorities eventually accepted Jack's testimony and, six months later, in March 1949, The Industrial Employment Board cleared him, overruling his suspension and reinstating his security clearance.

To Jack, the fearmongering and paranoia of the political witch-hunt were symptomatic of the authoritarianism inherent in the Judeo-Christian values that underpinned the whole country. A belief system that upheld racism and the subjugation of women and persecuted free thought. It only reinforced his efforts to see the whole venal edifice brought to its knees. To that end, in the guise of his magical alias, Belarion Armilus al-Dajjal Antichrist, Jack pledged himself to the *Manifesto of the Antichrist*, a self-penned polemic that pitted him against the evil forces of the "Black Brotherhood," Crowley's rather darling term for the Christian Church.

In its written judgement, The Industrial Employment Board advised that Jack be rehired by North American Aviation, but instead of returning, he took a new job at Hughes Aircraft Company, working as a group leader in the research and development lab, in charge of propellants, propulsion and launching groups.

As if the jolt to his professional life hadn't been worrying enough, cracks were beginning to appear in Jack and Cameron's marriage. Before they wed, Jack had insisted on an open marriage, but there were times when he didn't know where Cameron was or who she was with, or even when she was coming home again. Furthermore, work was taking him away for extended periods of time. As a consequence, after barely three years of marriage, the couple began contemplating divorce.

Conversely, the further they drifted apart as lovers, the closer they were coming together as a magical partnership. When Cameron became bedevilled by bouts of catalepsy – a mild form of epilepsy characterised by muscular rigidity and loss of bodily control, often brought on by extreme stress and emotional shock – Jack wondered if it was a side effect of the surreptitious magical workings he had performed with her, and suggested she use the trance-like states to go out on the astral plane. He introduced her to the writings of Sylvan Muldoon, a fellow sufferer, who catalogued his own spontaneous out-of-body experiences in his book *The Projection of the Astral Body*. To aid such journeys and alleviate her symptoms, Cameron became a habitual user of hashish, a drug known for its mental stimulation and endorsed by prophets and poets alike, from Madame Blavatsky to Baudelaire. Her consumption of the drug became so rife that Jack's ex-wife, Helen, began to blame her munchies-inducing usage for contributing to Jack's middle-aged spread.

Though she remained unconvinced by Crowley's philosophy and had not consciously fulfilled her role as her husband's Scarlet Woman – Crowley's appellation for a priestess of sex magick – Jack was gradually bringing Cameron around to his magical way of thinking. With work commitments taking him away to New York, Washington, D.C. and Alabama until the summer of 1950, he was forced to carry out Cameron's education as a correspondence course, and between October 1949 and February 1950, he wrote a series of letters guiding her through the occult arts.

Nurturing his spouse's interest in tarot cards, Jack taught how their purpose was not to facilitate clairvoyance but to help illuminate the path of the metaphysical journey on the Kabbalistic Tree of Life, an ancient Jewish mystical system, consisting of ten sephirot or principles, each one embodying a quality that makes up the spiritual body of God. The practitioner aims to bring about the sexual union between both the male and female aspects of God, through sacred deeds and ritualistic actions: to actualize God, so that it may rain its grace upon the adept and the world.

Like any good teacher, Jack supplied his wife with a recommended reading list. Alongside works by Crowley, it included Sir James George Frazer's *The Golden Bough*, widely held as a cornerstone in the study of religion and magic. *The King and the Corpse* by the Indologist Heinrich Zimmer and *The Hero with a Thousand Faces* penned by Zimmer's former student, the mythologist Joseph Campbell, a work Jack praised for simplifying Jung's concept of the hero. For Jack, simplicity was the key to winning the war of spiritual ideas. He fretted that magick was presently mired in too much claptrap in the way it was presented. He drew parallels with Gnosticism, whose spiritual truths proved too complex for the peasant mind to grasp and, as a result, lost ground to the far more comprehensible story of Christianity. Most importantly, Jack began to shed some light on the Babalon Working, feeding Cameron information on a piecemeal basis. Though much of it remained shrouded in mystery, containing secrets he claimed he could never impart, he described Babalon's coming in wholly Crowleyan terms as a spiritual Armageddon that would result in the destruction of the monotheistic Gods.

Claiming his magical invocation with Hubbard had succeeded, Jack suggested Babalon was already nesting somewhere on Earth, in a human host, and would manifest in time to unleash her prophecy. A sense of triumph and tragedy seemed inextricably bound up in the tenor of Jack's words regarding the Babalon Working. Having explained how the Enochian rituals were used to woo the Goddess Babalon, Jack warned that such rites were fraught with danger and, as proof, mentioned how he had recently suffered some vicious astral attacks relating to them. To underline his point, he cited Crowley and a roll call of his votaries, who had all trodden the perilous path that he, himself, was now on, and had either died recently or seen a serious deterioration in their physical condition.

In the event that he was next in line, Jack passed the Babalon baton on to his wife, his only hope in the event of his demise. Arming her with the requisite rituals and magical techniques, Jack made it clear that Babalon was the Great Work that linked them together. The prophecy came with an ominous caveat, however. As if struck by an awful premonition of a calamity to come, Jack feared that, if his magick work was mishandled, it could spell disaster for both of them. Having projected a seven-year incubation before Babalon broke free and made her presence in the world felt, Jack anticipated that on the day of her manifestation, he would be "blown away" by his accomplishment, a choice of words destined to take on an eerie significance.

By tapping into Crowley's spiritual current, Jack's magical invocation anticipated the revolutionary zeitgeist gestating just around the corner. Rock 'n' roll was all revved up and ready to be unleashed on the world, its wild, unbridled spirit, ripping asunder sexual, racial and religious barriers, in an era bestrode by a pantheon of new pagan archetypes. Marilyn Monroe, an Aphrodite for the atomic age. James Dean, a Luciferian angel rebelling against the father figure. And, at its centre, the Dionysian Elvis Presley, whose ecstatic mix of gospel music and the diabolic blues transformed him into a groin-thrusting embodiment of sacred sexuality, feared by the Bible Belt as the Devil incarnate. The second half of the 20th century was about to be rocked by a Babalonian earthquake but, tragically, Jack would not live to see that vision realised.

Jack Parsons mansion and headquarters for the Agape Lodge captured on April 3rd, 1946. Despite what the writing says, Jack actually purchased the property four years earlier. (Courtesy of the archives, Pasadena Museum of History.)

Jack with the Cameron clan. El Monte, 1947. From L to R: Mary Lou, Robert, Carrie, Hill, and Jim. (Courtesy of the Warburg Institute.)

While in Miami that Summer, Hubbard managed to drum up some publicity about himself via a puff piece for the *Miami Daily News* and he was pictured with Betty sailing in one of the schooners he purchased with Jack's money.

Jack and his "elemental" celebrate their nuptials. October 19th, 1946.
(Courtesy of the Warburg Institute.)

Aleister Crowley, Magus of the Machine Age, making the sign of Pan. (Courtesy of the Warburg Institute.)

Jack and Cameron with Delphine Haley and her children, George Haley Jr and Delphine Haley. 560 South Orange Grove, Pasadena. 1947. (Courtesy of George Haley Jr.)

"The Concrete Castle" on Redondo Beach where Jack lived while Cameron sojourned in Mexico.

Julie Macdonald, the bohemian socialite.
(Courtesy Alex Macdonald II.)

Julie Macdonald. (Courtesy Alex Macdonald II.)

Buddy Anderson at work.

4 - Occam's Razor

> "It is sometimes an appropriate response to reality to go insane." – Phillip K. Dick, *Valis*.

In its January 5th, 1948 edition, *Life* magazine featured a three-page spread on an artist colony frequented by American veterans in the picturesque town of San Miguel de Allende, Mexico. Buoyed by the success of their much-lauded muralists, Diego Rivera and David Siqueiros, Mexico had undergone a cultural renaissance in the arts and, using the G.I. Bill to fund their stay, San Miguel de Allende became a magnet for thousands of artistically inclined Americans, looking to escape the buttoned-down life back home for a more leisurely existence. With its colonial architecture, azure skies and warm, welcoming people, the town was an aesthetically pleasing setting to study art and, in May 1949, Cameron became one of the many who answered its siren call when she enrolled at the Universiteria de Bellas Artes. She went with Jack's blessing and his offer to financially set her up down there.

San Miguel's reputation as a fiesta town was well-founded, and Cameron threw herself into the hedonistic swing of things, reputedly enjoying fabulous flings with a Mexican bullfighter and a local nobleman. She also made some exciting new artsy friends, like the European émigré Renate Druks. Born in 1921, and raised in Vienna in a moneyed Jewish-Austrian family, Druks was a former student of the Vienna Art Academy for Women. One day, during the Nazi occupation, the teenage beauty was asked for directions by a German officer and agreed to take a ride in his car to show him the way. When her parents saw her getting out of the vehicle they were terrified, and immediately married her off to Dr. Harry Pincus Loomer, on the proviso he'd whisk her away to a safe new life in America.

In 1940, they settled in Brooklyn, and Druks took some classes at the Art Students League of New York. They then moved to Nebraska, where Loomer was stationed for the duration of the war. In 1943, they had a child together, Peter, and, after the war ended, they relocated to LA, but, by 1950, the marriage had fallen apart. With a sense of adventure equal to Cameron's, Druks took off for San Miguel, where she continued to hone her romantic realist painting style. Although there remained something of the grande dame about her, she was a committed, albeit well-off, bohemian who enjoyed the affections of her young, blonde, live-in lover Paul Mathison, an American who was then going by the European-sounding surname Andre to compliment Druks' continental background. Mathison possessed a puckish personality and loved to boast about his golden tail, which was partly true, in that he had an extension of the spine. Though he was gay with bisexual leanings, Druks was deeply in love with him and masochistically savoured the "agonia" of his distracted affections.

While Cameron was living the lush life across the border, Jack had vacated their Manhattan Beach house and moved into an apartment in a baroque folly situated on the seafront of Redondo Beach, known locally as "The Concrete Castle." According to George Frey, his friend's pad was adjacent to one belonging to a TWA pilot, whom Jack suspected was spying on him for Howard Hughes: "Jack couldn't speak freely in front of other people and he kept hazardous chemicals there, too."

With his wife away doing her own thing, Frey introduced Jack to a girlfriend of his, Gladys Gowan, a simple if highly-strung dame, whose main interest was dancing. "She was kinda difficult to deal with because she would cry and get emotional a lot," Frey recollects. "It was a short relationship, only a month or so." Regardless, Gowan lost no time in putting up curtains and building a nest for herself and her new man, even though it was clear that, for Jack, she was purely a plaything and he had no intention of getting serious with her. There was none of the mental stimulation he enjoyed with Cameron, but she was a pleasant distraction until his wife returned.

Cameron, meanwhile, had vacated San Miguel, following a murder that had taken place in the building where she was staying, and abandoned her art classes for another voyage to France. However, a new life studying art in Paris didn't pan out for a second time, and she shipped back to Mexico not long after. She eventually returned to the States in late spring of 1950, leaving Freya behind with friends. She complained how she'd run into financial difficulties while abroad, though it was noted that she arrived toting six or seven pieces of expensive leather luggage and a considerable quantity of pricey Mexican lace.

Back in California, she reunited with Jack, and one of the first things she did was compliment the alterations Gladys Gowan had made to his new digs. "In typical Candy fashion, she said, 'I like it! She gives the house a nice feminine touch,'" Frey recalls.[1] Cameron's cool belied a genuine anxiety over the possibility of losing Jack, and they both began to reconcile their marital differences. Soon all talk of divorce dissipated, and they put on a united front that September when Jack's actions brought them both under further scrutiny from the FBI.

The previous federal investigation in the wake of his suspension from North American Aviation had left its mark on Parsons. Though cleared, as a proud civil libertarian, the intolerable atmosphere and uncomfortable inquisition into his political and religious beliefs went against everything he stood for, and he began contemplating leaving the country to work abroad, just like his left-wing colleague, Frank Malina.

With that in mind, he contacted his old mentor, Theodore von Kármán, who put him in touch with Herbert T. Rosenfeld, president of the Southern California chapter of the American Technion Society, a company composed of technologists, scientists and businessmen who'd been designated by the Israeli government to recruit technical experts in the United States for the benefit of the newly established State of

Israel. At that time, Rosenfeld requested that Jack draw up a proposal for an Israeli chemical plant, which he duly submitted, but heard nothing back. In August of 1950, Jack made a second application for employment with Rosenfeld, who this time asked him to submit a proposal for a jet propulsion development programme. Considering Jack had once worked on a similar project for Hughes Aircraft, he borrowed some documents pertaining to jet propulsion motors and rocket propellants to help him calculate the costings. His papers were then given to Blanche Boyer, an acquaintance of Jack and Cameron's, to type up as a brochure, but when she saw the confidential nature of the files and learned the proposal was destined for a foreign power, she panicked, due to the current political climate, and contacted the Air Provost Marshall, who in turn alerted the FBI. When it was discovered that Jack had removed the restricted files from company premises without the proper authorisation, his employment at Hughes Aircraft was terminated and an investigation into charges of espionage was launched.

The following day, on the 27th of September, Jack went voluntarily to the FBI offices in Los Angeles to explain his actions. He admitted to making an honest mistake but stated that he'd been used to borrowing documents of a classified nature while working at JPL, and made it clear that he planned to use the data and prepared proposal with the approval of Uncle Sam.

An addendum to Jack's expanding FBI file included a profile of him and Cameron, provided by Boyer and her husband, who had known the couple for five years by then. It described them as "an odd and unusual pair in that they do not live by the commonly accepted code of married life and are both very fascinated by anything unusual or morbid, such as voodooism, cults, homosexuality and religious practices that are 'different.'" Subject seems very much in love with his wife but she is not at all affectionate and does not seem to return his affection. Both have had 'affairs' with other people, since their marriage, with the other's knowledge, and this apparently has been an accepted practice."

Cameron had long felt her husband was still tied to his mother's apron strings, and her independent spirit had, by Jack's own admission, helped wean him from the wet-nursing of women he was used to. Yet, focusing on the dynamic between the couple, the second part of Blanche Boyer's summary rather implausibly painted Cameron as the initiator of any wrongdoing. "(Cameron) is the dominating personality of the two and controls the activities and thinking of the subject to a very considerable degree. It is the opinion of Boyer, that if (Parsons) were to have been in any way wilfully involved in any activities of an international espionage nature, it would probably have to be at the instigation of his wife."

Boyer expanded on this, and revealed how Cameron confided in her that she was removed from her position working for the Joint Chiefs of Staff, and transferred to the Photo Lab, due to her association with a suspected German espionage agent, which cast a rather different light on her role in the honeytrap she claimed she was recruited for. When it subsequently emerged that it was Cameron who personally handed the sensitive documents over to Boyer for her to type up, she was dragged into the investigation too and questioned by special agents on December 2nd. Cameron admitted she was aware that her husband was preparing a proposal to be used as an application for a position in Israel, but added that she had not known the source of the material and had only been proofreading his proposal to check the spelling and grammar (as Jack was dyslexic).

The Boyers described how the Parsons had both been "extremely irritable, nervous and hard to get along with" the night those documents were typed up. The couple appear to have realised the seriousness of the situation, too, for Blanche Boyer relayed how Cameron had been visibly shaken and exclaimed, "Oh, my God," repeatedly when she informed her that the Feds had collected the material she typed. And then, when Cameron telephoned Jack to notify him about what had transpired, he decided not to leave work as it might appear suspicious.

All this notwithstanding, in a character sketch, Blanche Boyer described Cameron in a complimentary tone, as an "intelligent, quick-witted and vivacious person," and shared a preview of her future dreams: "She is an admitted liberal, having stated dissatisfaction with this country, and a desire to raise any children she may have in some other country, where the children will have the freedom to do as they like. In this regard, she has mentioned Mexico and Israel as two desirable countries."

Boyer further blabbed about Cameron's hectic sex life and repeated how Cameron had mentioned that during her European jaunt, she was propositioned by an American news reporter, but the name she gave her was not Arthur Krock's but somebody called "Bob." Whether this was, in fact, Krock and Cameron was deliberately concealing his name, or whether it was a different American newsman entirely remains a mystery, but, according to Boyer, this individual formed part of the retinue that joined Cameron on what was now believed to have been a group trip to England and Switzerland.

Someone Cameron hadn't physically rejected was George Tane (his surname spelt phonetically), another man, like George Frey, that she'd met while moseying on Manhattan Beach one day. They'd enjoyed a brief affair, with Jack's knowledge, but when the FBI learned he was not a US citizen, and constantly told stories about being a member of various underground organisations during the war, including one where he spoke at length about a trip he made into Russia "resulting in a fiction-like escape," they began to look into him. Tane was described by Boyer as being 33 years old, 5 ft 8 inches in height, with sandy coloured hair, a weather-beaten face and a Central European accent, though it was never clear what country he actually hailed from or what underground organisations he worked for. His features suggested he was a Swede,

Dane or North German, but the Feds' LA office could find no record for him in the telephone directory, registrar of voters, immigration and naturalisation service or police records, and his dalliance with Cameron summarily ended at Jack's insistence.[2]

The Feds then tracked down Cameron's wartime roommate Jean Selby, who told a similar story to the one shared by Blanche Boyer, which reamplified how Cameron admitted to her that she'd gotten into difficulty at the Joint Chiefs because of an affair she was having with a suspected German agent, though she never revealed his identity. When pressed, she described Cameron as "unstable, morbid, irresponsible, intelligent but easily influenced and fascinated by intrigue," and confirmed she'd been court-martialed on numerous occasions, though mostly for minor infractions. On a far more serious note, Selby alleged that Cameron did associate with a number of individuals believed to be pro-communist, although the only member of this group she could recall was Gene Kelly. A pattern was emerging. And the investigating agents recorded that during her time in Paris, Cameron associated with "a well-known communist editor of a Paris communist newspaper." His only identity, Lannellon, was spelled phonetically, but, despite following up on this, the agency could find nobody even approximating that name or job description.

With the pending investigation hanging over his head, and unable to secure employment in his chosen field of expertise, Jack was forced to look for alternative employment and, for a while, he was reduced to pumping gas for a living. According to George Frey, his friend was pragmatic about it: "Jack's whole feeling was, 'You do what you gotta do.'"

While Jack was eking out a living working menial jobs, L. Ron Hubbard's fortunes had taken a major upswing following the commercially successful publication of his book *Dianetics: The Modern*

Science of Mental Health. The book extolled a self-empowering process that aimed to "clear" an individual of debilitating "engrams" – a mental image of a traumatic memory stored in the reactive mind during a state of unconsciousness, whether in a past life, during childbirth or throughout adulthood – via an auditing process. Hubbard's bestseller proved to be a more easily digestible route to self-realisation than Thelema, and it brought its author the attention of the national media.

This was a bitter pill for Jack considering that many, including Cameron, believed Hubbard had cribbed some of his ideas for the book from what he'd learned during his time kibitzing with her husband, as well as genning up on the initiatory system of the O.T.O. and the Crowley titles in Jack's library. Cameron later recounted to friends how she once caught Hubbard going through the dumpster at the back of the house on 1003, trying to retrieve papers Jack had thrown out. Hubbard certainly didn't conceal the influence of Crowley on his thinking and even falsely claimed that he had known The Great Beast, even though the two men never met and Crowley regarded Hubbard as nothing more than a confidence trickster.

Still, *Dianetics* came at an opportune time. The war had created monsters, and Hubbard claimed that some of his early research focused on helping psychologically ravaged POWs and those dehumanised by conflict. For many suffering from neurosis in the post-war period, there was still a prevailing stigma about visiting a psychiatrist, so a self-help book provided a far more appealing option. Carving out a grey area between religion and psychiatry, *Dianetics* laid the foundations for the future Church of Scientology, whose perpetual pay for endless grades made a profit turning reality out of Hubbard's dream of starting his own religion "because that's where the money is." Jack at least found some consolation when Hubbard's bigamist marriage to Betty dissolved in acrimony, their karma doling out its own form of justice for him.

In March 1951, Jack and Cameron returned to Pasadena, moving into the coach house quarters of the old Cruickshank Estate on 1071 South Orange Grove, barely a block down from Jack's old place at 1003. While Cameron converted the loft above their living quarters into an art studio, Jack used the laundry room on the ground floor level as a makeshift laboratory, where he stored his chemicals and kiln, in violation of the local fire ordinance. In May, he set up his own business, Parsons Chemical Manufacturing Company, and began to take on work for the Bermite Powder Company, making explosives and pyrotechnics for the Hollywood film industry.

The return to Pasadena reconnected Jack and Cameron with an old neighbour, the sculptor Julie Macdonald, and a hip, new social scene that revolved around her. Macdonald was Pasadena's very own Auntie Mame, a free-spirited aesthete whose moneyed background afforded her the freedom to pursue her two great loves: jazz and art. Standing at six foot 2 inches, the statuesque socialite was a habitué of jazz clubs and well-known as the West Coast mistress of saxophonist Charlie 'Yardbird' Parker, whose improvisational brilliance helped break the sound barrier of jazz.[3]

Macdonald's house on Alpine Street was the King of Bebop's home away from home, and for her daughter, Judy, it was a charmed childhood: "Mom would take us to nightclubs on Sunset Boulevard and we wouldn't get home until two or three in the morning, so she'd write us notes for school. She had a very sculpted face, elegant body and demeanour, but when she got drunk and wasted it went into the back seat [laughs]. Bird was the first father figure in my life. He was a gas! He rehearsed in the garage and would invite people over. I'd come home from school and find Art Blakey, Ella Fitzgerald and Sarah Vaughan hanging out at the house."

Her mother had been introduced to Parker by Buddy Anderson, part of a group of African American jazzers who lived nearby at 958

Worcester Avenue: "We had a club called 'Emanon' – no name spelt backwards – and then we called ourselves the 'Po-bos,' which was ghetto for poor boys. That name originated from a jazz party we threw where the 15-year-old sax wunderkind Frank Morgan played his first paying gig. We were a totally underground group. We were avant-garde types that had to appear like regulars on the surface. The group included Buddy Collins from Kansas, my very best friend Robert Morgan, a carpenter, and Leroy Booth who I was very close to and shared several residences with. He was a professional student, always taking classes. We called him "Gramps" 'cause he was prematurely balding."

Anderson made beautiful jewellery out of ebony and ivory and was famous for his roach clips: "I only sold jewellery and clips to friends; you had to know me to buy some. I wouldn't sell to you if I didn't like you." These jazz mavens soon became regular guests at the parties thrown by Jack and Cameron at the coach house. "Julie took me to meet Jack and Cameron first," Anderson recalls, "they seemed like a normal couple but they had an aura about them. My first impression of Cameron was she was a very interesting person, very deep and somewhat possessed. I liked her very much. She was always nice and polite. Jack, I knew not as well, but he seemed an ordinary guy. He always dressed straight in a white shirt and tie. I remember he would mix a tub of punch with absinthe in it. It was so beautiful. It was the first psychedelic I ever had. Cameron took an interest in our little group. I could never figure the connection out. We were just devil-may-care."

For Cameron, the jazz scene bonded together people who felt a common disillusionment; individuals who were, as she later described it: "…alienated from the culture. The public, in general, was not as sophisticated about the Second World War as most of the people who had been in it, and coming back we didn't find much sympathy or interest. We kind of hung together as a group. Jazz afforded an opportunity to get to know and identify with the black man. I think that probably we were all interested in the underdog. We felt that we were the underdog also and, of course, the black musician was the obvious one."4

The irony of how black American soldiers, who had fought in a segregated army against white supremacists only to face racial discrimination back home, was not lost on everyone, and on his popular radio show the nation's pop idol, Frank Sinatra, articulated the thoughts of many: "Speaking of tolerance, neighbours, every one of us knows this: that God never meant for any man to fight for freedom and have any part of that freedom denied him by the country for which he fought."

When returning black G.I.'s were beaten up and in some cases even lynched by racist mobs for their military heroism, a huge gathering of black and white Americans met at the Lincoln Monument to protest and put an end to such evils. A stellar delegation led by Albert Einstein and Paul Robeson lobbied President Truman in person to enact an anti-lynching bill, only to be rebuffed by the Commander-in-Chief, who feared a political backlash from powerful Dixiecrat senators.

Such as it was, despite the popularity of swing bands with a wartime audience, the déclassé status of blacks prevailed. The racist reaction by some in the community towards the host of musical luminaries that turned up at Julie Macdonald's house, for example, proved that Pasadena's polite veneer really was only skin deep. "The neighbours weren't pleased with having all these black people around," Judy Macdonald recounts, ruefully, "and I couldn't have girlfriends over 'cause their parents didn't want them around niggers."5

With Julie Macdonald at her side, Cameron began frequenting the jazz clubs on Central Avenue, where she caught sets by the trumpeter Wardell Gray and became friendly with Percy Heath, soon-to-be bassist with The Modern Jazz Quartet. She also attended poetry readings given by Robinson Jeffers and the jazz poet Kenneth Patchen, whose novel, *The Journal of Albion Moonlight*, she found especially praiseworthy.

Another noteworthy jazz fiend playing a key part in that scene was the 25-year-old, zoot-suited artist Wallace Berman, who had designed the cover of Dial Records' *Bebop Jazz*, a compilation album featuring the debut recording of his hero, Charlie Parker. Through Macdonald, Berman met John and Patti Carruthers, popular figures on the L.A. art gallery scene, who subsequently introduced them to Jack and Cameron. "I was like this guy that pulled groups together and would introduce people from Los Angeles into the Pasadena scene," John Carruthers reminisces. "When I first met Jack and Cameron I thought, these are some interesting people, I'd really like to know them. They were dynamic! They were part of a group of people that Julie Macdonald called 'The Left Bank of Pasadena.'"

Berman was one of the lucky souls the Carruthers brought over to sample this swinging Pasadena scene, and he arrived accompanied by his gaminesque girlfriend Shirley Morand, a young woman destined to become his wife and muse. "I met Cameron and Jack in 1951, a year before Wallace and I married," Shirley Berman recounts. "The Carruthers took us to a Sunday afternoon party at the coach house that was mostly JPL people and artists. It was a very strange combination; all these crazy, strange, young scientists. There was lots of jazz music and people talking and drinking a lot of wine. It was beautiful. Jack was movie star handsome, just gorgeous, and such an interesting man. He and Cameron had one of those relationships where one would start talking and the other would finish their sentences. He would sort of appear, like a vision in a doorway, and then everything would quiet, she went quiet, that kinda thing. They were just lovely. He told us when he met Cameron he knew instantly that she was his mate."

John Carruthers was one of many who couldn't help but pick up on the sexual aura the charismatic couple exuded: "Jack was this laid-back guy whereas Cameron was more flamboyant, though not a particularly lovey-dovey person. She was very male that way, with an angular face and a voluptuous body, gorgeous breasts. They were both bisexual so, for Jack, Cameron was part of what he wanted to be."

During their first visit, Wallace Berman presented Cameron with a copy of *Steppenwolf* by Hermann Hesse, a novel in which a suicidalist seeks salvation, firstly through the pleasurable indulgence of sex and drugs, then by purging his neuroses in a hallucinatory magic theatre of his minds own making. This metaphysical journey of self-discovery was a recurrent theme in Hesse's work, and his writings kept Cameron captivated. In return, Cameron showed the Bermans some of her artwork up in her studio, including fashion illustrations she'd contributed to local department stores. "She admitted to it almost as a secret," Shirley Berman recollects. "She was not proud of doing it. She just did it for the money once and a while." Cameron also told Shirley about the art classes she'd been taking at UCLA. "Cameron knew a couple of people that my husband knew, artists like Zorthian, who had a hillside ranch in Altadena with this great, big swimming pool."

Jirayr Zorthian was an eccentric, Armenian American artist, renowned for his public murals and erotic paintings, and for his love of throwing wild parties at his 45-acre spread.[6] Cameron visited the residence with Jack, and separately on her own when the diminutive artist was away and Julie Macdonald was house-sitting for him, and several of her pictures ended up hanging on his walls. One particular party at the Zorthian ranch became a part of local legend. The artist had invited Charlie Parker to provide the evening's entertainment and, during his spot, the saxophonist stripped off and continued playing in the nude. "Almost everyone followed suit, except this guy from Africa who was appalled and insulted that people in a civilised country like America would do such a thing," recalls Buddy Anderson. "He said he'd come to this country to get away from behaviour like that." Anderson doubts Jack and Cameron were present that infamous night, though Bird did come and jam at their coach house on another occasion. One can imagine what Pasadena society thought of it all. "I've always been suspicious of Pasadena society," Shirley Berman muses. "My sister grew up in Pasadena, so I have a different kind of view. I think they're all loons! They're all freaks! Free love reached Pasadena first before it came to LA."

One conscientious practitioner of free love was Jo Anne Price, who worked as an artist model at the Pasadena Institute of Art and sat for various artists like Julie Macdonald and Zorthian. Price's very sexual air and zaftig figure got many hot under the collar and she quickly became Jack and Cameron's bedmate. "Jo Anne Price was beautiful and a total nymphomaniac," Buddy Anderson recollects fondly. "She weighed 205 pounds but had a perfectly proportioned figure." Anderson first connected with Price at one of Zorthian's parties, and she was soon spending a great deal of time over at the Emanon's hangout. "Nobody could last with her. It was over in seconds. That's the way she was. If she met a guy and they looked good to her, she'd go for it. She was a classic little cherub."

Another desirable girl sampling the delights of the coach house was Joan Whitney, a Junoesque blonde who, along with her va-va-voom gal pal, Mamie Van Doren, harboured dreams of breaking into Hollywood. Whitney's entrée also came courtesy of John Carruthers and, after meeting Jack only a couple of times, the starlet found she had a strange rapport with him. "Jack was such a knowledgeable person, and it was almost like you knew someone and you didn't say anything because he knew what I was thinking and I knew what he was thinking. It was very, very strange."

George Frey often made trips over for Jack and Cameron's Friday night soirées, attended by the likes of Renate Druks and Paul Mathison, who'd moved back to California from San Miguel to set up home in Malibu. "Very interesting people would show up," Frey recounts. "Cameron and Jack never provided refreshments. Everyone attending was expected to bring their own favourite beverages like wine, beer, or thermos containers of hot coffee or tea. The thought was that, because tastes were so diverse, guests would never be disappointed if they brought their own. We'd sit on benches around this large redwood table, which could accommodate approximately sixteen guests, and the room was lit by a series of black candles placed lengthwise down the centre of the table. Jack and Cameron's numerous friends never seemed to run out of fascinating stories and, when new guests would arrive, there would usually be an earlier guest recounting an interesting past experience. It was understood by everyone that the speaker should ignore any newcomers and not be interrupted. So any new arrivals would quietly seat themselves and place any refreshment they may have brought with them on the table. Then, when the current speaker had completed his story, Jack or Cameron would introduce the new arrival to any other guests they might not know." Gazing down on the guests from the wall was Cameron's life-sized oil portrait of Joan of Arc, brandishing her battle standard in one hand and a bloody lance in the other.[7]

Thirteen months after the investigation into espionage was launched against him, the case against Jack was finally dropped and it was decided that no further action be brought due to a lack of sufficient evidence. The offending documents were deemed innocuous and the ruling vindicated Jack's testimony, that he had not intended to use any of the information to injure the U.S. or advantage any other nation.

For a few golden months, peace of mind was restored; however, the New Year brought fresh bad tidings when The Industrial Employment Review Board revoked Jack's security clearance once and for all, stating that, in light of the recent investigation, he "did not possess the integrity or discretion and responsibility essential to the security of classified military information." This, to all intents and purposes, put an end to Jack continuing his career in the defense and aeronautics industry in America and made the lure of working abroad all the more crucial.

In February 1952, Cameron took Jack and their neighbour, Phillip Gronquist, on a round-trip to San Miguel de Allende, to expose them to the marvels of the town and to scout a temporary new home there. It worked wonders because as soon as they got back to California, Jack and Cameron began making plans to return to Mexico again that summer. In early June, Jack signed the lease of the coach house over to Sal(vatore) Ganci and his partner Martin Foshaug, two young arty friends Cameron had previously met in San Miguel de Allende, who were now working at the Pasadena Playhouse. One of the first things the new owners did was to offer the ground floor room next to Jack's laboratory to Jo Anne Price. And inspired by the former leaseholders, Foshaug painted a red devil's head on the wall above Price's bed, with his mouth hanging open, which made her pink chenille bedsheet look as if Old Nick's long tongue was poking out.

In the meantime, Jack and Cameron moved in with his mother, Ruth Parsons, who was house-sitting a nearby property at 424 Arroyo Terrace for elderly friends who were vacationing in Europe. They were scheduled to leave on the 17th of June, and the night before they left Jack met with George Frey in Exposition Park where he spoke about the impending trip: "Jack wanted to visit the Inquisition prison there, which was said to be haunted. He wanted to shake up the ghosts."

As far as Cameron was concerned, the idea was to have some R&R in Mexico before travelling on to Israel, where Jack could pursue new job opportunities. But their departure plans were pushed back the next day when Jack received a last-minute order from the Special Effects Corporation to provide an explosive for a forthcoming motion picture. Jack figured that, if he hurried, he could get the job done while Cameron was out shopping for provisions, and they could still get away in time.

At around 4:30 pm, Jo Anne Price looked in on Jack and saw him busy mixing chemicals. A half-hour later, Sal Ganci dropped by and chatted with him briefly, while Jack waited for his concoction to heat up in the kiln. Parting, Ganci joked: "For God's sake, Jack, don't blow us up!" Jack chuckled and told him not to worry.[8] Then, at approximately 5:08 pm, the fulminate of mercury that Jack was mixing in a coffee tin slipped out of his right hand. Instinctively, he reached down to catch the incendiary mixture, but it eluded his grasp and exploded as it hit the floor, ripping off his outstretched arm. With a deafening boom that was heard all over Pasadena, the explosion ignited the rest of the chemicals in the lab and set off a secondary blast. Upstairs in his room, Sal Ganci was thrown into the air by the shock waves. Despite being discombobulated, he knew exactly what had happened. Pulling himself together, he staggered downstairs to investigate. A ghastly scene awaited him.

What used to be Jack's laboratory was now a blown-out shell, enveloped in an acrid air of chemical fumes. Gingerly, Ganci ventured in, searching for Jack, who was not visible at first. Skirting the gaping hole in the middle of the debris-littered floor, he found him lying half-hidden beneath a large, upturned washtub. Lifting the tub, he reeled from the gruesome sight of his friend's burnt and mutilated body. Jack's right forearm was missing, and the skin on the right side of his face was torn off, exposing his jawbone and teeth. Mercifully, he was semi-conscious but making a godawful groaning sound, unable to speak due to his facial injuries. Ganci managed to prop him up, aided by his partner's mother, while Martin Foshaug called the emergency services.

Ganci's first thought was to notify Cameron, so he drove to Arroyo Terrace only to find Ruth home alone. At first, he played down the severity of Jack's injuries, not wanting to cause his mother too much shock but, after a while, he admitted her son's condition was extremely serious and that he may not live. At the news of this, Ruth sunk in her chair and began sobbing. Ganci did his best to comfort her, but then left promising to send back word when he knew more. By the time he arrived back at the coach house, an ambulance had already spirited Jack away to the Huntingdon Memorial Hospital where, at 5:45 pm, he was pronounced dead. When Cameron pulled up at the house she scrambled to make sense of what she was being told. Meanwhile, her brother Robert arrived at Arroyo Terrace fresh from the hospital and broke the bad news to Ruth that Jack was dead.

Hearing this, Ruth became hysterical and blurted, "I'm going to kill myself. I can't take this!" Helen Rowan, her invalided housemate, was called in to look after her, and Ruth's physician sent a bottle of Nembutal over to the house to sedate her. Rowan also telephoned a neighbour, Mrs. Nadia Kibort, to aid her, but while Kibort was in the kitchen, Ruth swallowed 40-45 pills, and the immobile Rowan could only look on helplessly as the tablets took effect and Ruth slipped into unconsciousness. She died at approximately 9:06 pm, less than four hours after her son.

Shortly afterwards, George Frey received an urgent phone call from Cameron, who was at her parent's house, relaying the dreadful news that Jack was dead. Still trying to take it all in, she asked him to come over. "She said her parents didn't understand and she needed to visit Jack's mother," he recollects. Driving as fast as he could, Frey arrived at the house and met the purchaser who had placed the order for the explosives Jack had been mixing. Like everyone else, the man was shaken by the news. "He expressed shock and sorrow, but Candy was not impressed, and told me the man was only interested in avoiding being legally implicated in Jack's death."

The two of them then headed over to Arroyo Terrace. "We went in and saw Ruth sitting in her chair, appearing to be relaxed and asleep. I didn't realize at first, but Cameron had a whole bag of pot on her, which she took into the bedroom and hid under the bed for safekeeping.

A short time later a policeman came into the bedroom and asked how old the deceased was. I told him 38, thinking he was referring to Jack, and he said, 'No, she must be older than that,' and then we knew Ruth must have committed suicide. Cameron simply remarked that she wasn't surprised."

Cameron's stoic reaction was partly explained by what she regarded as a more pressing matter at hand: how to get her 3lb bag of pot out of the house without the cops noticing? "The tricky thing was that when Ruth died Cameron and I were no longer lawful inhabitants, and when the police came to investigate Ruth's suicide, they assumed responsibility for the house and its furnishings," Frey recounts. "They told Cameron and I that we would have to vacate the house with our personal belongings before they could leave and secure the premises, and they wanted to inspect everything we removed. Jack and Cameron's suitcases were in the hallway ready to be loaded into the car for the trip. Now Cameron didn't have any concern with the police inspecting her clothing and toiletries, but she didn't know how to get the bag of pot out. The answer she came up with was clever. She telephoned Julie Macdonald and asked her to come by as soon as possible, bringing with her the largest purse she had. Julie possessed several and, when she arrived, she put Cameron's stash in her purse and departed without incident."

Cameron was snapped by news photographers as she left the house shortly afterwards, looking ashen-faced but composed, and before they parted company that evening, Frey overheard his newly widowed friend sigh, "Who will take care of me now? I don't know how to make a living." Having been told of the appalling injuries he'd sustained, Cameron understandably declined to view her husband's body at the hospital, and there was a closed casket at the funeral home. Mourners were told to remember Jack the way he was. "Nobody officially identified Jack's body," George Frey explains. "I'm sure it was him, but later some of Jack's devotees pondered if it was another person."

Cameron spent the night in Laguna Beach, at the home of Netta and Dorie Worthington, artist friends she'd met in San Miguel de Allende. The next day, in best film noir tradition, she split town and headed for the Mexican border, driven by her brother Robert. The getaway gave her the chance to flee any uncomfortable questions and the lurid newspaper headlines, such as 'Slain Scientist Priest in Black Magic Cult' and 'Sex Madness Cult of Pasadena Scientist Revealed.' The latter story appeared in the *Mirror* newspaper, whose front page was dominated by a press photo of Jack and an exotic image of a turbaned Crowley in Eastern garb, smoking a meerschaum pipe. One rag even plastered a macabre, Weegee-style photograph of Ruth Parsons, slumped dead in her chair on its front page, while her dog sat loyally at her feet, staring forlornly at the camera.

The *Pasadena Independent* dredged up Jack's past reputation as a cult leader who "dabbled in intellectual necromancy," and claimed Ruth had been drinking heavily and threatened to end it all by using a gun stashed upstairs, but both these assertions appear extremely unlikely. As does the *Daily News* contention that Cameron herself dug through the debris to retrieve Jack's body. Cameron was quoted by various newspapers: in one she claimed their plan to travel to Mexico was purely "a pleasure trip," whilst other articles reported Jack was preparing to travel there with the intention of setting up a fireworks or explosives factory. Weirdly, both Cameron and her brother Robert were quoted as saying that, while he was there, Jack "planned to conduct secret experiments." Why they would mention Jack was doing *anything* secretly remains puzzling, but this seems to have been a convenient cover story. Judging by the large amount of luggage that was waiting in the hallway at Arroyo Terrace, together with Cameron's paints and canvases and Jack's fencing and archery equipment in the car's trailer, it was plain the couple were going away for a long time and not planning on coming back anytime soon.

Before she split, Cameron asked George Frey to take care of Jack's cremation: "The mortician asked if I wanted to bury Jack's mother too. He said social security would take care of half the bill, which was $300, and said if I could find someone to pay the rest for her funeral, he'd do Jack's cremation for free. So I gave him the name of Ruth's sister. Jack's ashes were placed in a bronze jar and I paid $5 to store them. Cameron eventually picked them up on her return." Cameron also left Jack's special black box, containing his magical manuscripts and paraphernalia in Frey's charge: "The box had a hinged wooden lid and a note on top of it that said: 'Don't go further or you'll lose your life,' and I gashed my thumb on the hinge when I opened it. I took it seriously and closed it up after that. I still have the scar today."

In Mexico, Cameron retreated to her beloved San Miguel de Allende, where she struggled to come to terms with what had just happened. In town, she met an English couple with artistic aspirations, Nancie and Bill Patterson. Bill painted and Nancie wrote poetry for fun, and both were disciples of the White Eagle Lodge, a spiritualist temple based in England. It was there, barely a week after her Jack's death, that Cameron conducted her first blood ritual, in a desperate attempt to reach her husband on the other side.

To shock her consciousness out of reality and into an altered state, Cameron took the drastic measure of slashing her wrist with a knife, only to find she'd, fortunately, struck it using the blunt edge, which left a cut but no gashing wound. While she was conducting Crowley's *Bornless Ritual*, partnered by Mrs. Patterson, Cameron was given a new magical identity, Hilarion, the sobriquet of one of Crowley's former scarlet women, often invoked in the pages of his aforementioned astral travelogue *The Vision and the Voice*. Jack had already purloined the name and used it as an alias for Babalon in his treatise *Manifesto of the Antichrist*, deeming it the feminine counterpart to his own magical moniker, Belarion. A week later, Cameron read about the fleet of UFOs that were recently sighted, hovering over the Capitol Building in Washington, D.C., and took it as a cosmic response to her husband's passing.

In his 1917 book, *Mourning and Melancholia*, Dr. Sigmund Freud wrote: "The act of grieving involves grave departures from the normal attitude to life," and diagnosed grief as "a pathological condition with the power to derange the mind." He could have been using Cameron as a case study. Back in California, after two months away, Cameron's heartache reached critical mass and she made another unsuccessful attempt at suicide in an abandoned house in Altadena. Once she recovered, she moved back into the coach house along with Bobo Jackson, a girlfriend of Foshaug and Ganci. In her room, Cameron immediately set up an altar with black candles. "She started dabbling in witchcraft and stuff like that," Ganci recollects.[9] At first, he wrote most of it off as "black magic posturing. Cameron had these weird fantasies as part of her role-playing mysticism. They made for conversation and amusement. She enjoyed her witch pretence. I always felt it was her attention-getting device." Over time, however, Cameron's occult practices became more serious and convincing, to the point where even Ganci concedes: "Cameron played at being a witch and exotic, and she finally became what she thought she was."

The catalyst for Cameron's conversion were the personal papers she discovered in Jack's black box. Reading them through, together with copies of her husband's letters, Cameron learned about the unwitting but pivotal role she played in the Babalon Working, during their first rampant period together. It appeared that Jack had performed some acts of magical gymnastics in his head, synced to the sexual aerobics in bed.

In a letter he wrote to Crowley at the time of the Babalon rituals, Jack described working with the girl who had answered his elemental summons but could not fully bring himself to explicitly name Babalon as the focus of his invocation, alluding only that he was in direct touch with the beautiful and holy one mentioned in *The Book of the Law*. In retrospect, it seems crazy that Jack would be so coy with Crowley, of all people, about the nature of his magical forays, but this was one of many ambiguous aspects of the Babalon Working, whose significance and purpose was open to a variety of interpretations. Jack's own writings on the subject often contradicted themselves and wavered from one explanation to another, suggesting he was still trying to figure it all out himself.

On one straightforward level, the ritual can be seen as a purely symbolic and metaphysical exploration which foretold the changing times and attempted to harness divine powers to awaken the libidinous forces that lay repressed in so many people. But some, including members of the Agape Lodge's inner circle, believed the invocation was meant to result in an actual physical birthing. That Jack was trying to create a moonchild, a magical offspring imbued with Babalon's lascivious spirit, that had been enticed down from the astral plane and incubated in Cameron's womb.

Jack's writings certainly encouraged this impression. In the selfsame letter to Crowley, he speaks in foetal terms, depicting himself as a guardian for an entity that is destined to be born into the world in nine months' time. He then goes on to explain that any breach of secrecy, or premature discussion of the birth cum revelation, might result in an abortion. But the idea that the Babalon Working was meant to result in an actual physical birthing seems highly doubtful, not to say improbable. Jack was adamant with both his wives that there would be no children involved in their marriages, *whatever* their origin. He wanted his family history to end with him. In fact, on more than one occasion, when a female lodge member fell pregnant by him, ergot, the medieval witches' root, was administered to help induce an abortion or, if that didn't work, a "friendly" local physician, Dr. Zachary Taylor Malaby, was called to perform the illegal procedure.

Crowley, at that time, remained flummoxed by what he was hearing and fumed to Karl Germer: "Apparently Parsons or Hubbard or somebody is producing a moonchild. I get fairly frantic when I contemplate the idiocy of these goats!"[10] He believed Jack was dabbling in magical matters without the proper training, and running before he could walk in his mad "lust for results." Thinking outside the box had reaped such high rewards in Jack's rocket fuel research and yet, ironically, it was the very thing that was bringing about such confusing and spurious results in his magical experimentation.[11]

But there is yet another strand to the Babalon Working, and it was one that Cameron personally subscribed to – that *she* was the chosen vehicle for Babalon's manifestation. She saw proof of this in another letter Jack wrote to Crowley, in which he anticipated Babalon coming to him bearing a secret sign. Now it turned out that during those first early weeks they spent together, Cameron spotted a silver, cigar-shaped UFO moving soundlessly in the sky as she sat out in the back garden of 1003.[12] When she mentioned the sighting to Jack, later that day, he remained silent on the subject, and it was never raised again. Now, sifting through his papers, Cameron discovered that he had indeed marked the momentous sighting, by drawing a symbol of the UFO – a circle with a trine set within it – in the marginalia. To her mind, this was the sign he'd been waiting for. Furthermore, if, as Jack liked to believe, Cameron was indeed an elemental, then according to elemental lore, it would theoretically mean that Cameron did not possess a soul when they first met. So who better than she to be ensouled with the spirit of Babalon?

When something out of the ordinary happens, people often seek and require extraordinary answers to explain it, and despite Jack's injuries being consistent with the coroner's report, Cameron wasn't the only one who queried the official version of events surrounding his death. Wilfred and Helen Smith, for instance, believed Jack had, on a subliminal level, committed suicide – not as a conscious act, but due to his inattention. Their view was that after all the heartbreak and disappointments he'd endured, Jack just didn't care anymore and wanted to avoid any further screw-ups and mitigate his karma. There was obviously a great deal of bias and bitterness behind a lot of this thinking, though, especially on Helen's part. She never really approved of Jack's second wife and, to cap it all, felt that her ex-husband's death had at least saved him from an even worse fate: a life spent with Cameron.

But, weighing it up, there's much to discount the theory that Jack committed suicide. His behaviour certainly did not suggest a man who had suicide on his mind. He'd actually come through many of the setbacks to his career and personal life; he'd reconciled with Cameron and, with new irons in the fire, the future looked bright. If the job in Israel panned out the way it promised, he would have become a man of substance again. Furthermore, during the desperate ambulance ride to the hospital, Jack reportedly murmured how he didn't want to die and that his work wasn't finished.

Renate Druks started spreading a fantastical story claiming Jack blew himself up while trying to create a homunculus! While some, including Cameron, were convinced he was murdered, with one particular suspect entering the frame. Back in 1938, during a trial that scandalised the city, Jack's expert testimony helped indict Captain Earl E. Kynette, head of the Special Intelligence Unit. Kynette was charged and convicted, along with two of his officers, of bombing the car of Harry J. Raymond, a private dick who'd been investigating alleged corruption between the LAPD and City Hall. Considering Kynette was paroled in the weeks prior to the explosion, suspicion fell on him as the mastermind who'd wreaked some overdue payback on Jack. During one of her astral projections at the time, Cameron pulled up the floorboards of Jack's lab and discovered a bottle of mercury planted there, which she pinned on Kynette, although one doubts her visualisation would have held up in a court of law. The scope of these conspiracy theories then widened to include the possible involvement of shadow government agencies. Jack's death would've proved convenient to those elements opposed to the establishment of the State of Israel, who could not conscience a one-man technology transfer like him falling into the laps of a country they did not support.

Yet, as the principle of Occam's razor states, based on what's known, the simplest, most straightforward explanation is always the most probable. As Jack's best buddy Ed Forman attested, Jack could be sloppy when it came to the preparation of chemicals. You don't have to look much further than his reckless and illegal storage of highly explosive materials to find an example of his cavalier attitude towards them, and even a great surgeon can sometimes leave an instrument inside a patient they have just operated on. The most plausible facts remain that, on a hot summer's day, in an oven-heated workspace, while rushing to get a job completed, and with his mind no doubt on the road trip ahead, Jack had a momentary lapse of concentration – most likely caused by a jarring or obtrusive thought – which resulted in a tin of explosive chemicals slipping from his sweaty hand with fatal consequences.

Bereft by the loss, Cameron continued to travel out on the astral plane, trying to make contact with her soulmate. She had a close shave during one flight, when a flaming figure came flying out at her, and she barely got back into her body in time. She later wondered if it was Jack trying to embrace her. One queasy repercussion from these astral projections was the sudden materialisation of maggots, which kept dropping from the ceiling onto the floor of her room with a soft plop. Maggots held a particular fear for Cameron, and she kept a vacuum cleaner by the door to hoover up the nasty little beasties. Perturbed by such psychic phenomenon, she consulted that astral authority Sylvan Muldoon, who told her she was caught in a confusion of astral planes and had brought an astral entity back from the future. With the experiences becoming increasingly disconcerting, Cameron refrained from any further astral excursions for the time being.

Instead, she vented her macabre side, repeating a joke about a man being sucked into a jet engine to anyone who would hear it. Perhaps the black humour was a coping mechanism, but in light of what had just happened to her husband, it seemed a strange subject for comedy. "Her sense of humour was bizarre," confirms Sal Ganci, who, up until then, had tolerated Cameron's squirrelly behaviour. But things took a far darker turn when she began threatening to put her dog Freya in the oven to asphyxiate her. "When Cameron said that to me I got extremely angry. I didn't want anything like that happening."[13]

By now, Cameron was barely functioning, and her grip on reality was unravelling. Personal letters suggest she may have been institutionalised during this period, and her fragile state of mind was all too clear to many of those around her. "It was a terrible shock when Jack died, and after there was quite a bit of talk by people who knew Cameron that maybe she needed to be institutionalised," Shirley Berman recalls. "She told me that she'd been having nightmares but she never went into what the hallucinations were."

As John Carruthers puts it: "Post-Jack it felt like it was a barely alive situation and losing him was a big thing for Cameron. Jack gave her life momentum. He was a solid post. He'd been her source for money and, as a person, she was too far-out to hold a job, so she lived a hand-to-mouth life. He was her centre – Cameron was his star. Now she was a single thing out in space."

It was probably a good idea that Cameron was forced out to live in a new environment. Having to walk past Jack's ruined laboratory every day was a constant reminder of her loss. So instead she recuperated at the homes of a string of friends, including Renate Druks, Netta and Dorie Worthington, and even Wilfred and Helen Smith who, though concerned, thought the poor girl had gone completely batty.

Cameron boarded at Julie Macdonald's too, and brought some of her artwork with her, which was a real eye-opener for Macdonald's daughter, Judy: "Cameron's paintings spooked me! The expressions on the faces and the eyes – I wouldn't want to have any of them. She wasn't a real kid-type person. She didn't know how to handle children, or how to interact with them. She could do it for 10-20 minutes and that was it. She'd say and do whatever she wanted. There was no governor on her mouth. She not only cursed but said what was on her mind. She was very opinionated; mom was too, but mom had humour. Cameron was witchy, and when she got into that mode I left 'cause it spooked me."

Moreover, Judy, and her brother, retain an even more unsettling memory relating to Cameron. As already mentioned, Julie Macdonald had known Jack and Cameron prior to their residency at the coach house. They had originally met when the sculptress was living in the Busch mansion, next door to them on Orange Grove, for a period in the late 1940s. There, she rented rooms for herself and her two young children. During that time, Judy Macdonald distinctly remembers: "There was a death of an infant at Jack's house. It died in a fire there. Cameron came running over to our house and she was a mess. It was never brought up again." At the present time, there are no further details about this incident.

After Cameron vacated Macdonald's home, the Po-bos welcomed her in, and there, just months after Jack's death, she began a romantic relationship with Leroy Booth. In a country still struggling to come to terms with even the *concept* of racial integration, this forbidden union broke what was then regarded as the ultimate sexual taboo on both sides of the racial divide. During her stay, housemate Buddy Anderson remembers an incident that made him step back and look at Cameron anew: "Cameron brought with her a small bird, a multicoloured finch, and she left the house one day and, as soon as she did, her bird fell down off its perch and lay dead in its cage. She was gone for several hours, and when she came back we told her the bird had died, and she got hysterical and had a fit, and she held the bird in her hand and stroked it gently with her finger, and within 30 minutes the bird was standing up again chirping."

If the high jinks at 1003 had brought attention from the authorities, it was nothing compared to the scrutiny placed on the house on Worcester Avenue. For one, Cameron's tenancy in a racially mixed residence violated the city's rooming house ordinance and, as a consequence, she and Booth kept their clothes in separate closets as a precaution. Secondly, as Buddy Anderson admits, "Cops were looking at me 'cause I had a lot to do with white chicks, and they assumed if blacks and whites were living together, drugs were involved."[14]

Such suspicions were borne out when the house was raided at the end of September, and Booth, Collins, Anderson and Jo Anne Price were arrested by the Pasadena Narcotics Squad. "The bust was big news in Pasadena," Anderson recalls. "It made the front page with a picture of Jo Anne and the headline '205lb Model in Den of Iniquity.' Another newspaper described how Price was discovered by the police "cowering in the nude," and reported, amusingly, how she claimed that she was only present at the house because she was "being instructed in jazz" by the three men. While a further article characterised her as "an apprentice priestess in a strange cult." Cameron managed to elude the bust, fortuitously, and charges were eventually dropped for Price, Buddy Collins and Buddy Anderson, who recounts how "Booth took the rap: 90 days incarceration for marijuana possession."[15]

That autumn, Cameron's mood worsened after it was announced that a hydrogen bomb test was scheduled to be carried out on November 1st at the Eniwetok Atoll in the South Pacific. Convinced that the California coast was going to crumble into the ocean from the aftershocks, she fled in distress to Catalina Island, with Jo Anne Price and Bobo Jackson, to wait the catastrophe out. When the test went off without incident, the trio returned home, but by now, Ganci and Foshaug were so alarmed at Cameron's mental deterioration, they would not allow her to move back in: "We refused to open the door. I said, 'Your stuff is downstairs in the driveway, pick it up, we don't want you here.' And that was the last we saw of Cameron for a few months."[16]

Jack, Cameron and their friend Georgia Blake in San Miguel de Allende, four months before Jack's death. February 1952. (Courtesy of the Warburg Institute.)

Front page of *Mirror* newspaper reporting Jack's death.

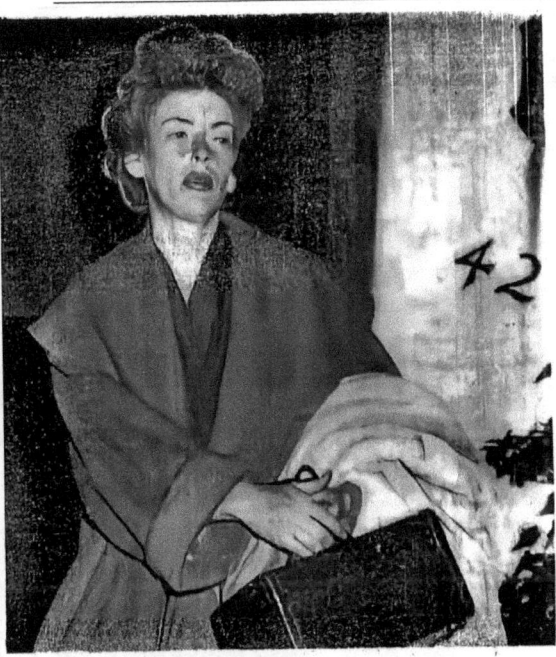

GRIEF-STRICKEN WIDOW
Her face clearly showing the grief of double family tragedy, Mrs. Marjorie Cameron Parsons, wife of blast victim, John W. Parsons, leaves home at 424 Arroyo terrace, Pasadena, where a short time earlier her mother-in-law, Mrs. Ruth Parsons, took own life.

Report continues. An ashen-faced Cameron is captured by press photographers.

Dead Scientist
'Black Magic' Cult Told

Behind the tragic explosion death of John W. Parsons, Pasadena rocket scientist, and the grief-inspired suicide of his mother, today was disclosed the strange story of how his brilliant mind wandered into mystic fields in unending search for a perfect way of life.

The 37-year-old jet propulsion expert, often an enigma to his friends, actually lived two lives, Pasadena police disclosed.

In one he probed deep into the scientific fields of speed and sound and stratosphere—

And in another he sought the cosmos which man has strived throughout the ages to attain; to weld science and philosophy and religion into a Utopian existence.

Old police files in Pasadena tell the story of how the quiet scientist, who died in the city-shaking explosion of his laboratory Tuesday night, lived his double life.

In 1942, Chief of Detectives Stanley Decker revealed, police received a letter from San Antonio, Texas. It was signed "A Real Soldier" and stated a "black magic" cult flourished at 1003 South Orange Grove avenue.

Detectives investigated and found the premises had been leased by Parsons and his wife, Marjorie. They were interviewed and frankly told of organizing a fraternal study group to discuss philosophy, religion, personal freedom and the mysteries of life and eternity."

There were, too, studies of the pseudo-psychologies, of fortune telling and seances.

Another news report on Jack's death. *Herald Express.* June 19th, 1952.

MYSTERY BLAST KILLS PASADENA JET SCIENTIST

Continued from Page 2

the ceiling under the upstairs living unit.

A heavy, double laundry tub was knocked over and Parsons is hurled to the floor under it. Still conscious, the scientist is taken to Huntington Memorial Hospital where he died thin an hour. Officers said he tempted unsuccessfully to tell them how the explosion occurred.

Mother Dazed by News

His wife, Mrs. Marjorie Cameron Parsons, 30, an artist, and brother, Robert E. Cameron, of 1254 N Raymond Ave., were present when Parsons died.

Cameron left immediately and broke the news to the elder Mrs. Parsons, who was staying at the home of friends at 424 Arroyo Terrace during their absence in Europe.

Mrs. Helen Rowan, an elderly companion who is crippled by arthritis, said Mrs. Parsons became hysterical after Cameron left.

"I'm going to kill myself! I can't stand it!" she said Mrs. Parsons wept.

Mrs. Rowan telephoned a doctor who had a bottle of sleeping tablets sent to the home. Another friend, Mrs. Nadia Kibort, of 320 Waverly Drive, arrived and Mrs. Parsons was given three of the tablets.

A short time later, while Mrs. Kibort was in the kitchen, Mrs. Rowan watched helplessly while Mrs. Parsons emptied the bottle of the 47 remaining tablets and swallowed them.

The two other women summoned a friend and nurse, Mrs. Nellie Smith, of 453 N Hudson Ave., who called Dr. J. R. Huntsman. When he arrived he found Mrs. Parsons dead.

The bodies of both Parsons and his mother were taken to Turner and Stevens Mortuary, Pasadena.

Investigators were mystified by the nature of Parsons' activity in the laboratory just before the explosion.

He and his wife were to leave at 10 a.m. today, towing a small trailer behind their car, for the trip to Mexico.

There was some speculation that Parsons, who was last employed by the Burmite Powder Co. in Saugus, was going on a secret assignment to conduct explosives experiments.

However, Mrs. Parsons insisted they were just going to Mexico for a rest. The trailer, packed and covered with a tarpaulin, contained only artist's supplies, archery equipment, fencing foils, a bed and a trunk.

A short time before the explosion Jo Anne Price, blond artist's model who lives in the converted carriage house next to the laboratory, saw Parsons at work.

Hurried Experiment

She said he told her he was conducting an experiment with some "very expensive" chemicals and was "in a hurry" to finish it.

Miss Price left, went up an outside stairway to the living quarters and then felt the blast rock the whole building.

Also upstairs were Martin Foshag, his mother, Mrs. Alta Foshag, and Sal Ganzi, all artists. They were uninjured as the floor, upset a refrigerator and broke a leg of a grand piano.

Police and Army ordnance experts from Ft. MacArthur found shattered bottles labeled "Explosives!" on the debris-littered floor of the laboratory.

They were searching the premises and also the Arroyo Terrace home today for any further stores of explosive materials which Parsons may have possessed.

His brother-in-law, Cameron, said he had been very close-mouthed about the nature of what he was going to do in Mexico. Cameron had the impression that it concerned Parsons' work with explosives.

Cameron pictured again leaving the house on Arroyo Terrace.

The Pasadena Independent described Jack as a cult leader who "dabbled in intellectual necromancy."

The macabre, Weegee-style photograph of Ruth Parsons slumped dead in her chair.

Ruth Parsons' invalid friend, Helen Rowan, who was unable to stop her suicide.

CRIPPLED FRIEND WATCHED HELPLESSLY
Crippled Mrs. Helen Rowan (right), who watched helplessly as Mrs. Ruth Parsons swallowed the deadly capsules, is aided from the house of death by a friend, Mrs. Nellie

The aftermath of Jack's makeshift laboratory.

Jack's mysterious black box.

5 - The Children

> "Every man and every woman is a star."
> – *Liber AL vel Legis* 1:3.

By December of 1952, Cameron was living in a ramshackle homestead at the end of Lambs Canyon Road, a former mining area on the outskirts of Beaumont, a sleepy hamlet 28 miles west of Palm Springs. It remains a mystery as to how she even found such a remote place. Most likely she was tipped off that the area contained a few abandoned properties in which she could live rent-free as a squatter. Having exhausted the hospitality of friends, at least she now had a place to call her own. Although she was forced to make do without electricity and running water, the locale afforded her the privacy and seclusion she was seeking, and its panoramic view of the night sky was ideal for sighting UFOs, which she now envisioned as the "war-engine" weaponry promised in the martial third chapter of *Liber AL vel Legis*.

Nestled in the shadows of the "beautiful mountain" range after which the nearby town was named, it was, on the surface, quite a comedown from the high-toned addresses of Manhattan Beach and Millionaires Row. Despite the meagre amenities, Cameron put her creative talents to good use and soon had the place spruced up and tastefully decorated. She lived alone at first, with just Freya and her pet bird to keep her company, but once friends tracked her down, they all came out to pay a visit, impressed by what they found.

"Cameron had a lot of Mexican things in her home," recalls Shirley Berman. "Beautiful, old wooden sculptures and carvings she'd got from an old church down there that had underground passageways. Of course, San Miguel was the silver capital of Mexico, and she had all these little silver boxes as decoration. She also had Mexican blankets in solid natural colours, reds and purples, but she used them as rugs instead of blankets. Her homes were always just gorgeous."

In the wake of Jack's death, Agape Lodge elder Jane Wolfe began to take a maternal interest in his young widow, and the two women commenced an illuminating correspondence. Writing to Wolfe that December, Cameron brought her up-to-date with what had been happening in her life since Jack's passing. In desperate need of some human warmth, and a confidante to share her inner turmoil, Cameron related how she'd been shunned as a madwoman and had spent the last six months living a wild, transient life, fraught with the perils her husband had once warned her of. In an attempt to make sense of what had come to pass, she shared her thoughts on the important magical ritual Jack embarked upon seven years earlier, describing it as the second instalment of the Babalonian force. The first was begun by Crowley, a man she now considered her spiritual father, who had bequeathed to her his greatest gift, Jack. Cameron contended that both Jack and Crowley died believing they'd failed in their magical missions, and believed she was the key to fulfilling them, and that her spiritual transformation into Babalon was close at hand.

The incarnation reminded her of a treasured poem she discovered when she was fifteen, Conrad Aiken's 'Tetelestai,' whose title hypnotised her and seemed to possess great importance.[1] The title was Greek, and its literal translation meant, "It is finished," a phrase most famously attributed to Jesus' last words on the cross. Aiken appropriated the term for his own meditation on life as viewed from death's door, and it now served as Cameron's own "Words of Triumph" as she became a living avatar on Earth.

The Argenteum Astrum, or Silver Star, was the magical teaching order Crowley conceived after leaving The Golden Dawn. Though independent of the O.T.O., *The Book of the Law* was still central to its creed, and its highest goal was the attainment of Knowledge and

Conversation of the Holy Guardian Angel, a discarnate projection of one's highest spiritual self. Initiates in the Silver Star were encouraged to work alone rather than in groups, aware only of those directly above and below them in the chain of instruction. In Cameron's case, this was Jane Wolfe, whom she both reported to and received guidance from on an informal basis. She also began to keep a record of her magical musings in a diary, a cathartic process that mirrored the redemptive qualities of her artwork, each reflecting a beauty and love that had hitherto eluded her.

From the very start, Cameron's artworks were the key to her attainment, to the point where they and her spiritual life became one and the same. For Crowley, who was a painter himself, the artist ranked above the magician on the totem pole of illuminism, and he considered poetry and art as precious tools for transmuting one's innermost psychic visions. To that end, Cameron's first undertaking was to illustrate *Songs for the Witch Woman*, a collection of poems Jack dedicated to her with the inscription: "In whom she is incarnate." Jack may have simply meant that the spirit of Babalon lay within his wife, as it did in all women, but, to Cameron, it provided further proof of her deification.

The title poem, 'Witch Woman,' underscored what an inspiring muse Cameron had been to her husband, and she repaid the compliment with a sequence of ink drawings that owed more than a little to the caricatures of Beresford Egan, whose Aubrey Beardsley-influenced portraits graced the cover of Crowley's novel *Moonchild* and Baudelaire's *The Flowers of Evil*. (They also resembled the art deco style sketches of Baron Hans Henning Voigt, whose work was published under the nom de plume Alastair.)

In a series of nude self-portraits, she depicted herself with long, windswept hair and flowery genitalia contemplating a small crucifix on the ground between her legs, and, in another image, kneeling while holding a bouquet of flowers, with the three crosses on the hill of

Golgotha in the distance behind her. And, in another variation on the theme, she pictured herself crucified.

Spiritual sacrifice was becoming a recurring trope in Cameron's artwork, intimately tied up with her identification and kinship with Joan of Arc. This was, once again, rooted in her late husband's works, particularly an essay entitled The Black Pilgrimage, in which Jack claimed to be the reincarnation of Gilles de Rais, the triumphant leader of the French army and Saint Joan's comrade-in-arms during the 100 Years War with England. Rais was persecuted by the Catholic church for alleged sorcery and the ritualistic raping and sacrifice of hundreds of children, and Jack was doubtless aware of Crowley's written defence of him, which he had intended to deliver in a lecture for the Oxford Poetry Society until he was deplatformed due to his controversial reputation. Crowley argued that Gilles de Rais was not the sadistic child killer of legend, but was instead, like Joan of Arc and the Templars, yet another high-profile victim who only confessed to such crimes under torture by the Medieval Inquisition, who were acting on behalf of politically motivated rivals seeking his estate and riches.

As part of her own spiritual crusade, Cameron inaugurated a loose-knit magical clique around her, which she christened The Children, in reference to the eleventh line from *Liber 49: The Book of Babalon*, in which Babalon enjoined: *"And gather my children unto me, for THE TIME is at hand."* Though Cameron took the lead role in the coven, both Renate Druks, who was slightly older than Cameron, and Paul Mathison considered it an equal partnership. Besides the cabal's outer heads, there was a floating cast comprised of Wands, primarily "strong male Negroes," and Pentacles, "white, healthy women," whose symbolism corresponded with two of the suits from the Minor Arcana of the tarot.

In her current squeeze, Leroy Booth, Cameron claimed to have found a representation of her male self, and, in Renate Druks, a female representation of Jack. Alongside Booth, Buddy Anderson and Robert

Morgan, other Wands included recent acquaintances Salvatore Torres and Eugene Bruito, Afro-Mexican affiliates of the Po-bos' drug crew, while Paul Mathison and Phillip Gronquist made up the white male quota of this multicultural mix.

Pentacles comprised Druks, Nancie Patterson and Joan Whitney, whom Cameron dubbed the Moon Maiden. Julie Macdonald was ennobled as the Queen of Swords, and Jo Anne Price was the Fertilizing Queen. Another convert, Evelyn Moore, was a newcomer to the group. Designated the Queen of Pentacles, she was an emotionally disturbed girl whom Cameron had taken under her wing. In the wake of the explosion that killed Jack, Moore became convinced that she was Faust and in league with the devil and had urged loved ones to keep her locked up so that she was unable to spread her evil influence. Cameron set about trying to channel the young woman's fears and quell her suicidal urges and, as a thank you, Moore presented her mentor with the gift of a pair of earrings made out of green shells, displaying Cameron's sign: a circle with a trine set within it.

In truth, it's debatable how seriously most of the participants took Cameron's venture, Druks and Mathison aside, but between the summer, autumn and winter equinoxes of that year, she orchestrated an ongoing series of sex magick rituals based on the Union of Opposites. Acting as mistress of ceremonies, Cameron paired up her Pentacles and Wands in a rite of magical miscegenation that aimed to create a new third race of Moonchildren, dedicated to Horus, whom Cameron viewed as the personification of all multiracial beings. This magical operation was symbolised by The Chariot tarot card, the 7th in the series of the Major Arcana, which depicts a charioteer harnessing the power of both positive and negative forces, represented as black and white sphinxes that he controls by will.

One major part of these operations centred around Cameron's obsession to produce Jack's magical child, whom she baptised the

"Wormwood Star." In an attempt to fulfil the legacy of her husband's one-man Armageddon, Cameron turned to his personal papers, in particular a segment titled Wormwood Star, which made up part of his Witchcraft manifesto. Hailing from an apocalyptic passage in the Book of Revelation, a star named Wormwood is one of the judgements of the tribulation – a period lasting seven years that befalls mankind during the reign of the Antichrist. This star, which could be interpreted as a dark, celestial being, is cast down from heaven and crashes to Earth, where it fouls a third of the planet's water supply, poisoning those who drink from it. Naturally, to Jack's mind, such a cataclysmic event was a cause for celebration, foreshadowing as it did the rise of The Great Beast and Babalon and the new Aeon of Crowleyanity.

To perform the task, Cameron corralled the services of four Wands: Booth, Anderson, Torres and Morgan, though not necessarily at the same time. Cameron began the sex magick ritual by consecrating her Star of Babalon. Then, during intercourse, she visualised sexual union with Jack on the astral plane and projected her psychosexual will on its conception, uttering "Abrahadabra" – Crowley's magical formula denoting the accomplishment of the Great Work – at the climactic moment. A little over a month later, Cameron's missed period confirmed the ritual had worked and she was pregnant with her magical offspring, which was due to arrive during the summer solstice of 1953.

Following her return to California from modelling duties for the House of Dior in Paris, Joan Whitney moved into the isolated residence with Cameron, who relished the companionship. During her time abroad, Whitney had acquired a more European outlook towards things, and Cameron's portrait of her playmate captured the chicness of a woman she praised as a perfect specimen of feminine beauty.

"When I came back from France suddenly everything looked different," Whitney chuckles, "so that's probably why I went to

Beaumont, because I was feeling different. We spent so many days together, so many hours, and we had one physical encounter together, but it wasn't like a big thing, we were just good friends."

Cameron spent evenings working on line drawings and writing by candlelight, and the two women enjoyed themselves by smoking their way through a bushel of grass that Cameron had smuggled back from Mexico in the lining of her jacket. "She was very good at sewing, so she sewed all these pockets and made this outfit that she could wear underneath her clothes so that the poundage wouldn't be noticed," Whitney explains. "It's not like today when you cross the border. So she came back with all this pot, and we smoked and smoked and smoked forever. It was like we could never get to the bottom of it. There was so much of it."

Cameron turned Whitney onto *The Book of the Law* and tried to include her in her sex magick project, pairing her up with Buddy Anderson, but Whitney didn't want anybody telling her whom she should bed down with and passed. Anderson would visit late in the evening and stay overnight, greeted by Cameron dressed in a toga or robe that she'd made herself. Even in the low light, he could see a marked change in her appearance and demeanour. "She had a very strange look about her, very mystical. Her hair was generally in disarray and she wore no make-up at all and her clothes made you take a second or third look. She was the kind of person you'd do a double-take to get a better look. I was only there at night-time and the place was so eerie. It was just lit by kerosene lamps and candles and it was very remote, not a single dwelling around. I saw some of her artwork but it was a little bit mysteriouso to me. It was like smoke moving about." Anderson had no interest in Crowley, but he did enjoy the sex and drugs that went with it. "I was young and all I wanted to do was get off quick, but Cameron was a joy, she always seemed to encourage everyone. We used to go up to the mountain at night and do peyote and mushrooms. We were so stoned, taking all the available medicines."

In January 1953, Cameron drove into Los Angeles and took in a lecture by the English writer and philosopher Gerald Heard at the Coronet Theatre on North La Cienega Boulevard. Heard was propagating the use and benefits of hallucinogens to expand human consciousness, a cause he was working on in conjunction with his compatriot and fellow author Aldous Huxley, who was about to drop his hugely influential book *The Doors of Perception*, that detailed his own spiritual awakening through the use of mescaline.

Huxley had crossed paths with Crowley back in the 1930s when the two men resided in Berlin, and some believe he may have been cast off on his voyage of mystical discovery when The Great Beast turned him on to peyote. The metaphysical experiences that Huxley and Heard spoke about influenced an array of notable artists and thinkers during the 1950s, and they became catalysts for the psychedelic sixties to come.[2]

The writings of these psychonauts certainly struck a chord with Cameron, who managed to obtain some peyote buttons by mail order from a botanical garden in Texas. Unsure of how to take them at first, she eventually cooked and ate them like vegetables, and later described how "The walls disappeared. What I got was Huxley's 'gray world.' Peyote causes a revolution in the unconscious. Once these things have surfaced and become conscious you have to adjust your life to it. You have to make tremendous alterations."[3]

Cameron had read how some Native American Indian tribes imbibed peyote to commune with spirit guides on the other side during their sacred vision quests, and, for her, it served as a convenient shortcut to the astral plane for sex magick rituals. An often recorded side effect of naturally grown hallucinogens, be it peyote, yagé or magic mushrooms, is the sexual desire they can arouse, and one extraordinary creation born out of this peyote period would, in time, test the bounds of what was considered artistic obscenity. Generally known as *Peyote Vision*, the sexually charged line drawing, created while she was bedridden, depicted Cameron on all fours being serviced from behind by an alien creature whose skin resembled the fungal camouflage of a peyote button. The picture packed a serious erotic punch and became a firm favourite among her intimates and fellow artists. On the downside, potent hallucinogens like peyote had a habit of making users prone to doomsday scenarios, and some of the jazz cats became increasingly perturbed by Cameron's apocalyptic pronouncements, and, slowly, one by one, they began to peel away.

Huxley's companion piece to *The Doors of Perception*, *Heaven and Hell*, warned of the schizophrenic side effects that could occur from such mind-altering experiences, and Cameron would have done well to heed his caution, for she had entered a state of being where the facts and fantasy of her life now seemed irrevocably blurred. Her peyote usage was an added tilt to her already precarious grip on reality, signs of which were readily apparent in her increasingly disjointed missives to Wolfe, which were full of idiosyncratic theories and fevered prophecies.

In one letter she warned of an impending dispute between Mexico and the U.S. over the Boulder Dam, which she anticipated the Mexicans seizing as a prelude to them taking complete control of America. She also predicted a race war in which soldiers from the continents of Africa, Asia and the Indies would soon rise up to conquer Europe, all under her command. Having witnessed a generation of white American manhood wiped out in the Second World War, Cameron brooded over the soldiers currently fighting in Korea; men whom she believed were seeking her kiss. But was this a kiss of life or the kiss of death?

Gripped by a messianic fervour, Cameron gave full reign to her Joan of Arc complex, portraying herself as a sword-wielding warrior, marching her victorious armies beneath the banner of Babalon. Like Saint Joan, she was beset by strange sounds in her head, auditory hallucinations (most likely a side effect from her peyote eating). By titling her body like an aerial, she found she could receive an intensely powerful frequency, akin to the hum of a telegraph wire, which seemed to be beamed into her by intergalactic intelligences beyond space and time. Joan Whitney witnessed such moments and recounts how Cameron would suddenly tune in and drift off into her own imaginings.

Cameron's flakiness and inability to fully connect was never more evident than in her relations with her family, and tensions came to a head when she visited them that February. With the zeal of a recent convert, Cameron tried turning her brothers on to *The Book of the Law*, regarding them as her own Cain and Abel, with whom it was her duty to reconcile. But when her mother presented her with a photograph of Aunt Nell, that showed her bedridden with a wicked gleam in her eye, Cameron flipped out. The picture dredged up some bitter memories and, as if purging herself, she accused her mother of conducting an extramarital affair and attacked the Cameron men for harbouring incestuous feelings towards her. Horrified at hearing this, Carrie charged at her daughter and forced her out the front door. Having been banished from her family's home, Cameron finally felt freed from their psychic grip, especially her mother, whom she regarded as a malign and destructive influence on them all and a death-dealing matriarch.

Confirmation of Cameron's new magical prowess came when she sent Renate Druks, Jo Anne Price and company to entertain Bob Hope at his home in nearby Palm Springs.[4] It seemed the famous comic was zeroed in on Cameron's wavelength, for when the ladies arrived his usual wisecracking manner was gone, replaced by a serious tone as he spoke of the recent sighting he'd made of a flying saucer. When the gals told him they were already well aware of their existence, Hope was taken aback, as he had feared he would be ridiculed for his admission. That evening, Cameron's sexy sirens enjoyed a kinky scene with Hope and a visiting priest who was defrocked, quite literally! Revelling in the sexual shenanigans, Cameron vowed that this was just the start of her infamy and that within two months her magical clique would become the scandal of the town. Then, within six months, they would be known to the whole world, as Babalon came into her own.

That said, the numinous side of Cameron's magical personality could not stave off the frequent bouts of depression that dogged her, or the nostalgia that accompanied it. When you're lost you go back, and she couldn't help but wallow in memories of a far happier past. She pined for her old love Sam Kelinson and was reduced to tears by listening to a recording of 'The Lovely Lass of Inverness,' as it conjured visions of Scotland, her ancestral homeland.[5]

And yet, by turns, Cameron's mood could swing from melancholia to fantastical plans for the future. That summer she dreamt of moving her base of operations to Catalina Island, where she would build a temple and raise her magical offspring, funded by the island's owner, chewing gum magnate, William Wrigley Jr. From there, Cameron pictured her chosen ones being transported to Mars via a flying saucer, a planet that she now considered her spiritual home. Most importantly, she foresaw the Earth being struck by a comet for real once her child was born, the explosion igniting a fireworks display that would light up the heavens with her seven-pointed star of Babalon.

Although personally convinced that she was the chosen vehicle of Babalon, Cameron sought validation from her fellow Thelemites, especially Crowley's successor, Karl Germer. Like other members of the O.T.O., Germer had never really taken to Cameron. He even mused that she may well have been one of those fascinating but shallow elementals whose prime purpose was to test, if not break, a practitioner of magick like Jack, to distract him away from his Great Work. Still, in echoes of Joan of Arc trying to prove her divinity to the sceptical court of the Dauphin, Cameron challenged Germer to visit her and bear witness to her incarnation, but he refused to engage and kept her at arm's length. Cameron did not take this well and made her resentment known to Jane Wolfe, blaming Germer's inflated ego for his inability to comprehend what Jack was trying to achieve with the Babalon Working. As a consequence, Cameron disregarded Germer's position, believing Jane Wolfe was now the supreme authority of Thelema on Earth.

The letters Cameron wrote to her were regularly shared among fellow O.T.O. adepts and they eventually fell into the hands of Gerald Yorke, a former Crowley devotee, who was amassing The Great Beast's archive back in England. Having read their contents, Yorke wrote to Karl Germer, and his sentiments echoed the thoughts of many in the order: "In medical language, Cameron is a lunatic. Elementals and forces and ideas like Babalon when uncontrolled are dangerous. She is now uncontrolled because Jack is dead. Her lunatic four or fivefold black and white moonchild operations, or attempted operations, are summarised by AC's comment: 'I get fairly frantic when I contemplate the idiocy of these louts!' (sic) I would insist on a vow of holy obedience and forbid all such workings. In my opinion, the poor girl is too far gone now to stop. You should dissolve and excommunicate her if she does not take and keep the oath. But when she refuses, as she will do, endeavour, through Jane, to get a copy of her letters and/or diary as a warning to others. She will be shut up and rightly so in a lunatic asylum as soon as she comes out in the open."[6]

Around the middle of February, Cameron left Beaumont for a two-week trek into the wilderness of the Indian reservation in Palm Springs. The trip presented problems from the outset, like what to do with Freya and her bird. Should she take them with her or leave them behind to starve? One alarmingly drastic measure she contemplated was to *slay* the dog and devour its heart and tongue. To carry out such an act, Cameron was focusing on something Jack once outlined to her in the Babalon letters, a few years earlier. Jack considered Freya a familiar spirit, an image of Cameron's animal self, that represented a source of power and danger. He warned his wife that someday she would have to destroy the dog and, in doing so, absorb her.

Unable to decide, Cameron turned to magick to make her choice. Taking Freya and her bird into her oratory, she closed the doors and opened the invocation with a banishing ritual, cleansing the atmosphere of psychic residue. Centring herself, she focused her concentration and performed the Hexagram rite, invoking Babalon. She then ate her Cakes of Light (a Eucharistic wafer mentioned in *The Book of the Law*, a mixture of meal, honey, oil and menstrual blood),[7] consecrated her air dagger with menstrual blood, held it aloft, and experienced a great universal power surge through her as she prayed and commanded Babalon to fill her with life. Once she felt charged up with Babalon's unholy spirit, Cameron closed the invocation, fed Freya one of the remaining wafers, and lay down by her side. She then fell into a peaceful sleep with a disk marked with the symbol of Babalon clasped in her right hand and a power charm in the other.

Mercifully, by the time she awoke the next morning, Cameron had decided it was best if Freya joined her on her journey, and she left extra food in the birdcage for her finch.[8] A good thing, too, because when she left the house it occurred to her that she may never return again. Her first stop in Palm Springs was to a clothing store to buy boots for her hike, but the excursion began to take on a strange, peyote-warped logic all of its own. Leaving the dog behind in the car, Cameron walked the streets as though entranced, passing a shop window that advertised Magic. Entering, she was drawn to a nude, kneeling, red-haired figurine with large breasts, wearing a red and white polka dot scarf. The vulgarity of the doll held a strange appeal, and once the shop's clerk demonstrated how powder shot out when the breasts were squeezed, Cameron purchased it.

With the boots bought too, Cameron followed a hunch and drove way up into Palm Canyon, a deep gorge on the mountainside from which crystal clear water sprung. With Freya at her side, she climbed over the waterfall, marvelling as she spied a seven-pointed star cactus haloed by the sunlight. After bathing her face and hands in the clear pool, she moved on to Andreas Canyon, another blissful oasis. There she came upon a white tree with the letters M and C etched into the bark, her own initials. Carved next to them were the letters H and B, which to her symbolised the magical monikers she and Jack had chosen: Hilarion and Belarion respectively.

Such episodes could be viewed as products of Cameron's magical thinking, wherein a magician trains themselves to see the magical consequence and significance in every situation, something Joan Whitney attests to: "Everything that happened to Cameron had a meaning. If you went to the store and someone said, 'Hello' to you, that had a special meaning, and so she lived every day like that. She read something into everything."

After bathing her feet in the stream, Cameron washed the figurine and placed it on a rock to dry in the sun. Perversely, she found herself falling madly in love with the saucy object, as if she'd been searching for it her entire life. Setting up camp by the side of the stream, Cameron bedded down for the night and slept under the stars. Looking back over her life, she contemplated how her romantic and idealistic inclinations had been corrupted and turned into fear and violence, murder and pain. Having shaken off her preoccupation with death, she now looked forward to reuniting with her soon-to-be-released beau Leroy Booth and enjoying a more positive, life-affirming existence.

However, by the following month, Cameron was at another low ebb, besieged by cramps and chronic pregnancy pains. The highly coveted birth of her magical child was not going smoothly and, having endured two previous miscarriages, she tried to convince herself this pregnancy would bear its strange fruit. For reassurance, she visited a clairvoyant in Palm Springs, accompanied by her concerned friend, Phillip Gronquist.

The psychic, a Serbian woman by the name of Madame Grey, seemed excited to meet her and informed Cameron she was of God and had great power to make men happy. She also seemed to divine that Cameron had known death and warned that she was now in the embrace of the Grim Reaper himself. She could see a black shroud in Cameron's life and predicted that she was about to die, only to be reborn a new person in the New Year.

A couple of days later, Cameron returned for a free, follow-up visit, this time noting the similarity in the medium's name with her first German Shepherd, Lady Grey. However, the second reading took a disturbing turn when Madame Grey revealed how a close relation had burned nine black candles and placed a black curse on Cameron at the time of her birth. The curse was responsible for all her current struggles, but the psychic swore she would lift it from her or else forfeit her own life.

At first, Cameron suspected her mother as the source of the curse, but then the spectre of Aunt Nell reared up to take her place. Cameron began to see herself caught in a death struggle between her own pagan calling and Aunt Nell's wish for a life in servitude to the teachings of The Black Brotherhood. When she returned home she replaced the black candles on her altar with pale green ones and meditated deeply. She then wrote to Jane Wolfe, asking her to return the photograph of Nell that she'd sent her. This was the very picture that had kick-started the set-to with her mother, and Cameron needed to destroy it to exorcise the curse.

Nature then dealt a terrible blow when, amid all the crippling pain in her womb, Cameron bled out and the birth of her expectant moonchild ended in another miscarriage. It didn't augur well for the rest of her magical master plan either. For while she was still trying to get over her own disappointment, Cameron learned that Julie Macdonald had already decided not to see the product of her own magical insemination through to fruition, and was further devastated when the twin progeny resulting from the Druks-Mathison magical union was also terminated after Renate had a change of heart and decided to have the foetuses removed. Having initially agreed to hand the twins over to Cameron, who'd already anti-christened the offspring Lucifer and Lilith in preparation, Druks' volte-face became the first of many disputes that drove a wedge between the two of them.

With Booth scheduled to be released from prison that spring, Cameron cogitated her next move and, after consulting the I Ching, she deemed a return to L.A. was the best course of action. Not everything made the trip back with her, however. A trunk secured to the top of her Packard containing household items and her Mexican artefacts was stolen while she stopped off at a highway diner to have something to eat. Despite that, and all the setbacks and heartbreaks she'd faced in Beaumont, she remained optimistic as she travelled onward.

In Pasadena, Cameron shacked up with Booth again at the Po-bos' pad on Worcester Ave. Evidently, the house was still under police surveillance, for in the early hours of Saturday, April 18, the residence was raided once again by vice squad officers searching for drugs. Although none were found, Cameron and Booth were arrested for violating the rooming house ordinance and taken into custody. Cameron wasn't even granted the option to dress and was still clad in her pyjamas when she was booked. She was, however, wearing the protective amulet Jack had made for her. It consisted of a six-inch piece of string with nine knots tied in it, a small piece of dark blue felt cut in a circle, two pieces of metal, one seed, a small piece of quartz, a deep blue stone and a phonograph needle. When a matron at the police station attempted to remove the amulet from around her neck, Cameron lashed out, kicking and biting until she was forcibly restrained and handcuffed. She was later released with Booth on $50 bail.

The arrest and subsequent fracas was covered by the *Mirror* newspaper under the headline: 'Pasadena Cult Widow's Amulet Fails in Raid.' The accompanying article rehashed the circumstances surrounding Jack's death and then went on to report how Cameron had refused to reveal the significance of the "good luck" amulet. There was a good reason for this. For only she knew it contained a sealed poison, which she had asked Jack to place there so that she could kill herself if her magical mission in the world proved too unbearable to carry out.

Cameron wearing one of her own creations. Circa Beaumont. 1953.
(Courtesy of Joan Whitney.)

Blurry shots of Cameron at her place in Beaumont, where she incarnated Babalon and conducted the Wormwood Star rituals. 1953. (Courtesy of Joan Whitney.)

Cameron's arrest as reported in *The Mirror*. April 20th, 1953.

Pasadena Cult Widow's Amulet Fails in Raid

The widow of the asserted high priest of a weird Pasadena cult was due to appear in Pasadena Municipal Court this afternoon on a charge of violating the city's rooming house ordinance.

Mrs. Elizabeth Cameron Parsons was clad in pajamas and an amulet when she was picked up with Leroy C. Booth, 28, by vice squad officers in Booth's home at 958 Worcester St. early Saturday, police said.

Mrs. Parson's husband, John W. Parsons, a pioneer in rocket and jet propulsion development, was killed in a mysterious blast which rocked the fashionable Orange Grove district 10 months ago.

Parsons was identified at that time as the one-time high priest of the Church of Thelema, and there was evidence at the time of his death that some sort of a cult still was operating in the old coach house where Parsons made his residence.

Mrs. Parsons gave police the same address—1071 S Orange Grove Ave. — when she and Booth were jailed.

She flatly refused to give up the amulet which hung around her neck when she was booked, and put up such resistance it was necessary to handcuff her. Matron Josephine Kehoe was kicked and bitten during the melee.

The amulet was found to contain a six-inch piece of string with nine knots tied in it, a small piece of dark blue felt cut in a circular manner, two pieces of metal, one seed, a small piece of quartz, a deep blue stone, and a phonograph needle.

She refused to reveal significance of the "good luck" piece.

Free on Bail

Both Mrs. Parsons and Booth were released on $50 bail for court appearance today.

Lt. Harold Thomas, head of the vice squad, said he had directed his men to the home to shake it down for narcotics. Booth and Jo Ann Price, 30, a buxom blonde identified as the prospective high priestess of the cult, were arrested at the address several months ago on narcotics charges that later were dismissed.

Officers Frank Repetti and D. C. Newland, who made the raid, said Mrs. Parsons had taken her German shepherd dog and a bird cage containing two birds to the Booth residence, and she carted them off to jail.

Joan Whitney, circa Beaumont period.
(Courtesy of Joan Whitney.)

6 - Welcome to the Pleasure Dome

> "We don't see things as they are, we see them as we are."
> – Anaïs Nin.

When her romance with Leroy Booth failed to rekindle, following his release from jail, Cameron found herself homeless and in reduced circumstances again. She sought refuge for a while at Renate Druks' home in Malibu and, when she departed some months later, she left a little present behind for her generous host. During a fitful night's sleep, Druks awoke to find a weird, astral apparition floating above her bed. An alien entity with a neon-coloured brain and a spinal column for a tail, that increased in size as it swooped down on her and then vanished before her eyes. Spooked, she consulted Jane Wolfe about the visitation, who immediately realised the spectre was the product of one of Cameron's conjurations, and she urged her friend to perform a banishing ritual for protection. "How naughty of her," Wolfe later mused with understatement.[1]

It was actually through Druks that Cameron was first introduced to the cosmopolitan inner circle of Samson De Brier, a flamboyant aesthete, whose home doubled as a salon catering to the more artistic and culturally savvy side of Hollywood. De Brier was reportedly born in China, in 1909, but grew up in Atlantic City where, so the story goes, his father, a corrupt politician, was stabbed to death by a jealous woman. In early adolescence he cultivated the pose of a Wildean dandy, draping himself in furs and jewels, and was a sartorial sight to behold as he promenaded along the boardwalk of a boomtown that prided itself on its reputation as "The Worlds Playground." As in Cameron's recent incarnation, it was a role he at first adopted then embodied wholeheartedly.

He clicked with a nightclub entertainer there, who squired him to Los Angeles so he could try his luck in the "flickers," but the only work he secured was as a body double for the actor Arthur Jasmine, who played the page of Herodias in Alla Nazimova's film adaptation of Oscar Wilde's *Salome*. When a career in Hollywoodland failed to materialise, Samson put his sixteen-year-old self on a steamer to Paris, where he fraternised with expat literati like Earnest Hemingway and Henry Miller, was deflowered by André Gide (an experience he would subsequently deliver in a detailed, blow-by-blow account), and was, allegedly, the model for Picasso's series of Pierrot paintings. On his American return, he hosted the *Gangplank* radio show for WMCA in New York, where he interviewed some of the biggest celebrities of the day, including Sonja Henie, Thomas Mann, and Noël Coward, with whom he shared much more than a passing resemblance.

After the war, he returned to Los Angeles, where he worked the night shift at Lockheed Aircraft Company and was employed as a male nurse in the psychiatric ward at the Veteran's Hospital. With his savings, he bought a Victorian-era duplex and moved it from its original location, at the intersection of Santa Monica Boulevard and Western Avenue, to Barton Avenue in West Hollywood. The duplex was rented out to tenants, and its small back garden led to a trailer-type dwelling where Samson himself resided. An adjacent carriage house was home to Roberta Haynes, a foxy actress who counted Marlon Brando amongst her visiting suitors. The income Samson accrued from his rentals provided him with the breathing space to live as a self-confessed "professional putterer."

The landlord's own home reflected his fondness for Art Nouveau décor and, as a collector of rare Hollywood memorabilia, it was festooned with costumes and props salvaged from modern-day masterpieces to long-forgotten silent classics. Visitors could view Glinda the Good Witch's wand from *The Wizard of Oz*, or Bugsy Siegel's derringer in a glass case, and with the house kept in permanent gloom, it felt like a dark museum. One later tenant, the producer Rick Nathanson, remembered: "Along with the film memorabilia, there were also portraits of Samson in the nude. It seems he had a portrait in the attic, too, because he never seemed to age."

It wasn't only the interior of De Brier's domicile that was steeped in old Hollywood, its ambiance hung over the whole neighbourhood. His house was just a block away from the Gower Gulch, a stretch of sidewalk where aspiring cowpoke actors once queued to work in the latest horse opera. And a little further beyond lay the Hollywood Cemetery, where Gods and Goddesses of the silver screen were buried or entombed in sterile mausoleums.

Over the years, Samson's salon drew some of the biggest names in the world of arts and entertainment, and the glitterati mixed happily with emerging artists and those trying to break into Hollywood. "Samson's house was just gorgeous and another meeting place," Shirley Berman recalls. "Anytime you walked by you could just knock on the door and it would be full of starlets. It was so weird to see these beautiful young girls prancing around the house, making tea for Samson, and he had all these famous friends like Tennessee Williams."

For the young, avant-garde filmmakers Kenneth Anger and Curtis Harrington, Samson's soirées were a rite of passage, and his house became a regular port of call. "Samson was an aesthete," asserts Curtis Harrington. "He had no career or profession. He was not a poet, an artist or an actor, he was simply a fascinating, multifaceted person who was extremely devoted to the arts. The kind of person you never hear about anymore. He invested all of the money he made in real estate. He was very clever that way, so he could live the life of a gentleman. He looked down on daily labours, he was superior to all that. He had enough money coming from rents that he could live the way he wanted to live, which was never to do anything that he didn't want to do. That's the exposed mystery of Samson; it's really very mundane."

Samson's association, however tenuous, with the stars of early cinema, endeared him to the two young filmmakers, who had been reared on the silent spectacles from that era. A golden age that produced their respective objects of veneration: for Anger, Rudolph Valentino and, for Harrington, the despotic director and Svengali to Marlene Dietrich, Josef von Sternberg.

De Brier also earned kudos from those around him for being openly homosexual at a time when it was still viewed by many psychiatrists as a mental illness and risked the threat of violence, arrest and incarceration. In this dangerous, clandestine climate, his home provided a sybaritic safe house, where his 'men-only' parties could swing away in private. It was a furtive, outlaw period that Kenneth Anger would, in later years, lament the passing of, for the risk (both legal and physical) of being busted by the cops or queer-bashed by a thug only heightened the eroticism of seeking sex in public encounters. In fact, this was the none-so-subtle subtext of his early film *Fireworks*.

As with Samson, self-mythological stories abound surrounding Kenneth Anger's early life, especially his time as an alleged child actor in Hollywood. A question mark still hangs over whether that is actually him playing the changeling prince in Max Reinhardt's enchanting version of *A Midsummer Night's Dream*. While his contentious accusation, that he was once on the receiving end of some paedophilic frottage from Walt Disney, walked an even more precarious line between fact and fiction. Such alleged glimpses into the nightmares lurking behind the dream factory would prove a rich seam for the filmmaker, who'd later find great success blowing the lid off some of Hollywood's murkiest secrets.

Anger would consequently paint himself as an errant son, born from a contraceptive mistake, who felt estranged from his Presbyterian parents, but found solace in his grandmother, affectionately named Big Bertha, a wardrobe mistress during the silent film era, who indulged his love for all things movieland. While still an adolescent, Anger appropriated his parent's 16mm camera and shot his first film *Whose Been Rocking My Dream Boat?* Just one of several examples of juvenilia that have subsequently been lost.

Curtis Harrington was equally precocious and had already completed his first version of his favourite Edgar Allan Poe story *The Fall of the House of Usher*, by the time he was fourteen. He first met Anger at the American Contemporary Gallery on Hollywood Boulevard, where rarely seen films from the silent era were screened along with European examples of experimental cinema by the likes of Oskar Fischinger and Man Ray. Inspired by these works, as well as the pioneering avant-garde films of Maya Deren, the two budding auteurs initially found an interest in their work abroad. Harrington toured some of his film shorts around Europe to some acclaim, and Anger made an even bigger splash with *Fireworks*, the previously referenced homoerotic wet dream of a film, which won plaudits from such illustrious figures as Tennessee Williams and Jean Cocteau, who awarded it the poetic film prize at the 1949 Biarritz Film Festival.

The film also completed a successful run at the Coronet Theatre on La Cienega Boulevard in LA. One intrigued audience member was the sexologist Dr. Alfred C. Kinsey, who was in town compiling interviews for his groundbreaking study into the sexual behaviour of the American male. His findings would controversially suggest that the sex lives of American men had far more in common with their Greco-Roman counterparts than might otherwise be suspected. Taken with this rare example of American homoeroticism, Kinsey immediately bought a print of Anger's film for his Institute for Sex Research at Indiana University and struck up a friendship with the intense-looking young filmmaker.

Buoyed by the commendation from Cocteau, Anger travelled to Paris where he worked as an assistant to Henri Langlois, co-founder of the Cinémathèque Française. He was called back home in 1953, following the death of his mother, and used the proceeds from the inheritance she left him (mostly Disney stock, ironically) to bankroll his next venture.

Tied in with their mutual love of classic cinema, Samson, Anger and Harrington also shared an affinity for the cultured styles of yesteryear. De Brier's fondness for Art Nouveau was clear for all to see from the décor of his home, while Harrington's heart yearned to return to the Belle Époch era. Anger's penchant was for the Yellow Nineties, a period in time to which his next film, *Inauguration of the Pleasure Dome*, became an evocative love letter.

Thanks to his relationship with Samson, Anger was invited to one of Renate Druks' costume parties held at her Malibu home, which she titled "Come As Your Madness." The event acted as a dress rehearsal for his new project. "It was wonderful to see that people's idea of madness, in Southern California and Hollywood, was to become principally dressed as Gods and Goddesses," Anger wryly remarked later.[2]

Thrown into this glamorous mix was Druks' close friend, the French-born diarist, Anaïs Nin, who was celebrated in bohemian circles for her erotic novels, as well as her patronage of her former lover, Henry Miller. Nin played up to her status as a wild, sexual adventurer by attending the party dressed in leopard print bodystocking, but her pièce de résistance was the birdcage she wore over her head and the roll of paper that spewed out from her mouth, bearing excerpts from her books. Pulling them through the open door of the cage, she tore off strips and presented them to her fellow guests as "ticker tape from the unconscious."

Anger attended the party as Hecate, Greek Goddess of the underworld, but hid in an adjoining room, brandishing a lit candle, waiting to make his big entrance. Unfortunately, busied with other guests, Druks forgot all about him, and when he did emerge, despondent, the candle was already burnt halfway down. In the following days, Anger told Samson the party reminded him of a dream he once had, and he captured it in a painting that later hung on his friend's wall. And his main aim was to recreate that masquerade on celluloid and bring his dream-painting to life.

Although it was initially conceived as a vehicle to showcase Anaïs Nin, who had already made a notable cameo appearance in Maya Deren's *Ritual in Transfigured Time*, Anger's plan went straight out the window the moment he met Cameron. Much to Nin's chagrin, the filmmaker had found his new star. Samson had taken great delight in firing Anger's mind with the legend of Jack and Cameron, and when he was first introduced to the much-gossiped-about Scarlet Woman, Anger reportedly gushed: "I've been waiting to meet you for a thousand years."[3]

Curtis Harrington, on the other hand, initially had reservations: "I didn't even want to know Cameron when I first met her because she had a very dark presence, very forbidding and intimidating. It struck me she was a bit mad but we soon got beyond that. I've certainly never known anyone like her before or since." (Indeed, seeds were sown for what would become a lifelong friendship.)

With Cameron painted as a usurper, the fallout was felt by all those present. "All of Anaïs' friends were quite disturbed and resentful," confirms Curtis Harrington. "There was tension on the set, mainly between Anaïs and Cameron, because Anaïs, being Anaïs, felt that *she* was the female star of the film. She considered herself a star in her own right, as an internationally known writer, and she could see that Cameron was taking over the production. Cameron was such a forceful presence that Kenneth kept giving more to her. Anaïs was more than a little piqued and jealous, so they were not on the best of terms." Witnessing how fascinated her co-stars seemed to be with Cameron, Nin admitted defeat and, in her journal, she described her rival in her best purplish prose: "Cameron (is) the dark spirit of the group... There is an aura of evil around her."[4]

Working like a ringmaster, over the weekends of December 1953, Anger primed, preened and prepped his ensemble, annexing Samson's dark, hallowed quarters to create the film's netherworldly setting. Completed the following year, the results demonstrated a marked maturation in his film craft. To encapsulate the dramatised derangement of the senses, the film needed an appropriate title. For that, Anger looked to the opening lines of 'Kubla Khan,' Samuel Taylor Coleridge's opium-infused reverie of Xanadu, the fabled, marble palace of the Mongol ruler from whose name the poem's title derives. At the time of its composition, Coleridge's vision was so startling in its scope that his fellow poet, William Wordsworth, refused to publish it, deeming the poem a dangerous, drug-induced gateway to madness. Its release came courtesy of Lord Byron who, having savoured the notoriety surrounding the stanzas, stepped into the breach and paid Coleridge handsomely for the honour of printing it himself. Anger's decision may well have been prompted by his new-found muse, too, for the poet was a particular favourite of Cameron's. If the title of the finished film seemed apropos, so did the score, Leos Janacek's haunting choral work, *The Glagolitic Mass*, set a spine-tingling tone for the spectacle to come.

Once the scrolling opening titles (beautifully hand-painted in the Art Nouveau style by Paul Mathison) have rolled, the film opens on Samson De Brier, lying on his ornate four-poster bed, in his opium den of a bedroom. With his fingers plastered in jewels, he portrays Lord Shiva in the first of his multiple roles. Sliding a necklace down his throat, he rises from his pit, exits his bedroom and enters his vanity room, where he preens himself in front of a triptych mirror. A demonic vision appears, rocking back and forth, twirling foot-long fingernails. It's Samson in a ghoulish guise that Anger would later dub 'The Great Beast,' in honour of Crowley. His monstrous façade, painted by Renate Druks, was made to resemble a cloth painting of Satan that was dug out from Samson's costume closet.

Shot from the feet up, Cameron materialises as the Scarlet Woman, draped in a shawl (claimed to have once belonged to Rudolph Valentino), with a Spanish *peineta* comb fixed to the back of her head. Under the intense colourisation of the lighting gels, her hair appears vermilion red, and with her spidery eyelashes, glittered cheek, and thick, garish red lips, she strikes an imperious pose. In a close-up shot, you can see her body palpably trembling from the intensity of her hypnotic gaze. There is an exquisite look of evil on her face as her lips part slightly and, from the palm of her hand, she proffers a tiny devil figurine to The Great Beast, that bursts into flames when he touches it. Cameron lights a joint from the flame and, as she inhales, the image of a turbaned Crowley (that was featured on the front page of the *Mirror* newspaper in the wake of Jack's death) is superimposed.

Joan Whitney appears as Aphrodite, resplendent in a Grecian gown and encased in another (superimposed) flickering flame. Brandishing a golden apple she approaches Samson who, in his third incarnation as Emperor Nero, accepts the fruit but turns away in disgust. Cameron reappears again, this time in the role of the Hindu Goddess Kali (now sporting a Cleopatra wig), and watches over an Egyptian set piece where the Goddess Isis, played by local sculptress Katy Kadell, feeds a plastic snake into Osiris' mouth (played by Samson again), who judders from the serpent meal. Renate Druks then makes her appearance as Lucifer's consort Lilith, a vision in orange chiffon. Framed by candelabras, she dips a glass diamond into Samson's mouth, who is now dressed as a fur-coated Eastern potentate. He sashays off camera, then reappears in the persona of the 18th-century occultist Count Cagliostro, sporting a whipped cream wig. He's filmed against the Venetian terrace backdrop painted on Samson's living room wall, and Cameron's Scarlet Woman sits in front of the mural, too, fanning herself as kabbalistic symbols are superimposed on top of her.[5]

Paul Mathison enters stage left as Pan, bearing the grapes of Bacchus. Bathed in smoke and looking almost albino, he strikes a magnificently malevolent pose. Beckoned forth by Lilith, Anaïs Nin makes her grand entrance as the Moon Goddess Astarte. Looking like a Dadaist astronaut, she reprises her birdcage number, her pretty face overlaid by a crescent moon. She stands swaddled in blue muslin and, once Samson has unwrapped her, performs a mime, drawing down the moon from the sky, symbolised by a series of silver orbs. She presents one to Lord Shiva who shrinks it to a marble and ingests it. Tweaking from the effects, he sprouts silvery wings that flutter excitedly.

The Great Beast and the Scarlet Woman reappear and conjure Cesare, the stone-faced somnambulist star of the German expressionist film *The Cabinet of Caligari*, portrayed by Curtis Harrington. He sleepwalks past Druks' painting of three Siamese cats and a superimposed portrait of an old crone, into an anteroom where Anger dwells, dragged up again as Hecate, his single eye peering out from a black-veiled headdress. Hecate presents Cesare with an amphora containing yagé and, acting as a butler, Harrington pours the elixir into lotus goblets which are imbibed by all.

This sequence became a major bone of contention between Anger and Druks, who objected when the director asked her eight-year-old son, Peter, playing Ganymede the cup-bearer, to dip his tongue into the goblet and fall into a trance. The fact that the cup was filled with nothing more harmful than sprinkles did nothing to mollify Druks' irrational fear that her boy would be poisoned, and she also baulked at the prospect of her son being present during the scene where Cameron, portraying Kali, flashes her breasts.

Druks was not the only one becoming increasingly disturbed during the filming. The performances were taking on a strange life of their own, and others also felt the make-belief was becoming all too real. In her diary, Anaïs Nin later fretted: "To see Cameron sitting with one breast uncovered and Peter tasting the elixir was to feel a chill of fear that her witches' milk might be the source of the goblet's contents."[6]

As soon as Count Cagliostro spikes Pan's drink, the ritualised madness begins and, as the nectar of the Gods takes effect, a truly bewildering array of multilayered images captures the tripped-out psychodrama. As the Gods and Goddesses of antiquity become increasingly hysterical, Anger creates a dazzling Danse Macabre, using double exposures and reverse shots, as well as footage of glittering, jittering ball gowns sampled from his earlier short film *Puce Moment*.

Lilith removes her Mexican Day of the Dead skeleton mask, only to reveal another death's head beneath. A Bosch-like creature haunts the set, while Anaïs Nin minces about brandishing a fishing net to ensnare Pan and, amid the melee, you can just about make out the lustful ladies manhandling Pan with sexual frenzy.

Anger also works footage from the silent film *Dante's Inferno* into the montage and bathes it in a red, satanic tint. As images of hell rebound around her, Cameron reappears, this time enthroned as Kali, exposing what Nin would bitchily describe as a "lifeless breast." (This breach is now viewed as one of the first incidences of female nudity in American cinema.) As everything descends into a bad trip, Cameron is a solitary point of calm amid all the delirium. The church organ section of the score becomes progressively discordant as the crescendo of music and images reaches a rapturous climax.

Paying tribute to the film later, Anaïs Nin wrote how it did indeed become a portrayal of their collective madness: "The reality and the madness mingled and that made chaos and confusion. The links were missing as in madness. There was a distortion. Love became hatred, ecstasy became a nightmare. Those who began with a sensual attraction, ended by devouring each other."[7]

Viewed today, in retrospect, a great deal of *Inauguration of the Pleasure Dome* plays out like a camp pantomime. Amongst the leads, Samson plays his theatrical parts well and is appropriately queenly, which shouldn't be all that surprising as it wasn't too much of a stretch for him. In contrast, there's nothing at all camp about Cameron who, amid all the skylarking and pageantry, strikes a very real note. Anaïs Nin, on the other hand, fails to live up to her raunchy reputation and is completely overshadowed by Cameron's magisterial mien. To her credit, Nin admitted as much: "At first Astarte was illuminated in the film and shed her light, but Cameron became a stronger figure as evil, a hypnotic figure, and the mood of decadence and destruction won out." Anger, however, spelt it out in black and white: "Suddenly Anaïs shrunk in the majesty that was Cameron because Cameron wiped her out!"[8]

Playing up its magical significance, Anger later cited his film for helping to plant Cameron's photogenic Babalon persona into the public consciousness, while Cameron came to see it as an important watershed for all of them together. It was "a chance to express our repression. We were what I call the Freudian generation. We were the children who suffered from the family scene undergoing such a big change. We were all literally abandoned children and this was our first opportunity to express it. I think we became interested in psychology first and that sort of released us, allowed us to talk about these things that had formerly been veiled in a literary context. We were able to be shocking."[9]

The film certainly serves as a great example to any aspiring young auteur as to what can be achieved with a limited budget, an ad hoc set, and a chichi cast. Boasting indelible images, beautifully syncopated to the music, and an effective use of superimposition, *Pleasure Dome* remains Anger's most skillfully realised "film-poem" to this day.

Stylistically, it owes a debt to the esteemed filmmaking duo Michael Powell and Emeric Pressburger, who were revered for the high artistic quality of their output, which so entranced cinemagoers, including

Cameron, in the post-war years. Their most recent visual masterwork, a dazzling adaptation of Jacques Offenbach's opera *The Tales of Hoffman*, affected her to such an extent that she began to believe that its story of malevolent forces conspiring to doom a poet's string of love affairs prefigured her own destiny.

The Crowley inserts permeating *Pleasure Dome*, that Anger added in the film laboratory afterwards, would later lead many critics to believe they were watching an enactment of a Crowleyan mass. Curtis Harrington, however, confirms the suspicion that the Crowley quotient came after the fact, as Anger got to know Cameron and, through her, Jane Wolfe.

Harrington was also thrilled to meet the former silent movie actress, having already read about her in the pages of John Symonds' sensationalist Crowley biography *The Great Beast*. "Jane Wolfe was an extremely interesting old lady. I knew that she'd been in Cefalu with Crowley from the Symonds' book, in which she is known as Elizabeth Fox, and it was difficult for me to reconcile this very sweet, old lady, who reminded me very much of my grandmother, being involved in all these sex rituals and orgies in Sicily. I could never reconcile that in my head. But she was devoted to Crowley and *The Book of the Law*. She was a true believer in Crowleyanity."

With few other biographical resources to draw upon, the Symonds biography was responsible for shaping a lot of people's perception of Crowley, Cameron's coterie included, and it perpetuated the still popular misconception of him as an arch Satanist, as Harrington recalls: "I remember once riding on a bus with Paul Mathison somewhere. He knew my imagination, and he said, 'Oh yes, I know of a certain house in Pasadena where they have secret satanic rites, and you have to go up into an attic and then they close the trapdoor and you can't get out.' I shivered, but I didn't know what he was talking about at the time, but now I know that he was talking about Jack Parsons."

Asked whether he believed Mathison and Parsons were once sexual partners, the filmmaker responds: "Paul was very bisexual and considering the fact that Crowley was also bisexual, and was Jack's role model, I wouldn't be in the least bit surprised. There was some kind of incident where Cameron expressed her jealousy towards Paul along those lines." Harrington stresses his own interest in Crowley is strictly intellectual: "I respond to Crowley as a personality. I find him amusing. I don't find him a figure of horror. I love his wicked sense of humour. I'd have liked to have played a game of chess with him."

Anger, on the other hand, took to Crowley and his Thelemic philosophy with unbridled relish, as he'd later explain: "As soon as I heard about it, something clicked and I said, 'This is mine!' I was never attracted to the church. My family tried to take me when I was 12 and I told them 'No!' I was the first child to do that. I refused to go to church on Sundays and I got my allowance cut because I was rebelling. But then they left me alone. So I had rejected Christianity at an early age. I find Christianity repellent. I don't like the story. I don't feel I need someone to get nailed to a cross to pay for my sins. It's ugly!"[10]

A little over a year later, Anger travelled to London and presented *Inauguration of the Pleasure Dome* at the ICA (Institute for Contemporary Art) in Dover Street. In the accompanying programme notes, the director described his film in strictly Crowleyan terms as: "A tribute to the Master Therion, the Abbey of Thelema, the evening on the sunset of Crowleyanity. Lord Shiva wakes, Madame Satan presents the mandragore and a glamour is cast. The idol is fed. The elixir of Hecate is served by the shade of the somnambulist. Pan's drink is venomed by Lord Shiva. The ceremonies are presided over by The Great Beast Shiva and the Scarlet Woman, Kali."

The film was reviewed by Paul Dehn in the *London News Chronicle*, beneath the headline 'The Scarlet Woman Shows Her Magic.'[11] In an article that was obviously prodded by Anger, Dehn described how the film revolved around Cameron, who was now billed as "Crowley's successor elect. The Scarlet Woman (who had) re-founded Crowley's Sicilian Abbey of Thelema at a disused ranch house in Paradise Cove, Malibu."

Crowleyites attending the screening included Lady Frieda Harris, who had spent the last decade of Crowley's life painstakingly designing his Thoth tarot deck to his exacting specifications. Despite Anger's claims that his film was a Thelemic work, on which Jane Wolfe had acted as an adviser, Lady Harris was having none of it, and after the screening she accosted the filmmaker in the foyer, berating him, according to fellow Thelemite Louis Wilkinson, "with all of the indignant loyalty of a disciple of Jesus vindicating the gospel to a deviationist follower of St Paul."[12]

"This is no tribute to AC – it's a sacrilege!" Lady Harris opened fire. "He would have derided it, all of it, from beginning to end!" Trying to placate her, Anger asked if they could discuss the matter later, only to be told they most certainly could not. "But, my dear," Anger pleaded. "Don't you say 'my dear' to me – I must speak now!" insisted her Ladyship. As the dressing down continued, Anger threw the present Lady Harris gave him before the screening on the floor and stormed off.

Not all of Crowley's British contingent were of such a low opinion, however. One avid admirer of the film, and of Cameron in particular, was the author Kenneth Grant, who wasted no time in contacting this glorious vision of Scarlet Womanhood, inviting her to England to join his newly consecrated New Isis Lodge. Cameron did not personally respond to Grant's overtures, for it seems she was put off by Jane Wolfe and Karl Germer, who'd soon excommunicate Grant for allegedly collaborating with an old adversary of his. But to Cameron's mind, the real reason for Grant's exclusion was because he'd sent her his official seal of approval, confirming her as the physical manifestation of the

Babalonian force. Though initially intrigued, Cameron refused to answer Grant's letters, but a year later she was urging Anger to meet with him, hoping he may still be of assistance to her if she followed Anger over to London. The filmmaker did eventually meet with Grant, though Cameron never did. In spite of this, she became a fetish object for him, a portal cum stargate to another dimension.

Cameron stealing the show in Kenneth Anger's film, *Inauguration of the Pleasure Dome*. (Courtesy of the Warburg Institute.)

The Scarlet Woman shows her magic

By PAUL DEHN

THE uneasy, black-magical spirit of the late Aleister Crowley—who, during his eccentric lifetime, styled himself Beast 666 of the Apocalypse and became High Priest to a dark little cult operating from Cefalu, Sicily, in 1923—is not yet wholly stilled.

An extraordinary film, to be shown privately tonight at the Institute of Contemporary Arts, Dover Street, by its 27-year-old American director, Kenneth Anger, introduces us to Crowley's self-confessed successor-elect, Mrs. Cameron Parsons, Californian widow of the Beast's own "godson."

Her husband, a genuinely brilliant scientist saluted by Americans as the perfecter of jet-fuel, dabbled before his death in alchemy.

Mrs. Parsons, a talented professional painter who prefers to be known among her acolytes as the Scarlet Woman, has refounded Crowley's Sicilian Abbey of Thelema at a disused ranch-house 20 miles up-coast from Hollywood in the somewhat unsuitably named Paradise Cove, near Malibu Beach.

The inner circle

Here (wearing a series of revelatory costumes and a small gold locket confidently held to contain a "condensed star") she holds ritual court over the inner circle of devotees who support her in Mr. Anger's picture.

They are: The new Beast 666; The Great God Pan; Astarte; Cesare the Somnambulist; Keeper of the Flame.

All these (and their equally vivid subordinates) have been filmed by Mr. Anger at their self-appointed ritual tasks, in livid, luminous colours.

Since the idiom is impressionistic, a valuable programme-note elucidates the action:

"Lord Shiva wakes. Madam Satan present the Mandragore, and a glamour is cast. The Idol is fed. The Elixir of Hecate is served by the shade of Cesare the Somnambulist. Pan's drink is venomed by Lord Shiva. The ceremonies are presided over by the great Beast-Shiva and the Scarlet Woman-Kali."

The film's most memorable figure is the Great Beast himself—made-up (one assumes with some foreboding that he was made-up) to resemble a demi-baboon.

Eccentric few

The bright and wickedly subtle violence of Mr. Anger's imagery quite terrifyingly conveys the ecstasy of the eccentric few to us, who are the unsympathetic many.

The Institute of Contemporary Arts are to be congratulated on showing Inauguration of the Pleasure Dome as a brilliant experimental work of art; but since a majority will hold it also to be a work of black art, the censor will certainly court equal congratulation if he bans it.

A scene from the black-magic film. The Keeper of the Flame hands the Golden Apple of Diana to Shiva

Inauguration of the Pleasure Dome reviewed by Paul Dehn. (*London News Chronicle*.)

7 - Sherry

Least could I tell you what is in my mind; seeing your face on mist I half forget. Half hope remembering the wind; stirring your hair of old regret. 'Autumn,' a poem by Sherry Abbott.[1]

In early 1955, Norman Rose opened Books 55 on La Cienega Boulevard, a bookshop specializing in art, mysticism and poetry. Rose was a slight, sparky guy with a generous spirit, who excelled in finding people jobs and places to stay, including Cameron, who bedded down in the back room of his shop, her *Peyote Vision* drawing tacked to the wall outside. "Norman had an interest in a lot of things magical, too," recollects Shirley Berman. "He was a strange character. He had just gotten out of prison. He was like a street hustler, but he was extremely intelligent."

Rose's bookshop drew a stream of gifted, young poets, like David Meltzer and Aya. Following the break up of his parents' marriage, Meltzer left his native Brooklyn with his jazz musician father to start a new life in California. The young Meltzer was a talented musician himself, who showcased his unique brand of rhythm and blues on the Horn and Hardart Children's Hour radio show. "I was a hip seventeen-year-old kid from New York so, of course, I knew everything," he quips. "What could these Californians teach me?"

Aya had abandoned the traditional life that was expected of her by escaping a loveless marriage to run off with her artist boyfriend, much to her family's disapproval. To curb her rebellious ways, her father and uncle plotted to have her committed to an institution to receive shock treatment. Luckily, her mother stepped in and advised her to get out of town and save herself. "Back in those days they tried to tame your mind and spirit," Aya expounds. "We didn't have a sisterhood then, so there was no coming together. And once they said God was a *he*, I was finished with the whole thing."

Aya helped Rose sell books at another hangout, Ben Shapiro's Renaissance Club on the Sunset Strip. The venue hosted the pioneering light shows of her new husband Elias Romero, and Aya also read poetry and gave tarot readings there. Eventually, through the scene, she met Cameron. "I admired her art, her magical proficiencies, and her liberated spirit," she explains. "We were on a similar path, although she was ten years ahead of me." As was her custom, Cameron presented the newlyweds with an artwork: a cubist representation of Isis, the Egyptian Goddess of healing and magic.

The Coronet Theatre stood across the street from Books 55, and its screenings included *Inauguration of the Pleasure Dome*. Cameron attended lectures and movie shows there when she could afford to, and became friendly with the projectionist, John Fles. "Cameron was a lively person, a free spirit, but people warned me about hanging out with her because of the black magick," Fles recounts. "Some people were wary of her, but I liked her as a person and her friends, like Wallace and Bob Alexander, were very supportive. Her artwork was the most impressive thing about her. I especially liked one piece where a picture was overlaid with other pictures on tracing paper. She was a really good artist and draughtsman."

To earn a bit of money on the side, to pay for her cinema-going, Cameron put her seamstress skills to work and started sewing clothes at a boutique owned by Donald Morand, Shirley Berman's brother. "Cameron was gorgeous but she didn't have a soft look. She made her own clothes and dressed beautifully; lots of style," Morand recollects. He also appreciated Cameron's dry sense of humour, and recalls the time she introduced him as a gay man at a party with the line: "You wouldn't think so to look at him would you? He looks like a baseball player!"

It was through Morand and Norman Rose that Cameron met the man who would eventually become her second husband, Sheridan Abbot

Kimmel, better known as Sherry, whom she would come to regard as her "tomb-mate."

"Sherry was a friend from Florida," Morand explains. "He'd been hospitalised and didn't work. I met him at Norman Rose's bookshop. Sherry and Norman had either been in the service or hospitalised together."

Like Cameron, Sherry was also a World War II veteran, having joined the Marine Corps Aviation, illegally, aged just 15. Not long after his mother Bess signed the papers for him, he was posted to Parris Island boot camp in South Carolina, notorious for its hardline regiment that proved too much for some recruits. Having survived that, he served as a tail gunner, just as Jim Cameron had done, in the hell of the Pacific Theatre. There he witnessed a comrade getting his head blown off and experienced his own baptism of gunfire when a piece of shrapnel lodged in his skull and became inoperable. Worryingly, it would shift like tectonic plates in his head, alternating his mood swings. Sherry left the service traumatised, suffering from what's known today as PTSD (Post-traumatic stress disorder). His injury and battle fatigue, along with his heavy reliance on drugs, transmogrified him into a real-life Jekyll and Hyde character. Prone to suicidal tendencies, he spent many periods in and out of Veteran Hospital psychiatric wards across the country.

Sherry's sister, Evie Kimmel, had been an ingénue actress back in the late '30s and was once engaged to dreamboat actor Tyrone Power. When she failed to hit the big time as a movie star, she did the next best thing and married one instead; actually two, first the character actor Keenan Wynn, then his co-star and chum Van Johnson, whom, as fate would have it, Cameron first met in the Photo Lab during the war. Wynn hated his oddball brother-in-law and referred to him, disdainfully, as "Sherry Ferblunget Abbott."[2] And Sherry was given the cold shoulder by Van Johnson, too, who dismissed him as a "fuck-up!"[3]

Their kids, on the other hand, adored him. "Sherry was a very otherworldly guy, extremely sensitive, not really made for this world at all," his nephew Ned Wynn recollects. "He introduced me to the music of Louis Jordan and the 'Hungarian Suicide Song' (better known as 'Gloomy Sunday'). He told me that while living out in the desert in Palm Springs, he rode in Martian and Venusian spacecraft and had sex with aliens. He wrote poetry, short stories and pornographic science fiction in which small, naked green women featured prominently. He also ate peyote with the local Indians and had a demonic, schizophrenic alter ego named Baal or Belial. He channelled Horus, who kept him awake at night with his automatic writings, urging him to take drugs. He was always into occult stuff. He had an illustrated book on Kabbalah and tarot cards and all that paraphernalia. Maybe that's how he and Cameron met." Or, more likely, that's what Cameron turned him on to.

Sherry's niece, Schuyler Van Johnson, also retains fond memories of her eccentric uncle: "Uncle Sherry had a great sense of humour. He was the first person I ever heard say "cool" and "stop bugging me" when I was about 7-8 years old. One night in our kitchen he got himself, Ned and some of Ned's chums hysterical, going on and on about Chicken of the Sea and asking why there wasn't a Tuna of the Sky. He was an avid sci-fi fan to the point where he would disappear for entire weekends, to go to the desert watching for UFOs. I think the Roswell incident in 1947 really affected him. He had a pet tarantula named Gar, and he bought me my first ant farm and we watched them designing their house for hours. He drove an old WWII jeep that he loved, and we spent many happy hours riding up into the Trousdale Estates, which was just being built then."

Ned also remembers riding shotgun in Sherry's jeep: "While driving he'd ask, sarcastically, 'How's laughing boy today? My famous brother-in-law?' He was referring to Van, who had become notorious in the family for his huffiness and sulks." Sherry loved to live up to the adage that the best of life lies nearest to death, as Donald Morand recalls all too well: "Sherry was very zany – way too nuts for me. I remember one time we went driving out to the desert and we were hopped-up on Benzedrine and he was driving so fast it was frightening. He sped over these unpaved roads and hit an animal; I got the hell out."

Sherry was repeatedly thrown out of national parks for starting landslides and, during one madcap lark, he ended up covered in sores from touching poison oak while throwing lit branches down the Dead Horse Mine in Yosemite. Though his love of danger struck fear in some, Sherry's surreal sense of humour endeared him to many and, after years of unhappiness, he made Cameron laugh again.

"Sherry was as crazy as a loon but everyone adored him," confirms Shirley Berman. "You couldn't sit in a room for five minutes without crying with laughter, he was so funny. I don't know what it was, it was just funny. He had a lot of demons, but he would even make fun of his demons. I know with Cameron it was terribly comfortable at first. She did love him." As did "the fags in West Hollywood," according to Ned Wynn.[4]

Sherry was a good-looking guy and, like Cameron, he'd been exposed to a wide range of sexual experiences. Indeed, on the surface, they seemed like kindred spirits. Two traumatised souls who used sex and drugs and the occult to explore the outer limits of reality.

That April, Cameron received a communication from her Holy Guardian Angel instructing her to cut her hair, deeming it a residue of her pride and vanity. Over the years she'd developed a real fetish about her crowning glory, and it became a recurring issue in her life, intimately tied in with her mood swings. It was felt by Karl Germer and others that such a sacrifice of her glamour was a deeply un-Thelemic thing to do, and not only took away Cameron's powers of fascination – so ably demonstrated in her appearance in *Inauguration of the Pleasure Dome* – but also smacked of the kind of pious action undertaken by nuns of The Black Brotherhood. There was much truth in this, for strive as she could, Cameron couldn't fully resist that recurring pull towards a cloistered life, and the resulting pudding bowl haircut made her look like a modern-day version of her mystical heroine, Joan of Arc.

Cameron's severe new image was captured by Wallace Berman's camera lens, and indicating the high regard he held her in, he used the resultant photograph for the front cover of his inaugural issue of *Semina 1*, a loose folio of poems and pictures that he printed up at home. For the time it was quite revelatory to see an image of such an androgynous-looking woman, and the photographer Charles Brittin, who worked on that first issue in conjunction with Berman, was enormously jealous of the shot Wally had taken.

"The photograph suggested she'd had some hard times. I think the drugs and the experiences had worn her down, and living out in the desert had taken its toll on her looks. There were a number of people who were very attracted to that life, but couldn't stand it for long." As stated earlier, Brittin was a fellow Iowan and felt it was understandable why Cameron periodically retreated from cityscapes. "We were amused because we both had perceptions of what being born in Iowa meant, and we both got out of there in our own individual ways. We both liked getting away from the distractions of urban life for the more simple life, and it certainly was a simple life, but hard."

Alongside poems by Berman's heroes, Jean Cocteau and Herman Hesse, and new verse courtesy of his compadres David Meltzer and Bob Alexander (aka Baza), *Semina 1* also featured Cameron's *Peyote Vision*, which had made its way from the walls of Norman Rose's bookshop into the Berman's home. Brittin, like many, was knocked out by the drawing but confirms Cameron kept the inspiration behind it to herself.

"She was mysterious about it. She had had something that changed her and I think she was suggesting it related to extraterrestrials, and I interpreted it as mescaline or peyote. The exotic sexuality intrigued me enormously. These really harsh, very hot sexy images she could produce. I was struck by the contrast between that and her other work, which was far more delicate and lacy and ambiguous. Some of the things were conceived when she was on different drugs. Some were definitely erotic and very hardcore-focused, and others were so dreamy, like *Alice in Wonderland*. You figure that out according to her different moods. She had such a range of different modes of impressions. I think of Cameron as producing scary things, inspired by all the mystical, religious things like Aleister Crowley, which to me was scary."

Berman took a special interest in Cameron and the creative bond they formed was noticeable to others. "When Cameron worked with Wally they had something going on that was private and much deeper than the rest," Brittin recollects. "She got the benefit of getting her artwork reproduced, and those from her most intimate group were really proud of it."

Cameron and Sherry enjoyed an on-off relationship to begin with; they weren't cohabiting, and she was pretty much still living an independent life. After a period lodging at Samson De Brier's, she spent May with Norman Rose at his cabin in the Sierra Mountains. Despite the support of friends, life was still proving difficult and she wondered if she was doomed to a living death. Numb, tired and burnt out from living hand to mouth, falling pregnant was the last thing she needed. This time there was no fanfare, as Cameron half expected to miscarry just like she had done before.

She remained a hostage to her see-sawing emotions, which catapulted from crippling lows to exalted highs. She was still disposed to the odd power trip too, behaviour that did not go unnoticed amongst those closest to her. Jane Wolfe was troubled by it and admonished Cameron for taking herself so seriously. Inhabiting the role of Babalon had brought Cameron delusions of grandeur, which, Wolfe urged, had to be brought under control so that her splendour and beauty could shine through.

Renate Druks also shared ambivalent feelings towards Cameron, as Curtis Harrington elucidates. "Renate once said to me that at a certain point, on an occult level, Cameron made a great mistake metaphysically because she was given a choice between love and power and she chose power, and that was her undoing."

One disturbing example of Cameron exerting her dominance like this is relayed by Joan Whitney. She recounts an unsettling trip the two of them made out to Loree Foxx's place in Joshua Tree. Foxx was a former girlfriend of Wallace Berman, who'd abandoned a Hollywood acting career to live a drop-out life. At her home, which included a menagerie, she threw peyote parties and entertained old Hollywood pals like the hell-raising movie star John Drew Barrymore, with whom Cameron developed a close friendship.

"Cameron was aware of the solstice and the time of year, and we went out to the desert on a certain night when there was a full moon. When we got out there she kept saying, 'Come on, let's walk out in the desert.' Now I have certain phobias and I'm certainly not gonna walk in the desert in the dark with scorpions and things, so I didn't go. So we visited Loree and then we drove back to L.A., and as I'm helping her unload the car, I see wrapped up in this blanket were all these really heavy, beautiful, elaborate daggers. There must have been a dozen of them, and I asked her about them and she said she was going to sacrifice me to Aleister Crowley, and that's why she wanted me to go out in the desert. I couldn't believe it because I never noticed them when she was loading up the car." Although Whitney is adamant Cameron meant what she was saying and wasn't joking around, in the end, it amounted to little more than one of her periodic psychodramas. Asked if she feared for her personal safety, Whitney admits, to her credit, "I dunno. I was kinda wild in those days and it didn't happen, so no."

Perhaps it was her Taurean bullish qualities, but Cameron seemed to make a habit of getting into power struggles with certain females. Foxx herself was a case in point. Though they seemed friendly on the surface, others couldn't help but pick up on the simmering rivalry between the two queen bees. "They both had a lot of style," Donald Morand explains. "Maybe I'm biased, but the way I saw it Cameron was competing with Loree. I remember her saying to Loree: 'No matter how much time I spend getting myself together, you always look better.' They both admired each other artistically. Loree did caricatures of all the people in Norman's bookshop, which were really great, but not particularly flattering. But Cameron was the artist. Loree was clever but didn't consider herself an artist or doing a show."

Shirley Berman was one of the few women with whom Cameron didn't display a competitive streak, but she remembers how other females on the scene did harbour bitchy attitudes towards her friend: "I'd say 'Cameron' and they'd say, 'What? You mean, *Marjorie*?' as a put-down. I could never understand that, and I don't know what that was all about except that a lot of men were attracted to her. Cameron was very comfortable around men. I mean, even just as friends."

As a case in point, Cameron was one of the few people who could handle John Drew Barrymore, who could become contentious with people, especially when high on speed and booze. He had a term that described it: "Love-Hate-Fuck-Kill" relationships," but, with Cameron, there was a demonic appreciation of each other.

When her pregnancy went beyond the first trimester, Cameron readied herself for the likelihood that, this time, she would go full term. Sherry assumed the expectant child was his, but Cameron's busy love life put the paternity in question. Although she told Aya that Crystal was conceived in a cave by a man with long red hair, others close to her at the time believed the most likely candidate for fatherhood was Ted Jacobi, one hunky half of an extraordinary-looking pair of identical twin brothers, whom Cameron met while lodging at Samson's.

"The Jacobis were famous for being beautiful," Shirley Berman explains. "They were these blonde Italians who looked like drawings by Cocteau. My brother lived with Ed, who was gay, but Ted, the other, wasn't. He was a gangster. They would come walking down the street and you would just stop cold. They looked like walking sculptures. They had blonde hair and big beautiful blue eyes, not in a pretty way but chiselled. So they were famous for the way they looked; and, I mean, there were *two of them*."

There were indeed, and Kenneth Anger would subsequently suggest that Cameron's conception was the result of a ménage à trois she enjoyed with *both* brothers. According to Aya, there may have been some forethought on Cameron's part, too: "That's how we did it back in those days; you picked a handsome man and said, 'OK, you're it!'"

For a while, the Jacobi twins had been Cameron's companions on the road, joining her in desert wanderings across California and the Hopi Reservation in Arizona, where, Cameron claimed, she learned to master the art of weather magic that had so eluded Jack. Like a gypsy, Cameron took off again that summer, this time to Mexico with a man named John Muir, a divorcee who paid her passage in exchange for helping to take care of his three children.[5]

Heavily pregnant, Cameron returned to Los Angeles to prepare for the impending birth, moving into a pad on North Normandie Avenue in the Los Feliz district.[6] Cameron's den was just a couple of blocks away from 1746 Winona Boulevard, where the original headquarters for the O.T.O. was located, and wasn't far from Jane Wolfe's place on Fountain Avenue, either. A good thing, as Cameron needed a close friend on hand because her relationship with Sherry was becoming increasingly corrosive. During one argument he slit his wrist in front of her. It was a case of *amour fou* – crazy love, with both parties adept at pushing each other's buttons.

Calculating Cameron and Sherry's astrological charts, Aya got an inside track on their dynamic. On Sherry's chart, she discovered the majority of his planets were stacked up in the 8th house. "To have your planets all in the 8th house, that's the house of going into the other world, the occult house," Aya explains. "So it's no wonder he was like that. It suggests he shouldn't really have been here. And he would take these huge bottles of pills; he wouldn't take one or two. It would kill you the amount he took. Sherry was a crazy visionary in his own way."

Cameron's own sign of the zodiac played a pivotal part also. "Cameron didn't pick stable people," Aya asserts. "She picked those that could tell you the mysteries, but there's so much destruction that goes with it. Sherry burnt her tarot cards, for instance. Cameron was Taurus, which is very conservative, and yet that's not who she was. But she also had Scorpio rising, too, so that accounts for her love of delving into the mysteries and her secretiveness. I think she was secret about different parts of her life, except for the magical moments she wanted to share. That's why it's hard to piece it all together. And then she had this Aries moon, so she had a volatile, emotional nature. Both houses of romance were empty, so there was heartbreak in that area. She really was very romantic, and she had these great flights of fancy about the different people she cared about, but they were just fantasies. She wasn't too anxious to jump into anything real. That's not who she was. She had a destiny beyond that stuff."

Cameron's magical path was a crucial element of that destiny and one which Kenneth Anger was hoping to fulfil. That fall, the filmmaker travelled with Dr. Kinsey to Cefalu, Sicily, to visit Crowley's Abbey of Thelema where he once conducted sex magick rituals in partnership with his Scarlet Woman, Leah Hirsig. "Kinsey was interested in Crowley's use of sexual energy," Anger later recounted.[7]

Before they could gain access to the former Abbey they first had to negotiate with the two brothers who owned the now derelict 18th-century farmhouse. This proved far more difficult than expected, as they found themselves caught in a farcical tug of war between the two siblings: one a Mussolini-loving, black-shirted fascist, the other a dyed-in-the-wool Communist. Once an agreement was brokered, Anger set about removing the whitewash from the walls, to reveal Crowley's erotic and demonic Gauguin-inspired frescoes beneath, which locals had covered up, deeming them blasphemous. (Crowley was eventually expelled from Cefalu by Mussolini, who feared Italy wasn't big enough for two megalomaniacs!)

That September, Anger wrote to Cameron and wildly exhorted her to come to Cefalu, to take her rightful place at the Abbey. He enclosed a manifesto, which he urged her to sign up to, pledging her to dedicate her life to magick and the Great Work of Thelema. But Cameron wrote back explaining she couldn't make the trip over because she was pregnant and had no funds, and was in great pain due to the appalling state of her teeth.

With dreams of enthroning Cameron in the Abbey, Anger also wrote to Karl Germer, asking him for money to save the site and restore it to its former glory. But his hopes were dashed when Germer balked at the price Anger had been quoted, and accused the owners of trying to bilk what they assumed was a rich American. Jane Wolfe, who actually helped decorate the Abbey, also questioned the whole venture, believing the Abbey had already served its purpose and was not worth re-establishing anew.

Furthermore, despite what Anger told Lady Frieda Harris, Wolfe wasn't exactly enraptured by *Inauguration of the Pleasure Dome* either and, in a letter to Karl Germer, asserted that, despite watching it three times, she could not discern any Thelemic connotation in it whatsoever. In fact, she compared it unfavourably to the productions of silent films she herself once starred in and chided: "There was no scenario. Like the old Mack Sennet comedies, they started 'shooting' and worked out a plot as they progressed. Interesting in spots, but the bacchanalia ending of the picture needed the hand of a Cecil B. DeMille – as I remember the movies."[8]

Cameron's coronation would have to wait a while, anyway, for on Christmas Eve, 1955, her baby daughter was born at the LA County Memorial Hospital. The hospital was so overcrowded, Cameron was forced to deliver in a corridor, alongside three black women who were all in labour, too. The newborn was christened Crystal Eve Kimmel, in commemoration of the day of her birth and as a tribute to Sherry's sister, Evie. Regardless of the questionable paternity, Sherry was named as the father on her birth certificate.

For Cameron, after so many miscarriages, the birth came as a sweet relief but, from the outset, she found the demands of a newborn baby impossible to deal with. She got so stressed-out one night, she showed up at the Berman's house in Beverly Glen in a dreadful state, begging them to take Crystal off her hands. "Cameron came to stay with us right after Crystal was born and they hadn't slept in two weeks, Cameron or Crystal," Shirley Berman recollects. "She asked if we could help her and we said 'Sure' and she brought Crystal over and stayed for one night and then disappeared for about five days and left Crystal with us. Crystal never slept; it was so strange."

It's doubtful there was any prenatal care on Cameron's part, and for someone in the habit of ingesting hallucinogenics, this could've explained some of Crystal's behavioural problems. Motherhood had not diminished Cameron's macabre side either. The Bermans were also celebrating the birth of their own child, Tosh, and when his uncle Donald told Cameron he was worried they were all going to freeze to death out there that winter, she presented him with a ghoulish watercolour of his newborn nephew dead in a cemetery. "It was genuinely frightening," Morand recollects. "But I felt responsible because of my stupid mouth. It was like she was interpreting visually what I was saying and gave me this horrible picture. What it depicted was horrifying and I tore it up."

In the autumn of 1956, Cameron was given her first art exhibition, a joint show with the artist Ed Kienholz, held at curator Walter Hoops' Syndell Studio in Brentwood. What should have been a cause for celebration ended, alas, in catastrophe, when the building caught fire and destroyed some of the artworks, including Cameron's.

Shortly after the exhibit, Cameron and Sherry travelled down to Florida to visit his sister Tess and her husband at their home in Hialeah. It was meant to be a happy family reunion, but it was marred by emotional meltdowns. It all started when Cameron suggested to Sherry that she'd like Kenneth Anger to be brought into their new set-up, for she regarded him, alongside her prospective husband, as her priests – one of the Moon, the other of the Sun. Sherry entertained the idea at first, but when she mentioned her plan of reuniting with Anger in Spain, he hit the roof and destroyed her passport, not only so she couldn't travel, but so she would also be forced to get a new one with his surname on it.

Furthermore, despite him being dead, Sherry remained insanely jealous of Jack Parsons, and the hold he still exerted over Cameron. He desperately wanted to replace him as her magical partner and, trying to break the spell, he tore up Jack's magical diary, as well as the journal Cameron kept of their time together, casting each ripped page into the sea.

This was not the first time Jack's materials had gone with the wind. His possessions had a bad habit of slipping through Cameron's fingers. For instance, in the period immediately after her husband's death,

Cameron left several hundred of his books, plus a briefcase full of his manuscripts, with the public librarian in Pasadena, before she left the city. When she returned to claim them several months later, she discovered the librarian had disposed of most of the books and the briefcase had disappeared. Then there was the time she sailed to Catalina, in the wake of her drug bust, and carted Jack's black box with her, only to leave it unattended on the quayside. She kept a watchful eye on the box from her hotel window, observing how the fishermen and members of the public walked past without seeming to notice it.

Cameron's kooky behaviour and mishandling of her husband's magical possessions was becoming a serious cause for concern for her fellow Thelemites, who felt Jack's precious papers were no longer safe in his widow's hands. Endeavouring to secure as much as possible, they requested that Cameron start sharing the remaining material or, at the very least, make copies of the writings before they were lost forever.

Cameron was willing to share the contents of the black box with Jane Wolfe, whom she loved and trusted, and these included the recordings Jack and L. Ron Hubbard had made while performing the Babalon Working. These fragile records were the kind used by secretaries to take dictation and were not built to withstand repeated plays, which is exactly what had happened to them; so, as a result, the audio was now virtually wiped clean. Cameron also sent Wolfe a painting: her rendition of a circle with the trine set within it which, she contended, was her sign to Jack that she was undeniably Babalon. Jack vowed that one day the painting would be priceless, but Cameron had always detested it and now wondered whether she should bury it along with the black box.

The disastrous trip to Florida made Cameron homesick for California, but before she could leave, she had to wait to collect on the insurance claim for her paintings that were lost in the Syndell Studio fire to pay for her return. Back in L.A., there weren't too many options on the table in front of her, and with her relationship with Sherry on the rocks, and weighed down by the responsibility of her baby, Cameron went to stay at her parents' home for a while. But she soon hit the road again after another row with her mother, who now regarded her daughter as the black sheep of the family.

The rift between Cameron and her mother was further exacerbated by the preferential way Carrie treated Mary Lou's own difficult child, which she babied as though it was her own; all the while remonstrating that she was unable to cope with Crystal. "When Cameron mentioned her family it was always negative," Shirley Berman confirms. "It was extremely dysfunctional. She didn't want to talk about them. She would mention them but then say, 'I don't wanna talk about those assholes!' and that was it." Cameron would never go into details, but Shirley Berman could tell it was based on some long-drawn-out issues: "She talked about growing up in Iowa and, to me, it sounded like she never had a happy childhood."

For a while, Cameron disappeared off the radar, but Sal Ganci eventually located her living in a shabby, little hillside house in El Sereno: "I visited her there and Cameron made some lunch for me, and Crystal was the nude table centrepiece. While she sat, knees folded, she urinated. No fuss or comments were made." When Ganci returned a week later, Cameron and Crystal had packed up and gone, and the house was deserted, except for the base and elaborately carved headboard of Jack's Italian Renaissance bed.

Cameron had moved on to a new place in the Highland Park district, south of Pasadena, a predominantly Mexican community. Afeared of the flame-haired witch in their midst, her #superstitious neighbours began leaving the heads of decapitated cats outside her door. "I stayed there with her for about a week and it was so sad," remembers Shirley Berman. "She said that stuff like that had been going on ever since she moved there. It was awful. I also remember there was a room there that was kind of private, actually. It had a panel that you had to push to get into this back room, and there were strange dolls in there and a lot of magick stuff, and I looked in there fast and I thought, that's a room I don't want to spend any time in. It had that kind of aura."

Around the time she visited, Wallace Berman had just published the second issue of *Semina*, which featured a contribution from Cameron, a poetic work in progress entitled 'The Anatomy of Madness.' Its lines were dedicated to Jack, whom she credited for magically creating her.

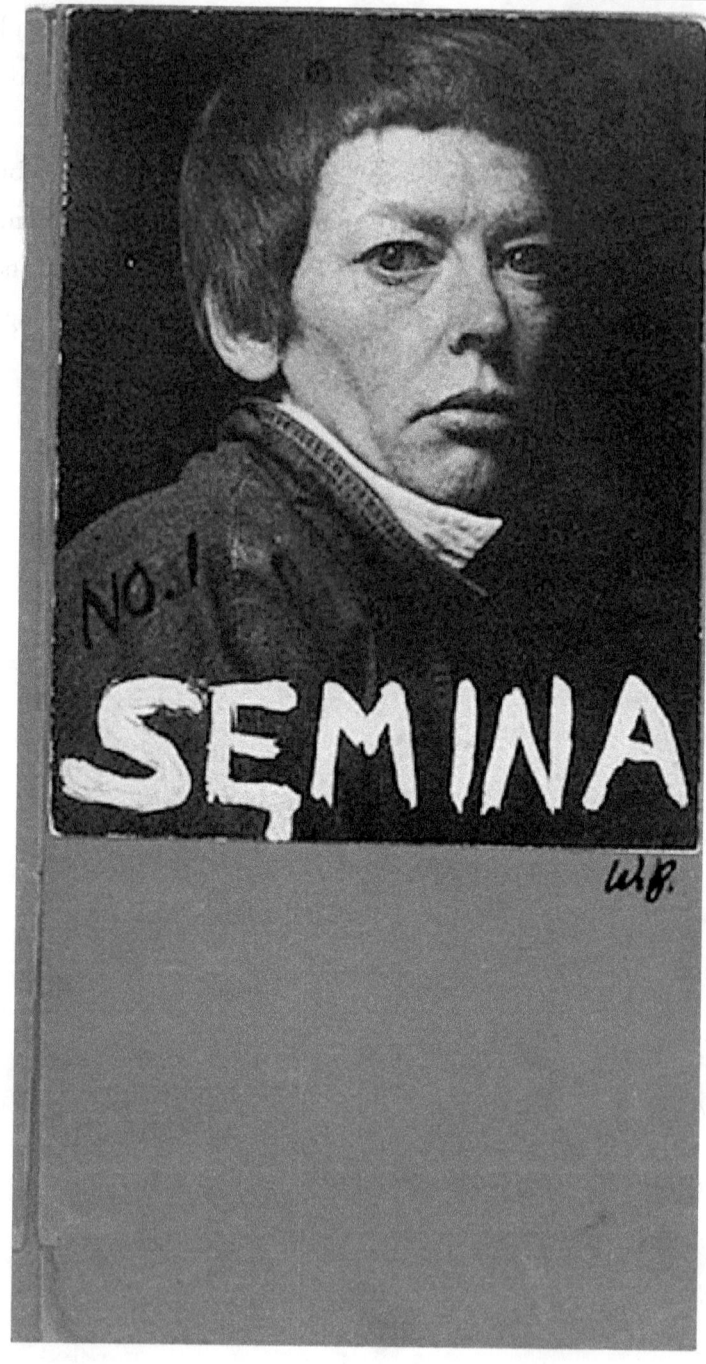

Cameron in Joan of Arc mode captured by Wallace Berman's lens. The photograph featured on the cover of his inaugural art folio *Semina 1*. (Courtesy of Shirley and Tosh Berman and the Wallace Berman Estate.)

Ed and Ted, the extraordinary-looking Jacobi twins. Both are rumoured to be the real father of Cameron's daughter, Crystal. 1955. (Courtesy of the Warburg Institute.)

Kenneth Anger and Dr. Alfred Kinsey in Cefalu, Sicily while visiting Aleister Crowley's Abbey of Thelema. 1955. Anger had dreams of re-establishing the Abbey and enthroning Cameron as its new Scarlet Woman. (Courtesy of the Warburg Institute.)

8 - The Wormwood Star

> "One must still have chaos in oneself to be able to give birth to a dancing star." *Thus Spoke Zarathustra* by Friedrich Nietzsche.

Prior to the ill-fated exhibition at the Syndell Studio, Cameron collaborated with Curtis Harrington on a short, poetic film study, dedicated to her artwork. "I admired her very much and *The Wormwood Star* is my personal homage to her work and persona," the filmmaker explains. "She was an intensely personal artist and she lived in her own imaginings. You can tell that from her poetry and diaries."

The film's title, of course, harkened back to the sex magick rituals Cameron conducted during the Beaumont days. "Before I made the film, I'd heard from Renate that Cameron had spent some time in the desert trying, through magical means, to conceive a child by the spirit of Jack Parsons without success. Cameron never spoke of Jack directly, but I do remember feeling sometimes when I talked to her, of her going off into a realm that I didn't understand at all. It was sort of an apocalyptic thing and it's there in her poetry."

The film was shot on 16mm Kodachrome in the Whitley Heights home of Edward James, the millionaire art patron and poet, who generously allowed the struggling young filmmaker to reside there while he was abroad. "Edward was a wonderful man and an extremely eccentric person," Harrington recalls fondly. "He never lived in this house, but he would visit on rare occasions. The house was filled with pieces from his own collection of surrealist art, so he had major paintings by Salvador Dali, Pavel Tchelitchew and lots of Eugene Berman. I was very privileged to live in that environment."

James' former wife was none other than Cameron's childhood heroine, Tilly Losch, and he was a major player on the Mexican art scene, who counted the surrealist painter Leonora Carrington among his protégées. Harrington sees a great affinity between the work of Cameron and Carrington, and it's been suggested that the two women may have actually met during Cameron's travels in Mexico. In hindsight, it's a shame that Edward James never made Cameron's acquaintance or appraised her work, for he might have provided some much-needed patronage. But, according to Harrington, the art connoisseur never even saw the fruits of his own labour: "There was no market for Cameron's art and no market for that film."

The indivisible line between Cameron and her artworks was increasingly evident to her closest allies. Shirley Berman describes how on entering Cameron's domicile: "You would experience the strangest feeling: Cameron *became* her paintings. It was just totally revealing and beautiful." The artistic expression of Cameron's spirituality was reaffirmed in the penultimate title card of *The Wormwood Star*, which signalled her mystical attainment in the Silver Star system: 'Concerning The Knowledge And Conversation Of The Holy Guardian Angel As Revealed To Cameron.'

The filmmaker admits that some of Cameron's more esoteric concepts were lost on him, but he could always rely on their mutual friend, Paul Mathison, to translate them. The multitalented Mathison also lent his skilled hands behind the scenes, dressing the set, drawing the opening title cards and Seal of Solomon pentagram, and designing the extraordinary costume that adorns Cameron at the end of the film. "Paul was not a painter, he was simply a designer," Harrington explains. "He had a great flair for dressing a woman. He could take a bolt of cloth and swirl it around, and that's what Cameron wore." For a soundtrack, Harrington turned to the percussionist Phillip Harland, a physicist by profession who, in collaboration with his wife, the accomplished artist Leona Wood, conjured a minimalist, Middle Eastern score that was improvised to a screening of the film.

With the chime of a gong still reverberating, the film opens on a white-walled atelier, decorated with figurines, decanters filled with potions and objet d'art. The ominous sound of discordant strings heralds Cameron's dramatic entrance. At first, Harrington shoots her from the waist down, tracking her movement as she sweeps into the room, trailing a crimson cloak and stepping past a Seal of Babalon star chalked on the red-tiled floor.

Cameron sits at a table, her face obscured, and strikes a theatrical pose, replicating the outstretched arm of the naked male statue in front of her. There is a mirror on the table and an open book, with a red rose and a key resting on its pages. Another occult book lays opened at her feet, and a stigmata wound is visible on her one barefoot. She sits perfectly still, dwarfed by the large Seal of Solomon pentagram on the wall behind her. Up until now, Cameron's face has not been seen, and when it is finally revealed her russet hair is cropped short and her eyebrows are exaggerated, so much so that her Vulcan visage bears an uncanny resemblance to the Australian artist, Rosaleen Norton.

Despite being born five years and a continent apart, the similarities between the two female artists was not just physical. Like Cameron, Norton's artwork explored phantasmagorical themes, and her erotically charged canvases were emblazoned with daemons, succubuses and serpent-tongued women. Both women invoked the Gods of wild sexual abandon to inspire them: Babalon and Pan respectively. And just as Cameron once drew pictures in the sand by the side of the road, as a young girl back in Belle Plaine, an urchin Norton earned chump change busking as a pavement artist. Unlike Cameron, though, Norton became a beloved and delightfully dotty celebrity in her lifetime, nicknamed "The Witch of King's Cross."

In a similar vein, Harrington likens Cameron's more delicate work to another queen of bohemia, the Argentine artist Leonor Fini, whom he'd known while living in Paris in the early 50s: "I think her line drawings are similar to Cameron's, they're very feminine."

Sat at the table, Cameron starts mirror-gazing, the meditative technique which allows an individual to communicate with spirits or glimpse visions of the afterlife. Harrington's camera follows Cameron's gaze as it disappears through the looking glass, reopening on the other side, where her macabre portrait gallery dwells: An astral vision of an electrified face with insane eyes. The masked facade of some strange, insectival entity. A wolfish devil with sly, satanic eyes.[1] Then, arguably the finest picture of all, a child with cracked eyes and frizzy hair based on a doll Cameron buried and then dug up.[2]

Cameron compliments this haunting display by reciting an ode to The Wormwood Star, Jack's apocalyptic heir, delivered in her *sotto voce* voice:

"Seven times I rap upon the mighty door of the subterranean vault. Open, open, I stand without in the drafty and dank corridor that approaches thy lair. Seven times resound my summons on this stony door, in the dead stern caves and curse the midnight hour. Come thou forth, I bear a lamp for this terrible darkness; thou shall behold that face known in dreams. Mine eyes are terrible and strange but thou knowest me. Behold my garments are of rich cloth and I bear the air of a land of bounty beyond the sea. Come forth, thou art in the shadow of the light I bear, and thy garments reek of the dead in this sunless place. We shall ascend the stair that is fraught with unwholesome things. The stone road before me and into the blazing vault of the night of nights we go forth as light."

Harrington's camera pans from head to toe to take in a full-length line drawing of an empress, clad in a hijab and swathed in silken robes. He then repeats this process on a demoness with an enormous mane and a fleshless body of blood vessels, pissing into a chasm. An image of a blackened phoenix with tattered wings brings this first collection of pictures to an end, and the screen fades to black, momentarily, before a blast of trumpets signals the next set of images: A travelling caravan of medieval armies brandishing heraldic flags, and Cocteauesque religious figures with gigantic mitres and wimples, riding bug-eyed steeds across the sky.

Harrington's lens roams the paintings, to a jangling soundtrack of drums and tambourines, picking out Viking warriors, African tribesmen, pink swans and childlike depictions of dinosaurs. Through thoughtful editing, the filmmaker manages to visually marry Cameron's pictures with her poetry. The best example of this is when his camera settles on a rendition of the Three Magi pointing to the Star of Bethlehem, symbolizing the birth of the most famous mystical cherub; and, as it does, Cameron's exaltation to her own celestial child, who has, in its own way, also been cast down from the heavens, reconvenes in perfect sync:

> "*Dark star I seek you in all the endless rooms of the universe. I have entered the maze of chaos and searched the promise of no end and no fulfilment but I have seen your helmeted head flashing gold from all the bloody triumphs and sunsets of the world. I have heard your voice singing lonely songs of desire in the world-womb. I remember the artistry of fingers that held the rose in wonder. Your musical flute sounding the hymn of love seeking since the birth in the crashing star nebulae. Sing limbs of muscle and star foam, pursued and pursuing radiant warrior, how long? In love of God, how long? How long? How long?*"

As her words trail off, the camera comes to rest on a tribe of Mongolians, wrapped in papooses and huddled at the death scene of Kubla Khan, a nod to Cameron's beloved Coleridge poem. Then, in a stunning finale, Cameron reappears, wearing an asymmetrical, gold lamé bodysuit. With her arms outstretched in a crucifix pose, she stands beneath a wreath of gold leaves, holding a sprig of gold leaves in her right hand. Harrington's symbolism is clear: "The thrust of the film is to present the artist as an alchemist who, through her creative work, becomes herself transmuted into gold."[3] The filmmaker captures this vision of beauty and power in a full-length shot that gradually zeroes in on Cameron's face, closing with a close-up of her patented witchy stare.

Looking back, fifty years on, Curtis Harrington remains justifiably proud of *The Wormwood Star*, but its artistic value would become all the more significant years later, when many of the paintings featured in the film, most notably the religious figures from the travelling caravan, which were rendered on parchment paper, were incinerated by Cameron in what the director describes as a "ritualistic orgy of destruction. I don't know why or what was in her mind but it was a great loss, so the only evidence of this work is in my film." Reflecting on their collaboration, he muses: "I think Cameron respected me for who and what I was. I'm just very happy I made the film because I think it's an important landmark as evidence of her work and her life. It was made out of love."

In June of 1957, Wallace Berman held his first exhibition at the recently opened Ferus Gallery on La Cienega Boulevard. Founded by Walter Hopps and the artist Ed Kienholz, the gallery featured an array of Berman's installations and sculptures.

Following a complaint that obscene material was being displayed, two plainclothes vice cops showed up to check the show out, totally missing the pornographic photo in a glass box hanging from the arm of Berman's crucifix sculpture *Cross*. According to Charles Brittin, the cops would have left without incident if Ed Kienholz hadn't retrieved a reproduction of Cameron's *Peyote Vision* from a pile of loose *Semina* pages at the foot of another Berman assemblage *Temple*, and waved it in their faces, taunting, "Is this what you're looking for?"

Motives differ as to what possessed Kienholz to do such a provocative thing. Some saw it as a misguided attempt to drum up publicity for the show, while others, like Shirley Berman, allege it was an underhanded ploy for getting her husband's show out of the gallery. Whatever the reason, Berman was promptly arrested on the grounds of obscenity and the show was closed down. Unable to pay the $100 fine, the artist was locked up for the night and only released when his movie star pal, Dean Stockwell, bailed him out the next morning. The whole sorry experience put Berman off from ever exhibiting in a commercial gallery again. While Cameron's subsequent claim, that Wallace urged her to fight the charges in court, is disputed by Shirley Berman, for as Charles Brittin points out: "No one even thought to contact The American Civil Liberties Union at the time, to defend the case under freedom of expression."

    This incident only seemed to reinforce Cameron's belief that her words and images had the power to stir up trouble. This sentiment was emblazoned on a flame-singed, magical journal she titled *Abraxas*, which carried a caution similar to the one that graced Jack's black box. In essence, that only those with a strong will and a pure heart would be able to handle its contents – the rest risked being destroyed by them.

    That September, as part of a group of poets that included David Meltzer, Cameron read from her journals at a poetry evening held at Bob Alexander's Stone Brothers print shop on Sawtelle Boulevard. In attendance that night was Berman's bailsman Dean Stockwell, who had been introduced to Cameron via that debut issue of *Semina*.

    "Seeing Cameron's image on *Semina 1* was like meeting her," Stockwell recollects. "She was wildly talented and hyper-unique. A very, very intense personality, but very fascinating. I was very concerned, at the time, with that part of humans that has to do with love, so we had a good friendship on that basis. My life's had a great deal of alchemy and magic, but I frowned upon Mister Crowley, a big dark frown. I think he was full of shit and, unfortunately, she didn't avoid disasters that pitifully go with Crowley. She once told me, and I agree, that some psychologist had told her it was a good thing she was an artist because if she wasn't she'd be a dangerous person."

Stockwell, in turn, introduced Cameron to his fellow actor and best friend Dennis Hopper. He, too, was awed by the scene's two leading lights: "Cameron and Wallace Berman, they had infectious personalities. It wasn't anything they said necessarily, it was just their presence. They were just someone that you knew were different and they had a magnetic quality that you wanted to be closer to. You knew they were special. They had a special aura about them."

Invariably, when someone acquires an alarming reputation, it tends to give others the license to embroider and embellish and, typically, over the years, the dark rumours swirling around about Cameron's past had become increasingly extreme and exaggerated, as Hopper attests: "The stories I'd heard before I even met Cameron: how she was a witch; how her husband blew himself up trying to do a Frankenstein number in the garage trying to bring a cadaver back to life or something; how they were followers of Aleister Crowley; how they drank blood and sacrificed cats. I'd heard that they'd had a black mass or something and some guy had fallen down the stairs and broken his neck, which gave him an erection and four women had fucked him before the emergency squad arrived [laughs]. Now whether these were true stories or not, they were the kind of thing you heard and you thought: who is this woman? These stories came together and you thought: Wow! [Laughs]. So you had that sort of going in."

Also sharing the bill with Cameron and Meltzer that night was the visiting Scottish author Alexander Trocchi who famously referred to himself as "a cosmonaut of inner space." In tandem with writers like William Burroughs and the poet Phillip Lamantia, Trocchi's work drew on his heroin addiction, a drug whose usage was glamourised partly due to the knowledge that hallowed heroes like Charlie Parker, Miles Davis and Billie Holiday had all been hooked on it.

"Trocchi was a transgressive hero, particularly when *Cain's Book* came out later, which is all about the romance of heroin," explains David Meltzer. "Wallace did the cover for Phillip Lamantia's anthology *Narcotica*, which shows him fixing. Whether it's opium or absinthe, there's always some drug or substance that becomes a trigger for great work, although William Blake did it without anything."

One person inheriting Blake's mantle was the New York poet Allen Ginsberg. Two years earlier, at the Six Gallery in San Francisco, he delivered his jeremiad *Howl* – a state of the (alien)nation address, whose publication threw down the gauntlet and signalled the arrival of a radical New Beat Vision. The literary term "Beat" was conjured by his friend and fellow Columbia University alumni Jack Kerouac, who'd heard the 42nd Street hustler, Herbert Huncke, using it frequently to describe how weary and beaten down he was. Huncke was responsible for introducing the uptown college boys to the dark delights of the Times Square demimonde, which Ginsberg memorably described as "A giant megalopolitan drawing room, where everyone would meet to discuss the oncoming apocalypse."[4]

In his roman à clef *On the Road*, Kerouac transformed the word beat into a soulful, "beatific" vision of America. Written to a Benzedrine-fuelled, bebop temp, his breathless prose reflected a young, romantic flip side of American society: a post-war gathering of malcontents lusting for life, meaning and mystical illumination amidst the hydrogen bombs, crass materialism and conformity. The book brought Kerouac overnight stardom, but being hailed as a "spokesman for a generation" became burdensome, and he'd spend the next decade drinking himself out of his predicament. By then, his torch had been passed on to the next generation, his legacy "having started an unprecedented worldwide cultural revolution," according to Burroughs.[5]

The older, erudite Burroughs was regarded as a mentor by Kerouac and Ginsberg, and the dutiful duo helped piece together his soon-to-be-released novel *Naked Lunch*, a collection of riotous routines inspired by the author's escapades whilst residing in the underbellies of New York, Mexico City and Tangier. Due to the homosexually graphic content of the book, the U.S. pressing of *Naked Lunch* was initially banned in America for obscenity, as was Ginsberg's *Howl*, but both rulings were ultimately overturned in pivotal decisions that helped turn the tide in favour of unfettered artistic freedom.

The incendiary work of this vanguard of writers inspired a burgeoning Beat subculture, and its flame burned brightest in its primary enclaves: the East and West Villages in New York, Venice in Los Angeles, and the North Beach neighbourhood in San Francisco. Wallace Berman felt a strong kinship with the Beats and became a solid ally, publishing excerpts from their work in subsequent issues of *Semina*. However, it's unclear what, if anything, the Beats meant to Cameron. In later years she would often be mistakenly labelled as a Beat artist, merely because she swam in the same waters. Born the same year as Kerouac, she was certainly a contemporary age-wise, but, artistically, Cameron was really a pre-Beat bohemian whose heart lay in Romanticism. Also, as Aya contends, the "boy's own" nature of the Beat's storytelling didn't always speak to their female constituents: "Kerouac wasn't my mentor. We women didn't have icons."

Still, it's easy to see why *Howl*, Ginsberg's meditation on madness, might have particularly appealed to Cameron. The original Olympia Press copy of Burroughs' *Naked Lunch* was certainly available to read at the Berman's house but, according to David Meltzer, the most likely candidate for her attention, if any, would've been the poetry of Ginsberg's protégé, the Shelley-inspired scapegrace, Gregory Corso.

One widely admired book that certainly did have an effect on Cameron, and the rest of the Semina crowd, was *The Outsider*, written by the precociously talented English writer, Colin Wilson. Using the lives of great artists, writers and thinkers (including Van Gogh, William

Blake, Franz Kafka, Ernest Hemingway, Herman Hesse, Friedrich Nietzsche, Albert Camus, Jean-Paul Sartre and T. S. Eliot) as examples, Wilson reasoned that the state of being an outsider in society was the natural home for any sensitive artist, and maintained that such individuals were particularly susceptible to manic depression, which accounted for their euphoric creative highs as well as their devastating emotional lows. These were sentiments that Cameron could certainly relate to, and many of her friends took solace from the book. "Anything remotely mystical like *The Outsider*, or Hesse's *Magister Ludi* (*The Glass Bead Game*), or the works of D.H. Lawrence were gobbled up," Aya attests.

In the winter of 1957, Cameron, Norman Rose and David Meltzer left L.A. for San Francisco, which was gaining a reputation as the West Coast Mecca for the Beat phenomenon. In reaction, *San Francisco Chronicle* columnist Herb Caen coined the term "Beatnik" in jest at these interlopers, who seemed as way-out to him as the soon-to-be-launched Russian satellite, Sputnik 1.

Soon after they settled, Rose found Meltzer a job at his book warehouse and turned his place on Larkin Street over to his two friends. "At first Cameron and Crystal lived with me," Meltzer recollects, "and then she moved into her own place, a cheap basement rental at 707 Scott Street in the North Beach district. There we had a brief dalliance under funny and unusual circumstances. It was spontaneous, natural sex magick. Cameron had moved into this high-ceilinged, Victorian-era apartment and bought gallons of army surplus khaki paint – she liked that colour – to decorate the walls. It was winter, so the windows were closed and two hours into the decorating the ether fumes from the paint filled the room and we arrived at one of those ether planes. When you're young and stoned, nothing is impossible. I've never forgotten it. I'm sure I should talk to one of the disciples of the O.T.O. as it was definitely a sex magick experience. It was nothing that I knew about.

Not that I was this hugely experienced stud – Cameron was – and she was doing things that struck me at the time as being supernatural. She was real when it came to that and I respected that."

When she wasn't having an enchanting effect on men, Cameron's day-to-day existence consisted of struggling to get by and make ends meet, or as Meltzer wryly puts it: "The mundaneness in between the satanic rituals! I was basically Cameron's confidant. We'd sit in the kitchen and drink coffee or chain-smoke pot, which was really terrible back then, so you had to smoke an awful lot to get its effect. We'd talk about literary things. Cameron loved the Bollingen series of books on Coleridge and she'd point out things she liked. She identified with anybody in the Romantic, anti-modernist tradition. Coleridge first, Keats and Shelley second. Crowley was more into Swinburne, and I think Cameron may have found him too hothouse. Blake should've appealed to her as he conversed with angels and painted metaphysical kingdoms in retaliation to the mechanised world. Joseph Campbell's *Hero with a Thousand Faces* really spoke to her, but strangely not *The White Goddess* book by Robert Graves that was out around the same time. Campbell already had synthesised many different traditions and narratives and mythologies but, in a sense, he gave a different kind of permission. It wasn't bogged down so much in the kind of male power structure that she had been involved in. It was kind of a comprehensive narrative that you could apply to both the male and female experience."

When it came to Crystal, Cameron made good on her previously reported intention to raise her children with the freedom to do as they liked. Meltzer got a taste of her hands-off approach when they went for a meal at a local Chinese restaurant and Crystal ran amok, and her mother refused to intervene when she crashed other people's tables and bumped into things: "Her attitude was, 'That's how she'll learn.'"

For Joan Whitney, Cameron's attitude was in accordance with the edicts of Crowley: "I think Cameron was more of the school of 'You don't say no,' and with Crowley, one of the things I learned in life to this day is, it's very hard to say 'I' because you had that thing that if you said 'I' you slashed yourself. So I think Crystal was just never told 'No!' Aya saw it as a case of like mother like daughter: "Cameron refused to be tamed and so she brought up Crystal that way... uncivilised."

During the period Cameron spent with Meltzer, she made little reference to her past, save for one key incident: "I remember walking together through a tunnel to North Beach and she admitted that it was the first time in years, since Jack's death, that she'd been able to walk with her head up and look people in the eyes again."

One such person was Edward Silverstone Taylor, a Pasadena-born pianist who used to frequent the parties she and Jack threw back in the coach house days. Since then, Taylor had become a well-known hipster on the North Beach Beat scene, organizing such events as the Collective Expressionism happening at The Six Gallery, where Allen Ginsberg and Jack Kerouac read poetry and participants destroyed a piano and many of the artworks on display.

Taylor also dabbled in film and devised the Lucitron, an optical projector that could be manipulated to create an endless variety of patterns and colours according to the skill of the operator. After the two of them became reacquainted, Taylor decided to train his visual eye on Cameron and made her the focus of his seven-minute, home movie-style film *Street Fair San Francisco*.[6] The Ektachrome footage captured Cameron hawking her artistic wares at the bustling street fair on Upper Grant Avenue. Crystal is seen briefly in the film too, holding a naked dolly, as are Wallace and Shirley Berman, who would soon take over Cameron's vacated apartment on Scott Street.[7]

Among the display of Cameron's paintings, two pieces really stood out. *Crystal* was a sublime depiction of her daughter as an elemental sprite, rendered on a discarded door panel, which gave the feel, if not the appearance, of the kind of assemblage art that was being made by some of Cameron's friends, like the junk artist George Herms. While a canvas, alternatively known as *The Beast* or *The Vampyre Woman*, depicted a borzoi-like creature with a vaguely human face, an arched spine and a mane of red hair.

Also featured in the footage were Taylor's friend and fellow filmmaker Dion Vigne and his wife Loreon, an enamelist who helped run the street fair. Like Ed Taylor, Loreon had also attended the coach house soirées in Pasadena but had only seen Cameron once since Jack died. "It was a few years after Jack blew himself up," she recollects. "Cameron came to visit me at my factory in West Covina, where I made ceramics. We were having a nitrous oxide party, and after she inhaled some she ran off with some young guy into the orange groves. I always wondered if that's how Crystal was born."

Loreon couldn't help but notice the change in Cameron since she last saw her: "She obviously cared a lot about Jack and was really depressed after he died. She had this dark aura, and I was aware of a certain amount of mystery around her. We'd hang out together, sit around and smoke pot and listen to music. I was impressed by her. I loved her artwork. It was slightly satanic, but she had a nice style. She was an amazing person. She was this very mysterious, very intriguing human being who always looked a little wild. She *was* a wild one."

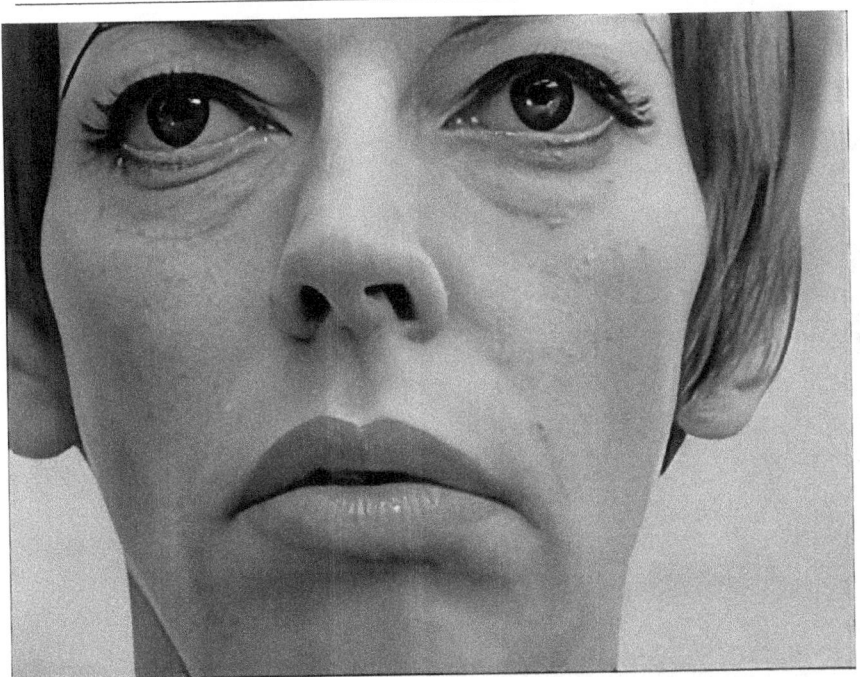

Close-up of Cameron from Curtis Harrington's film *The Wormwood Star*. (Courtesy of Curtis Harrington.)

A still of Cameron from the finale of *The Wormwood Star*. (Courtesy of Curtis Harrington.)

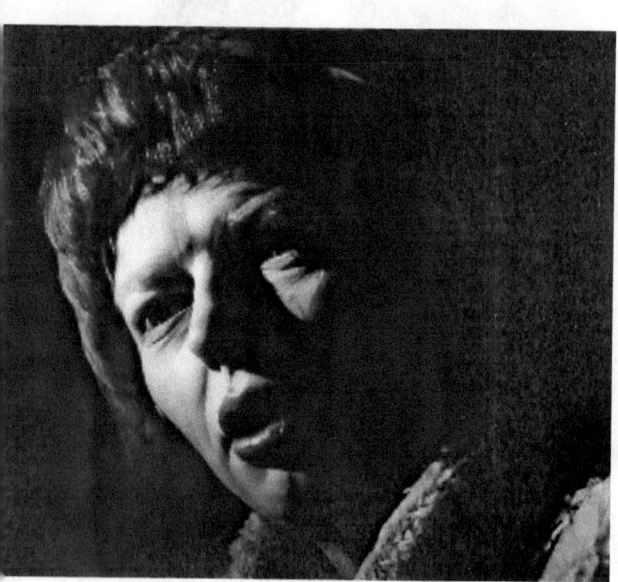

Cameron photographed by Joan Whitney around the time she starred in *The Wormwood Star*. (Courtesy of Joan Whitney.)

Cameron takes a dram. (Photo courtesy of Joan Whitney.)

David Meltzer LP cover. 1958.
Around the time he and Cameron moved to San Francisco.

The actor John Gilmore. "Cameron was like Jimmy Dean ... they both took risks and made discoveries." (Courtesy of John Gilmore.)

Stills of Cameron from Ed Silverstone Taylors film, *Street Fair San Francisco*.

Right: Shirley Berman, smoking a Sherman's cigarette, in a still from *Street Fair San Francisco*.

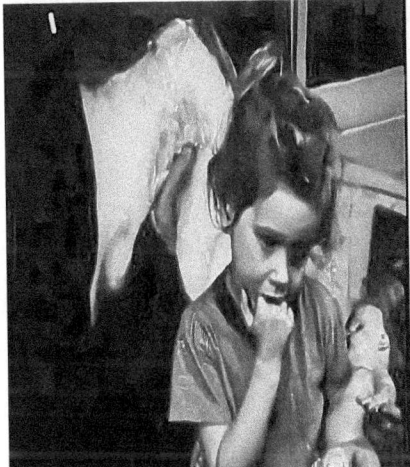

A still of Crystal from *Street Fair San Francisco*.

A still of Wallace Berman from *Street Fair San Francisco*.

Cameron with Crystal and her second husband Sherry, one week before they were married. Sherry had recently been released from the VA Psychiatric Hospital in Florida where his head had been shaved. Pasadena, 1959. (Courtesy of the Warburg Institute.)

9 - ERONBU

"We Jews killed Christ and, if he comes back, we'll kill him again." – Lenny Bruce

Following her twelve-month stint in San Francisco, Cameron returned to Los Angeles and, on April 13, 1959, she finally tied the knot with Sherry in a civil ceremony down at Santa Monica City Hall. Sherry had only recently been released from the VA Psychiatric Hospital in Coral Gables, Florida, and had driven across the country to join his intended. In the months leading up to the marriage, Cameron had undergone a hysterectomy, a procedure she'd put off for some time, fearing it would have an impact on her nuptials by making her sexually unresponsive to her husband. While she was hospitalised, Cameron described her fiancé to a social worker as a talented, sensitive and high-strung writer whom, she felt, could thrive in the right environment. But she also admitted to feeling a deep-rooted anxiety that she could no longer bear children for him, and would be caught in the middle of a tug-of-war battle between her husband and her daughter for her affection and attention. Cameron's gloomy forecast proved accurate, for the honeymoon period truly didn't last long, and the two separated soon after.

Due to an untreated peptic ulcer, allergies to certain foods, and rotten teeth that made it difficult to eat, Cameron was becoming increasingly emaciated and existing on a diet of just milk, honey and cottage cheese. She was also suffering from a damaged liver, which she believed was the result of the serum hepatitis she'd been given when she was mustered out of the service. Raw-boned and sunken-cheeked, her spectral presence became a prominent fixture on Hollywood's emerging coffee house scene.

In 1957, Herb Cohen and the actor and folk singer Theodore Bikel opened the Unicorn Café on the Sunset Strip, the first real Beat hangout in the city, where people could read, play chess, smoke pot or listen to visiting poets like Allen Ginsberg. It was, according to Victor Maymudes, who built the joint, "A place where rebellion had a place to grow."[1]

"In the interim time after the war, people didn't know what to do," Cohen recollects. "A lotta guys got out of the Army trying to figure it out. No one thought of "Beat" as a movement. It soon became mythologised and refined. Within a year or two there was an explosion of 60 coffee houses in L.A."

Increasing numbers diluted the initial hipness, and the so-called Beat Generation was swiftly codified and stereotyped by the mainstream media as a bunch of goatee-sporting, beret-wearing, bongo-bashing goofs, with even the target of Cameron's temptresses, Bob Hope, lampooning the craze on television. "By that time it was tourists and weekend beatniks," Cohen explains. "Beat had changed already by 1959. It was exploited. Shops were selling black leotards and berets. Kerouac to me was like Bob Dylan later, they both wrote about people who were doing it. They articulated it. They were the messengers. Times they are a-changing, but *they* didn't change the times – *Cameron*, and people around her, were the ones who were doing it."

This is quite an accolade from Cohen to one of his former patrons, someone who still makes a big impression on him to this day: "Cameron was so striking and people were wary of her. She was not approachable. She didn't sit down and have conversations; she wasn't a garrulous, outgoing personality. She walked around in her own space and place. She was spacey – in her own world. She was a few years ahead, more hippy than Beat. Cameron was before all this. She was the real thing."

The Unicorn became so popular that the two proprietors opened another establishment, Cosmo Alley, a venue with a more musical emphasis, that showcased such talents as blues-folk queen Odetta, a then-unknown calypso singer named Maya Angelou, and the superhip, iconoclastic comic Lenny Bruce.[2] The entertainment was served up to a racially mixed clientele that included a new generation of young Hollywood actors, all under the thrall of those maestros of "Method," Marlon Brando and Montgomery Clift. Their most famous acolyte was a certain James Byron Dean who summed up his own popularity with the pithy bon mot: "In this hand, I'm Montgomery Clift saying, 'Please forgive me,' and, on the other, I'm Brando saying, 'Fuck you!'"

The handsome young actor John Gilmore was a confidant of Dean's and, in the spring of 1955, the two of them paid a visit to Samson De Brier's house. They were both interested in meeting the alleged lover of Andre Gide, as Dean had played the part of Bachir, the flirtatious Arab houseboy, in an adaptation of Gide's *The Immoralist* on Broadway.

Through Samson, Gilmore met and became a close friend of Curtis Harrington who, in turn, introduced him to Cameron. "Cameron was extremely intense and very insightful and had an animal-like magnetism that was extremely attractive," Gilmore recollects. There was a big sexual charisma about her. She was very strange-looking and had a witch persona. She was extremely thin and strikingly pale with long red hair and long, flowing robes with like a train on it. She was like an ageless being, totally beyond anything ordinary, and she despised anything ordinary and mediocre. She seemed to be able to see beyond what you were seeing. She was strange and could isolate herself into a trance."

A keen artist himself, Gilmore particularly admired Cameron's watercolour *Lady of the Lake*, her finespun take on the Arthurian legend. "I told her it reminded me of Ophelia in *Hamlet*, muttering before she sinks after she's poisoned herself, and Cameron smiled and said, 'Well, that's close.' The actor also dug an oil piece, along a similar theme, titled *Death Boat*, in which a female figure lays dying, while her dog sits at the prow looking back at her. This, too, appears to have been rooted in her love of stories set in medieval England; in this case, Lord Tennyson's ballad 'The Lady of Shalott,' which tells the tale of Elaine of Astolat's infatuation with Sir Lancelot, and ends with her lifeless body floating down the Thames towards Camelot. "Her delicate drawings had a hypnotic, magical quality I loved," Gilmore enthuses. "We discussed painting and Cameron also seemed interested in hearing about my childhood. As a boy, I had practised stage magic and put on shows and was avidly influenced by Houdini and Blackstone. She was interested in them but was far more concerned with Crowley who, frankly, I was never drawn to or impressed with, though Curtis was, and we talked many, many hours about that period of history. Curtis had an intellectual interest in Crowley, but you don't make discoveries that way."

One particular childhood story Gilmore told seemed to especially resonate with Cameron. "One thing I spoke to her about was how, when I was a child, I used to dig holes in the garden. It was a secret important place to me. I told her how I tried to dig all the way to China, and she said it would never be possible because of the centre core of molten lava." For years, Gilmore wondered why this tale held such a strange fascination for Cameron, oblivious to her own childhood hole to Hell.

James Dean was destined to die in a terrible car crash, leaving behind a mangled Porsche and three memorable movie performances that immortalised him as an enduring icon of cool. As with his pal Jimmy, Gilmore could sense a disastrous, fatalistic element in Cameron, too. "She was a very gentle person, in a very urbane way, but I felt she could be easily taken advantage of. I did not reach out for her because I knew her being was somehow encapsulated by its own inner chemistry. I remember her saying to me that she could see into me, and she kind of moved her hand as if focusing a lens. She said something like: 'You're like me and unless fortune smiles you'll be all alone,' and I took it as a defensive comment. But only like 900 years later have I understood what she was saying to me."

Gilmore also draws parallels in the similar way Cameron and Dean approached life – they both walked it like they talked it. "Cameron was like Jimmy in that they both took risks and made discoveries, propelling them through their migrations. Cameron was an explorer and there's danger when you do that. It's like in the film *The Fly* when the little boy asks Vincent Price why his father died and Price says, 'because he was an explorer and you go to places where no one else goes and put yourself in harm's way and sometimes you perish.' Cameron was an explorer going into uncharted territory. Her creative drive governed her life; there was no compromising whatsoever. Cameron's work was not viewer-friendly, it was viewer-disturbing. Her art was like, 'Enter at your own risk!'"[3]

By the time Cameron encountered fellow artist Burt Shonberg, he had already acquired a circle of admirers due to his eye-catching murals that graced a number of the city's most popular coffeehouses. After graduating from the School of the Museum of Fine Arts in Boston in 1953, Shonberg entered the military and became a radio operator at Fort Huachuca in Arizona where, in an echo of Cameron's prom hall decorations, he painted murals in the mess hall, and was similarly recognised by his peers as a creative talent. After he left the service, in the summer of 1955, he travelled to Los Angeles and enrolled at the Art Centre using the G.I. Bill. For several years he eked out a living as a commercial illustrator, and then, in 1958, he formed a partnership with the then-unknown science-fiction writer George Clayton Johnson, and together they opened a European-style coffeehouse in Laguna Beach called Café Frankenstein.[4]

The joint was popular with the Art Centre students and the burgeoning folk crowd but also attracted the unwanted attention of the authorities when members from the local Ladies' Church League objected to Shonberg's faux stained glass painting of Frankenstein's monster that adorned the café's bay window. They deemed it irreligious and tried to rally the straight-laced community to have "the den of iniquity" closed down. But when the artist threatened to erect a crucified dummy of Frankenstein's monster outside the premises in its stead, they backed away.

During his first year in Los Angeles, Shonberg had a life-changing, mystical experience, which he later recorded:

"I had my first dramatic experiences beyond the limits of so-called ordinary, everyday consciousness. This was not induced by any chemical means or yogic-type efforts on my part; it came by itself and took me by surprise. Every day, for seven years straight, I was hit by a number of widely separated, momentary blasts of unexpected light. These initial experiences of being unexpectedly and mysteriously shanghaied out of moving time and into The Eternal Now were of such a nature, that I saw all the usual, generally accepted notions of what this world is all about as being sheer imagination. Also, the quality of these experiences was such that I knew that what I was seeing – strange and shocking as it was – was unquestionably true. At that time I had been wholly unprepared for this robbery of my dream state, and so my initial reaction to this experience was stark terror. During these first awesome unveilings of where we are and how it is, I witnessed the undeniable truth of our situation in ordinary, worldly life, and this was so frightfully staggering that I no longer had any choice in my life concerning what to be serious about. I knew I had to experience that Great Light again, somehow, but also I knew I had to be able to withstand the great shock of full consciousness. It was at this time that I actively began to search for A Way."[5]

Since boyhood, Shonberg had been an ardent believer in UFOs and extraterrestrial forces, so with all they had in common, it was only a matter of time before he and Cameron touched souls. Inspired by his new mate, Burt replicated her habit of ritually burning his own art to prove how unattached to it he was. It was art made to communicate; not to be decorative. And Cameron also introduced her new lover to the writings of Crowley, as a guide to help him find "his way."

"Cameron gave birth to Burt's mysticism," confirms Shonberg's buddy, Ira Odessky. "He was like this square from Boston and Cameron just turned him around, turned him on and, as a result, all this other stuff happened, but she was responsible. It's a helluva story. It's like an epic, like a *Gone with the Wind* type of thing, it's big! Cameron didn't turn Burt crazy – he *was* crazy! It was too much a part of him, she just let it out."

Another amigo, Darryl Copeland, agrees: "Cameron showed Burt the way [laughs]. He was born in the wrong era. He should've been born a few hundred years ago. Burt was something else, powerful. He was a charming, handsome guy. A great painter and a powerful presence."

"He was a towering giant," Odessky chimes in. "People who don't understand say, 'Oh, it's too cartoonish' or some shit. His strokes are so brilliant. Each one is a jewel. You just sit and look at it and go, 'Gee whiz!' Each of his strokes were coloured with the rainbow, according to what colour he wanted to bring out and fast – you've never seen anybody move so fast! It's like he knew exactly what to do, like red here, gold there. It was amazing. Burt could paint an incredible piece overnight, and in the morning he'd take three or four amphetamine pills and they were like champagne. Burt had the energy to begin with, but he loved these pills and he'd work all night and create a masterpiece. He'd look at it for a while, and then he knew when it was time to quit. Calling his work 'psychedelic' is putting him in a box, so they can put a price on him. I don't know if words can describe this amazing soul. The film *The Day the Earth Stood Still* was a big influence on him. He had a series of drawings on music paper which makes reference to the movie. In the film, Klaatu, the highly evolved alien played by Michael Rennie, looks at Professor Barnhardt's chalkboard and tells the boy the maths is all wrong, so he solves the equation, which is his calling card for the Professor. And this was what Burt was doing – leaving these pictures as calling cards."

One of Shonberg's most admired paintings was *Seated Figure and a Cosmic Train*, a self-portrait rendered in his mosaic style, depicting the shirtless artist sitting on a chair in his studio next to an open patio door. His face is bathed in a dappled beam of light shone from the front of a streamliner that's breaking the crest of the mountain in the distance, while the disembodied head of an American Indian chief hovers in the sky above.

"If you looked in the beam you could see the energy that's in the air. Burt could see forcefields," Copeland asserts. "He was a walking mystical experience. Everywhere he went – fires would break out. I remember taking peyote at the pad where he lived and it was just too weird. Suddenly this fire started and it was definitely a vortex of some kind of psychic energy there – and Burt was definitely the magnet."

Odessky had a similar experience with him: "One time, I was in a very strange place after taking some hallucinogen and I'm tweaking, and I see these blue lights coming off Burt, and his aura and spirit drifted up, and I was worried that he was gonna split, and I go, 'Burt, don't go! Burt, don't go!' But Burt was one of the beautiful people. If you had a bad trip he would hug you and rock you in his arms to get you through it."

Ledru Shoopman Baker III was not long out of high school when he first met the artist: "I was told about him by a cousin of mine who raved about how intelligent and talented he was, and when I met him I was blown away because he treated me with dignity, as though I was someone, and I was only twenty years old. I was in The Fourth Way system of Gurdjieff, and he was totally involved with the Gurdjieff system.[6] In The Fourth Way, you're not required to go to a monastery but practice wherever you are. Burt writes about being hit by several blasts of light, these mysteries of consciousness. There were no drugs involved. He knew there was only one thing to be serious about – a higher state of consciousness, everything else was illusion. Burt had studied and applied Gurdjieff and came up with the ultimate formula, an equation: G (The pyramid of all objective consciousness) + 777 (The Law of Crowley) = all of everything. There was a mirroring of the two systems, though they shouldn't be mixed."

When Shonberg introduced Ledru to Cameron she did not disappoint: "When I first met Cameron she was wearing a cape. She was a formidable presence. She had a witchy appearance but not that vibration. She had the eyes of a werewolf, where if you flinch or look away, there's something lacking in you. She was a wondrous beauty. Burt said Cameron was part of the high society scene in Pasadena, where she was introduced to the teachings of Aleister Crowley, which became her life's focus. Burt and Cameron had an attitude of impersonality and being as objective as possible. Objective consciousness is where you see the truth of whatever you're seeing, hearing or thinking about. With certain experiences, you have to get back there and verify it. It's like you build a light bridge to the top of the pyramid of the all-seeing eye. It's only when you're at the tip of the pyramid that you can see all four sides at the same time."

The two artists found a ranch out in the High Desert territory to live in, which they named ERONBU, as in camERON+BUrt.[7] Historically, the desert has always been a traditional place of pilgrimage for those seeking spiritual experiences and California's prehistoric landscape was no different. Aya hung out at the ranch and fell in love with the charged atmosphere of the surroundings: "The impact of nature out there, the starkness. You don't feel a storm in the city like you do out in the desert, with the crackling of thunder and the animal energy going around. That's what the natives understand – that everything is *alive*. To Native Americans, of course, the Earth is *she*, and Cameron really respected that."

The desert was conducive to Cameron's mental well-being and, after all the sturm und drang that punctuated her time with Sherry, she was now in a relatively stable relationship. Shonberg took on a fatherly role with Crystal, too. "Burt loved children. He felt they were the most important thing you have," Odessky confirms.

The Joshua Tree National Park was especially rich in mysticism. Seekers there found great significance in the fact that the eponymous Joshua Tree itself was famous for growing in only two places on Earth: the Southwestern states of America and the Holy Land. It was also a hot spot for UFO activity and, while they were out there, Cameron and Burt befriended George Van Tassel, a pilot and alleged alien contactee, who hosted the annual Giant Rock Spacecraft Convention. Giant Rock was an enormous free-standing boulder, revered by Native Americans as a sacred landmark, and Van Tassel lived beneath it in excavated living quarters that served as his family's subterranean abode.

Back in 1953, while he was operating the Giant Rock Airport, Van Tassel claimed he was taken aboard a Venusian UFO, where extraterrestrials telepathically imparted to him knowledge on how to rejuvenate human cell tissue. The following year, at the behest of these "Space Brothers," he began constructing the Integratron, a 38-foot high domed structure built, he claimed, on an intersection of powerful geomagnetic forces. Utilising the technological know-how allegedly imparted to him by the extraterrestrials, as well as the left-field theories of the inventor Nikola Tesla, Van Tassel installed a Multiwave Oscillator device to harness these electromagnetic energies and use their frequencies to recharge and rejuvenate human cell structure.

Due to the popularity of his story, Van Tassel initiated his own UFO cult, based on the channelled revelations, but even some believers, like Burt, were wary of his boosterism. "Van Tassel was so enthralled with contact but Burt warned him, saying he was getting involved with astral forces that were dark forces from lower planes," Ledru explains.

Cameron was also drawing up plans for her own space-age construction: a Temple of Thelema consisting of five interconnecting pods, built on stilts, jutting out from a mountainside. And her ambition was to expand ERONBU into an art colony, based on the San Miguel de Allende model. Such creative ideas seemed to flow like water while she was in the desert. "Cameron had her visions out there," Aya attests, "and she was going through all that spiritual messaging, and even seeing saucer sightings, and just feeling the energy of the ships and lights following you out there – that was just part of what she was searching for. It had to do with time travel and getting into the other dimension, which we're so sure is there, but you don't know how to reach it."

Having not communicated with Kenneth Anger for a year, Cameron wrote to him from the desert and relayed how her appearance had changed since they last saw each other. After 13 years of cropping her hair, she'd decided to let it grow long, rebelling against the monastic inclination to sacrifice her locks and looks. Life seemed on hold for the moment, and she wondered if her future lay entwined with her exiled friend.

At the time, Cameron could often be seen bombing around the desert in a black hearse she acquired, and she used it for trips back into town, where Burt had mural commissions to fulfil. John Gilmore ran into the compelling couple at Pandora's Box, on the Strip, where Shonberg was applying his unique talents to the décor.

Herb Cohen also featured paintings by Cameron and Shonberg on the Unicorn Café walls. "Burt was a good artist and did a lot of things that got destroyed," Cohen recounts. "He did a mural for the 7 Chefs restaurant which burnt down a month after it opened. I later ran The Purple Onion restaurant that had his famous Purple Onion mural also."

For Cohen, the two artists were well suited: "It was a strange relationship. Burt was very strange all the time, but that's the way he came to us and that's the way Cameron was too."

One of Cohen's waitresses, Dianne Rico, was the daughter of the famous comic book artist Don Rico, as well as John Gilmore's ex-wife. Known as "Deadly Dianne," she was also pals with Burt and Cameron, and after she knocked off work, they would spirit her back to ERONBU in the hearse, where they'd all get high and paint the rocks.

Cameron also got her rocks off at the sex parties thrown by John Franco, a Hollywood set designer whose house just off Melrose Place was known as the Honey Hole, due to the carnality that took place there. With pot, booze, peyote and mescaline laid on, the evening's festivities would sometimes heat up into full-blown orgies, featuring a bevy of established actors, starlets and scions from the Hollywood film industry. (Maila Nurmi, who'd since lost her gig as TV's glamour ghoul, Vampira, worked as a maid there, and had the unenviable task of changing the bedsheets.)

John Gilmore regularly attended these shindigs: "Luana Anders was there, as was Errol Flynn's teenage girlfriend, Beverly Aadland." But, most notably, he recalls seeing Cameron enjoying herself there with a wild child actress whose Lolita-like sexploits incurred the moral opprobrium of those old matrons of movieland virtue, Hedda Hopper and Louella Parsons.

Despite their rampant libidos, Gilmore never personally got it on with Cameron: "I knew Cameron was coming onto me, but I was never really attracted to her physically. She was just too lean and hungry. A beautiful soul but unreachable and untouchable, with such intrinsic magnetism that it repelled as it attracted; and, if you seized upon it, it felt like you were taking advantage of her. She was a very sexual woman, and her creativity was tied in with her dark sexual energy. That's what the exchanging between us was. Her eyes glowed like a cat, and I could sense myself being devoured. I don't know what she had in mind, but she would stare at me and our eyes would meet like a cat looking at you and something's transmitted. There was an energy between us but it was a forbidden pleasure. I'm sorry we didn't connect in a more intimate way but somehow the time or chance or inclination didn't jive, there was some barrier."

Gilmore got another glimpse of Cameron's lesbian leanings the night Curtis Harrington threw a party at his apartment in honour of Maya Deren, who was in town to deliver a film lecture at Club Renaissance, which Cameron attended. Deren's discourse was littered with curt barbs aimed at Hollywood's superficiality and commercialism: "I make my pictures for what Hollywood spends on lipstick," she would famously say, and Cameron took one comment she made to the audience that night – "You're all beautiful! Everybody in Hollywood is beautiful!" – as a sardonic dig on how "Hollywood is the one place in the world where beauty becomes anonymous."[8]

Deren had recently immersed herself in the voodoo culture of Haiti, filming ceremonies there and penning an account of her spiritual awakening entitled *Divine Horsemen: The Living Gods of Haiti*. She was used to being the centre of attention, and was in a typically hoydenish mood that evening, dancing wildly on a table in Curtis' apartment while Gilmore and fellow actor Russ Tamblyn banged away on bongo drums. In a telling image, Gilmore recollects catching sight of Cameron at the party, hunched up and smoking in a corner, studying Deren intently. Babalon may have been eclipsed by the Vodoun Queen that night, but she didn't leave the party without planting a goodbye kiss on Deren's lips when she left.

Entrance to the ERONBU ranch. (Courtesy of Aya.)

Aya at the ERONBU ranch: "Cameron had her visions out there." (Courtesy of Aya.)

Cameron with her artist boyfriend Burt Shonberg and Crystal at the ERONBU ranch. (Courtesy of the Warburg Institute.)

Cameron and Crystal at the ERONBU ranch with the hearse. (Courtesy of Aya.)

10 - Night Tide

> *"And so, all the night-tide, I lie down by the side of my darling, my darling, my life and my bride. In the sepulchre there by the sea, in her tomb by the sounding sea."* 'Annabel Lee' by Edgar Allan Poe.

Over the summer of 1960, Curtis Harrington brought Cameron's fey, forbidding persona to bear on his first, full-length, directorial debut, *Night Tide*. The screenplay was based on a short story he'd penned called 'The Secrets of the Sea,' a modern spin on the Greek myth of the sirens luring sailors to their doom, which he'd been inspired to write after reading a collection of short stories by Truman Capote. In a role custom-made for her, Cameron was cast as an ethereal sea witch. "Cameron's presence and image was so powerful and strong that she had to be this figure of mystery," the director explains.

The film was shot with a budget of a mere $50,000 and, because of this, Harrington was forced to rely on non-union talent and production prudence: "All the main players were paid screen actor's minimum scale, which back in 1960 meant $350 a week." Prior to filming, the director turned down an offer from members of mobster Mickey Cohen's gang to finance the picture: "They were very charming men, but I had visions that if the film didn't do well, I'd end up at the bottom of the LA river in a block of cement."

Instead, Harrington hustled seed money from more benign sources, including the ever-reliable Roger Corman, who assisted on the finance and distribution side of things. Because the film was being made with mostly non-union talent, it didn't qualify for the IATSE (International Alliance of Theatrical Stage Employees) stamp, which was required for a film to be shown in a commercial cinema theatre. To get around this, Harrington hired Floyd Crosby, a union-certified cameraman, to shoot some interior scenes for a few days, which was just enough to obtain the IATSE seal of approval.

There were other nebulous powers to overcome too. When Harrington's astrologer landlady heard about his new project, she asked her tenant what day the filming was going to commence. When he told her she warned him not to start on that date, as it was Mercury Retrograde, a very bad time to start a project. "I asked her what Mercury Retrograde meant, and she underlined the fact that if you do something under Mercury Retrograde, you'll have to do it again."

Unfortunately, Harrington had already rented the jazz club where the first day of shooting was scheduled to begin, so he went ahead. "We shot the club scene and got it in the can, and the next day we were shooting down on the beach and the production manager came running up and, I'll never forget, he came running across the sand with a terrible look on his face and said all the film from the club scene was fogged so we have to reshoot it. So I had to reassemble the club and the band and the flute player and Dennis and Cameron. That converted me to a belief in astrology for life!"

In his first starring role, Dennis Hopper played Johnny Drake, a fresh-faced sailor on leave in Santa Monica who falls for Mora, a raven-haired beauty played by Linda Lawson, who works as a mermaid in a sideshow attraction.

The film centres on Hopper's journey to discover the truth about Mora's real identity and mixed up in a mystery he can't quite fathom, the young actor drew upon his small-town, Midwestern upbringing to portray an endearing and earnest character; a far cry from the darker, unnerving, psychopathic roles for which he would become synonymous down the line.

"I thought he was a wonderful young actor in the James Dean school of acting," Harrington asserts. "He had seen my short avant-garde films and liked them very much. That's why I approached him about doing *Night Tide*, and he said he'd love to work with me." As he was new to working with trained actors, the director relied heavily on Hopper's film experience, as well as seasoned old troupers like Gavin Muir and Marjorie Eaton.

Linda Lawson came courtesy of a friend's recommendation. After graduating from high school, Lawson visited her sister in Las Vegas in hopes of pursuing a singing career. With her sultry looks and silky vocals, she got her break singing in the production line at The Sands Hotel, then Frank Sinatra's own personal fiefdom. Despite her relative inexperience, Lawson plays her role well, and the early awkwardness of Mora's and Johnny's slow-burning romance is beautifully done.

Lawson was more than a little wary of her female co-star, however. "Curtis told me Cameron was a practising witch, so I was very nice to her [laughs]. I didn't want any spells cast or anything. But she had a wonderful look about her." Although oblivious to Cameron's life as a painter, Lawson concedes, "Her aura was very artistic." Although they were bound together by the storyline, there was no womanly chitchat off-screen between the two women which, in the context of the roles they played was perfect, as Cameron's water witch exerts an unspoken, telepathic hold over Lawson's character.

Their first scene together takes place early on, in the aforementioned jazz club, where the audience grooves to the laid-back sounds of the jazz flautist Paul Horn. The sequence was shot at The Manne-Hole on North Cahuenga Boulevard in Hollywood, a nightclub owned by the jazz drummer Shelly Manne. This sprung from Harrington's desire to emulate some of the film techniques of French New Wave cinema, that were very much in vogue at the time, where footage was shot in real locations using non-actors in some scenes. Many of the patrons at the jazz club were enlisted from Harrington's circle of friends, for instance, including Paul Mathison, sporting a blonde buzzcut, who served, once again, as Harrington's set designer.

Unlike other Hollywood films that went woefully over-the-top when they tried to capture the beatnik jazz scene, Harrington's take, based on his observations at the time, was far more naturalistic. As Johnny tries, unsuccessfully, to chat Mora up, Cameron appears dressed in a black gothic getup. She saunters over to the couple and addresses Mora in Greek (which she learned to speak phonetically), promising her: "Soon you will be among your people, my love. Oh yes, really soon we will meet again."

Agitated by what one assumes is a dressing-down, Mora splits and Johnny leaves soon after in pursuit. Just as he leaves the club, he looks back to take another look at the mysterious woman in black who broke up his scene and, as he does, the camera zeroes in for a stunning close-up of Cameron, who turns her head to give the full blast of her evil eye.

Mora remains remote and distant at first, resisting Johnny's romantic overtures because, we later learn, she is haunted by the irrational fear that giving herself sexually to someone will ignite repressed, homicidal urges within her. But as he walks her home, Johnny's boy-next-door charm thaws the ice and, after he steals a kiss, she agrees to meet him the next day.

The following morning, Johnny visits Mora at her apartment above the carousel on Santa Monica Pier, and they take breakfast on a terrace. (Framed with Santa Monica Beach in the background, it's easy to forget that it was still relatively novel to see real-life happening within the dramatic structure of a movie.) He then escorts her to her work, where she introduces him to her gregarious guardian Captain Murdock, ably played by the veteran character actor, Gavin Muir. Johnny and the sea captain bond over their shared seafaring experiences, and he invites the young sailor to enter the sideshow and view the mermaid exhibit. Inside, Johnny is left speechless as he marvels at the dreamy sight of Mora in repose at the bottom of her aquarium.

As the couple's romance blossoms, their dates include a midnight beach party out at Paradise Cove in Malibu. There, Mora performs a Balinese dance to a bongo beat before a group of teenagers, while Cameron, black-veiled and standing on a nearby rock, looks on. Mora becomes entranced by the music, and the spell is only broken when she catches sight of Cameron's wraith-like silhouette and faints.

After another visit to Mora's apartment, Johnny meets the daughter of the carousel owner, played by Luana Anders, who informs him that two of Mora's previous boyfriends have washed up dead. Strangely, a telephone call comes for Johnny, despite the fact that no one knows he's there, but when he picks up the receiver, the line is dead. Just at that moment, he spies Cameron storming across the boardwalk and decides to follow her, journeying through Venice – and its canals, bridges and oil derricks – looking for answers.

One of Harrington's role models was Orson Welles, and he was partly inspired to use Venice as a location having seen Welles' crime thriller *Touch of Evil*, which used the beach town as a backdrop a few years earlier. "It's terribly gentrified now," Harrington recounts, "but then Venice was a wonderfully run-down, ramshackle area, far from the glories of its past, and history of the man who invented it because he wanted to recreate another version of the Italian city."

Venice's crumbling environs mirror Cameron's own fading glamour, but Hopper vouches that such wear and tear did not affect all areas of her body: "She had a very old, wrinkled face, but it had no relation to her body at all. Her body was that of a young woman. We had a very wonderful, very intimate relationship. We were very close, but there wasn't a lot of talking involved. We had a physical relationship, maybe three or four times, but it wasn't like a long process."

The full extent of Cameron's facial deterioration is seen clearly in a close-up when she stops at one point to check her pocket watch – Harrington's homage to the white rabbit in *Alice in Wonderland*. (The timepiece she holds may well have been the one Jack was wearing when he was killed, which was still in her possession. The hands of the watch still stopped at the time of the explosion).

Just like the white rabbit, Cameron rounds a corner and disappears, leaving the bewitched, bothered and bewildered matelot standing outside the home of Captain Murdock. The number of the captain's address, 777, was painted on a lifebuoy by Cameron as a nod to Crowley's cabbalistic compendium. "I sprinkle little occult references throughout my films, just as a little conceit that some people will pick up on," the director explains.

His tongue loosened with drink, the sea captain drops the bombshell that Mora is no sideshow novelty, but is, in fact, a real-life descendant of the mythical sea creatures. He warns Johnny that he is in mortal danger if he continues seeing her, but the smitten sailor refuses to believe it, even when Mora corroborates this truth to him back at her apartment. She further explains that the woman in black is also a sea creature, and is here to take her back home to her people.

Confused, Johnny consults a fortune teller, melodramatically played by Marjorie Eaton, who cautions him that he is in great danger, while Mora is caught in a "vortex of evil." In a dream sequence, Mora reveals her scaly tail to Johnny, who awakes to discover she's missing. Scouring the beach, he finds her tethered to a wooden stanchion beneath the pier and rescues her from the lashing waters. With her boyfriend still unwilling to believe the truth about her, Mora takes him on a scuba dive. They tussle underwater and a knife is drawn, but it's not murder Mora has in mind. Instead, she cuts Johnny's air supply and sends him to the surface, while she drowns herself to "embrace the rapture of the depths."

That night, Johnny dreams of Mora and discovers her as a mermaid on the rocks, gazing into a mirror as she combs her hair. The mood changes as she tries to pull him into the sea and Cameron materialises, momentarily, her laughter mocking the sailor's desperate plight. Johnny wakes and returns to the sideshow where he finds Mora's lifeless body floating in the tank. Suddenly, Captain Murdock bursts in and blames Johnny for her death. He brandishes a pistol but misses his target and, as Johnny ducks for cover, he inadvertently tips the tank of water over, spilling Mora's corpse onto the floor. The sea captain is arrested and confesses all at the police station. The story of the sea people was simply a ruse he was using to string Mora along to keep her wedded to him, and he admits that he is the culprit responsible for the double murders. However, in a fitting twist, he swears no knowledge of the mysterious woman in black, so Cameron's role in everything is left suitably ambiguous.

Although it was initially promoted as a horror flick, *Night Tide*'s ambiance and visually arresting sequences are far more redolent of a *film noir*, albeit one with a supernatural undercurrent. Particularly impressive is the way Harrington synthesizes the Santa Monica Pier with the amusement arcades and carnivals at the (now demolished) Long Beach Pike and Pacific Ocean Park Pier, to create one seamless, magical milieu.

Linda Lawson pays tribute to him: "I think Curtis is the most extraordinary cameraman. The mood in that film is incredible and you can't do that with colour and the film they have today. It has to do with the darkness and the lighting and the shadows. It gave it this whole feeling of constant, ominous, terrible things about to happen."

Dennis Hopper agrees and recalls fondly: "It was amazing shooting that little film, a terrific experience." Actually, the actor was so upset at the prospect of the shoot ending, he got drunk on the last day of filming and ended up having a motorbike accident. Having been a consummate professional throughout the production, Harrington feels Hopper's behaviour was born out of his unconscious resentment that their time together was coming to an end.

In July 1961, *Night Tide* premiered at the Spoleto Film Festival in Italy, where it garnered glowing reviews from the Italian press, while *Time* magazine described it as "a forest of fearful, briny enchantment" and included it in their top ten list of films to see that year. Unfortunately, due to a dispute with one of the film's financiers, it would be a further two years before it was given a general release. When it was finally made available to the public, it played, fittingly enough, in a double feature alongside Roger Corman's film adaptation of Edgar Allan Poe's *The Raven*. The delay hit the film commercially, though. "It was what the French call a *film maudit* – a cursed film," sighs Harrington today. While Hopper points out: "We had the film reviewed by *Time* magazine but nowhere to see it [laughs]."

Despite those setbacks, *Night Tide* has become a bona fide cult classic, beloved by a select band of film buffs, including Kenneth Anger's former boss Henri Langlois at the Cinémathèque Française. Like *Pleasure Dome* before it, Cameron's presence dominates, which is all the more remarkable when you realize she is only on-screen for less than five minutes. (It echoes the film-stealing cameo of Orson Welles as Harry Lime in Carol Reed's classic *The Third Man*, as it's Cameron's elusiveness and mystique that commands the picture and helps define the trajectory of the main characters in it.)

Looking back today, the film's star credits her for lending an extra special quality to the project: "Cameron was just fascinating and I loved working with her," Dennis Hopper enthuses. "But she was strange. She was always well-mannered. I never saw her lose her cool, but you could sense that there was something very sensitive about her. This isn't to say she was helpless or vulnerable, she was always in control, but there was this sensitivity. She wasn't a talker, but when she did speak it was in a low-key way which made her presence in the film all the more powerful."

Cameron in a still from *Night Tide*. (Courtesy of Curtis Harrington.)

Cameron, Dennis Hopper and Curtis Harrington while filming *Night Tide*. Summer of 1960. Cameron's painted 777, Crowley's Cabbalistic symbol, on the lifebuoy. (Courtesy of the Warburg Institute.)

Cameron gives the evil eye in the jazz bar scene in *Night Tide*.
(Courtesy of Curtis Harrington.)

11 - Black Pilgrimage

> "If there is still one hellish truly accursed thing in our time, it is our artistic dallying with forms, instead of being like victims burnt at the stake, signalling through the flames."
> – Antonin Artaud, *The Theatre and its Double*.

In the spring of 1960, Burt Shonberg was one of several artists chosen by the psychiatrist Dr. Oscar Janiger to participate in a study probing the effects of LSD-25 on the creative process. By the end of the experiment, Dr. Janiger was so impressed with the artist's offerings he bought some of his canvases, while Shonberg was left with the realization "that the significance of art resulting from the psychedelic experience could possibly reach to actual magic and beyond."[1]

Regrettably, Shonberg's mind expansion came at a terrible cost and carried some very public side effects. Friends would see him walking down Sunset Boulevard in the throes of a psychotic episode. "He'd kinda stand there and howl," Ira Odessky recounts. "Or Burt would blow 'Shhh... ' in your ear, with a message, and talk like the wind," adds Darryl Copeland. Dennis Hopper was also a pal of the painter and admired his artwork, but remembers: "You'd see Burt around all the time, talking to space people or having a conversation with himself while he was walking. He sort of went over the edge. It seems like a lot of men Cameron lived with went over the deep end [laughs]. Maybe they were over the deep end when they moved in with her and came out the other side totally mad!"

While Cameron was bestowing her otherworldliness to *Night Tide* that summer, Shonberg was sprinkling some of his own artistic magic on another Roger Corman project, his film adaptation of Edgar Allan Poe's *The Fall of the House of Usher*. He was hired to create the macabre Usher family portraits seen throughout the film, a couple of which were snapped up by the star of the picture, that well-known art connoisseur, Vincent Price.

Soon after their respective film experiences, Shonberg and Cameron parted ways, though they remained on good terms. "There were no tears in their parting," Ledru confirms. "That was way beneath them. Burt would say: 'Our friendships are eternal; we don't make temporary friendships.' That was one of his mottoes."

In August 1960, a solo exhibition of Cameron's work took place at the Paull Five Gallery on North Larchmont Boulevard. The gallery was owned by one of Cameron's girlfriends, Anita Paull, a beautiful, former fashion model who sold artwork, jewellery, candles and other objets d'art on consignment. "Anita would exhibit individual pieces of art, little sculptures, drawings, watercolours and paintings," Charles Brittin explains. "When she visited somebody and saw something she liked she'd say, 'Can I show that?' or 'Would you like me to try and sell that?' with the idea of giving artists the chance of letting people see their work."

To advertise the event, Cameron designed a poster consisting of a black ink drawing of a disembodied arm, a macabre reference to Jack's severed limb, beneath what could be construed as a fragment of a falling star. Even greater publicity was generated when she received her first professional review, courtesy of Henry J. Seldis, the art critic for the *LA Times*. In a small but glowing write-up, he described her as "an artist possessed. With a peculiar mystique and outstanding skill of draftsmanship, she presents us with a fantasy world filled with horror and ecstasies. In spirit, though not in style, this contemporary Los Angeles artist recalls Bosch and late Goya."

"It was a beautiful exhibition," Brittin recollects. "Cameron's work was very handsomely displayed. There were many small pieces, mainly the ink drawings, and a few things with a slight watercolour tinge to them." Bad luck seemed to dog Cameron when it came to exhibiting her work, however, and the hoodoo continued when four of her pieces were stolen.

While she was still perceived as a rarefied artist by some of her friends, the Brittins were privy to the more rough-spun, down-to-earth side of Cameron's life, as a broke single mother trying to get by. Cameron's bare-bones existence and itinerant lifestyle had certainly taken a toll on her, and Brittin remembers how, while contemplating yet another move, she muttered ruefully to him: "We never really escaped the Depression did we?"

"Cameron desperately wanted company and, I think, seemingly normal company," Brittin asserts. "She didn't want any more hype. When she came to us, she just wanted to have a cup of coffee and a cookie and talk about raising her child. She knew that I was in the art world so we didn't need to talk about art, we could just psychologically hold hands. She was a sweet person with a great personality – not the way some of her friends wanted to picture her to be. They wanted to see her the way she may have been at certain stages of her life: being the Goddess and doing all the black magick, more dangerous, more hazardous things. We were lucky not to see that side of her. She didn't have any glamour then, she dressed roughly, she didn't use make-up. Often she was sort of starved and harsh-looking, and that was marvellous. She wasn't flirty, she wasn't trying to make an entrance. I'm sure she could establish her persona. Of course, in *Night Tide* you see her playing a role, and you can see she can do it. But we were closer to her in everyday life."

Cameron so enjoyed her time filming *Night Tide* in Venice, she stayed on, moving into apartment 2 at 49 Wavecrest Avenue. The beachfront neighbourhood had burgeoned into a beatnik bastion, with its own louche and rackety scene, and was home to some familiar faces. For instance, one of its most popular spots was the Gas House, run by man-mountain Eric "Big Daddy" Nord, who'd been an initiate of the Agape Lodge back in its heyday.

A this juncture, a new friend, Joan Martin, entered Cameron's life. Having returned to collect her daughter Jessie from a supervised play area on Venice Beach one afternoon, she found her child in the company of Cameron and Crystal, who'd been picked up by the police for running away. "I'd gone for a walk with the artist Fred Mason," Martin recollects, "and when we got back there were these cops with Cameron and our daughters. Cameron thought it was all funny and very significant. We had daughters of a similar age and right there and then we became friends. Crystal was wilful and did as she pleased. She didn't want to go to school and Cameron admitted she didn't know what to do with her. She semi-jokingly referred to her as 'post-literate.' She believed in letting your kids run free."

While Joan Martin enjoyed a friendship with Cameron built on their shared domestic lives, her painter husband, Don Martin, bonded with Cameron as a fellow artist. "Cameron considered Don one of her teachers; they talked about art. With me, she discussed domestic things as women and mothers. It was like the Gertrude Stein and Alice B. Toklas thing, where Alice doesn't get to talk to the interesting celebrities. Our relationship was a social one. Cameron was into the tarot and astrology and had the Crowley deck. She'd talk to Don about Crowley but he didn't like him. He thought he was just for blue-haired old ladies. I think Cameron would have liked to have had Don as another one of her conquests. If Cameron was attracted to someone she made the move. It was all very 'Love under will' [laughs]. She had a very active social life. She had her reputation: 'Oh, the witch! The witch!' people would say, but our relationship was based on an aspect of her life that was peripheral to her public persona. Don and I were a rest from all that. Don used to say, 'Cameron's a farm girl at heart,' and I found her interesting and generous and liked being with her and talking with her.

We had a nice time together, and it was a friendship we could pick up where we left it. Cameron and my other daughter Rachel were very fond of each other, too."

Cameron was less enamoured by some of the other Venice artists and poets, though: "The only Venice people Cameron liked were Fred Mason and Don," Martin confirms. "She couldn't stand Stuart Z. Perkoff and the others – she thought they were assholes! Perkoff and I were very close, but I don't know why Cameron didn't care for him. Maybe because that group used hard drugs."

In 1958, Perkoff opened the Venice West Café on Dudley Avenue, a major hangout where Wallace Berman graffitied his axiom *Art is Love is God* on the walls. At the time there did exist two opposing camps among the Venice poets – the mystics vs. the lumberjacks – but Joan Martin doubts this had anything to do with Cameron's dislike as her husband Don was a coal miner's son; so, if anything, he belonged to the lumberjack crowd.

According to another local friend, Marsha Getzler, Cameron's antipathy towards the Venice poets may have been because she found them "too raw and in-your-face, or dare we say… uncouth." If so, she wasn't alone in that view at the time. Aya had also migrated down to Venice and she, too, had little time for the "boy's choir" of poets. "Stuart was a pushy Leo and not that cuddly, and what they had to say wasn't speaking for me and I don't think for her either. He was a fine poet, and now I understand that, but, back then, he wasn't in our circle of aspiring metaphysicians."

One reason for Cameron's animus against Perkoff may have been a piece he wrote on Aleister Crowley that he contributed to the literary publication *Mendicant*. Drawn from his journals, the poet seemed hung up on the assumption that Crowley was an embodiment of *EVIL*. Having read John Symonds' *The Great Beast* biography, Perkoff confessed that he sometimes felt the same evil inside himself, so it's entirely possible

Cameron may have taken umbrage at this and felt the poet was unqualified to talk on the subject.

After another stint in the VA hospital, Sherry came back briefly into Cameron's life. She brought him along with her one day to meet Joan Martin, who marvelled at the special effect Sherry had on her kids: "My eldest daughter adored him. She just sat there on the floor staring at him." Martin also noticed how intense Cameron and Sherry were in each other's company and picked up on the strong sexual attraction between them, though they didn't hold hands or snuggle.

Ned Wynn also met the couple around this time and was initially bowled over by Cameron: "I found her beautiful and entrancing." But he could only see trouble ahead for little Crystal: "Even though I was pretty young at the time, I knew intuitively that Crystal was going to have a troubled life. The minute Sherry told me about her I just figured… poor little girl. Cameron was incapable of parenting and so was Sherry. Though he could love her to bits, he could never be strong enough or straight – clean and sober – enough to make a difference." For Crystal, Sherry was an unpredictable character: okay with her one minute, throwing her allowance in the Venice canal the next. Over the years she was made aware that he was not her real daddy, as her mother tried to ingrain in her the belief that Jack was her true father, in a spiritual sense. One quirky story even had Cameron driving her daughter down South Orange Grove and pointing to a tree in the backyard of the former grounds of 1003 and declaring, symbolically, "*That's* your father!"

Sherry's attempts to ingratiate himself with his family became increasingly desperate and violent, though the violence was usually turned on himself as he tried to emotionally blackmail his wife with grand gestures of suicide. "Cameron's reply was 'Go ahead!'" Joan Martin recollects. "He'd tried it so many times before."

The Christmas period proved particularly difficult for him. It was not only a traditional time of year for family get-togethers, but it also marked Crystal's birthday. So when Cameron refused him permission to see his daughter that year, Sherry took an overdose and was rushed to hospital to have his stomach pumped of the 60 phenobarbital pills he'd swallowed. He was released eight hours later, only to be found hovering on the ledge of the roof of his apartment building in East Hollywood, near to where Cameron used to live on Normandie Avenue. He was stopped from jumping by a brave policeman and the whole psychodrama was covered by the local newspapers and TV news. The *Los Angeles Examiner* relayed the story under the headline: 'Policeman's Ruse Foils Death Try. Writer Saved 2nd Time in 8 Hours.' In an article marred by factual errors, Sherry was billed as "science fiction writer Sheridan Kinnel (sic), 24," and the piece went on to explain how police officer Donald E Davis, 28, was dispatched to an apartment at 4013 Sunset Boulevard following a call Sherry made to the long-distance telephone operator, announcing his intention to commit suicide. According to Officer Davis: "Kinnel (sic) met me at the door and told me his room-mate was sick, but when I went inside he swept past me and raced up to the roof." The police officer found Sherry teetering on the ledge, holding a cement ornament. Trying to coax him away, he offered him a cigarette. "I got as close to him as I dared," explained Davis, "and, when he took the cigarette, I started to light a match for him, inching towards him as I made believe the match was burning my fingers." After a couple of unsuccessful grabs, the officer eventually managed to pull Sherry back from the ledge to safety.

Before he was returned to Central Receiving Hospital for the second time that day, Sherry admitted to reporters that he was "depressed because his estranged wife Marjorie had refused him permission to see their daughter Kristle (sic), who was five years old on Christmas day." While the *LA Times* article covering the incident quoted him as saying,

"If I can't have the kid I don't want anything!"[2] The *Examiner* concluded, with further factual inaccuracies: "Kinnel (sic), a Korean War veteran with a silver plate in his head, is scheduled to report to Sawtelle Veterans Hospital on January 17 for psychiatric observation and treatment." In the accompanying photograph, Sherry appeared agitated but dangerously handsome, in a sweaty Kerouac sort of way. He gazes intensely at the press camera as he's led away, while Officer Davis looks off to the side, posing with his pocketbook in hand, pretending to write up the incident.

"Sherry was one of the things we could not believe," Charles Brittin recounts. "We held our breath every time he came out of the mental hospital. What terrible thing was gonna happen? We felt this was a couple who shouldn't be together, but they drew off something in each other. They needed each other somehow. People just thought it was too bad."

Later, Sherry spun a very different story to his nephew Ned Wynn, claiming he'd feigned the whole suicide trip and had actually gone up onto the roof to hide his stash of Benzedrine pills behind some bricks in the chimney stack, fearing the cops would search his pad. "Uncle Sherry told me he had threatened to jump or they would have found the bennies, so instead of going to jail, they sent him to the VA hospital for observation. I remember him saying, 'I don't know what's worse: a cell full of pissed-off spades or a room full of guys who think they're Studebakers!'" To corroborate this version of events, Ned admits, "He and I got high on some of the pills a few days after he got out." Ultimately, Sherry realised it was splitsville with Cameron, and, with no chance of reconciliation, he left town and returned home to Florida for good.

While Cameron was starring in a movie informed by the French New Wave, Kenneth Anger was languishing in Paris, struggling to get a string of projects off the ground, including his plan to make a film version of the S&M novel *The Story of O*. When these failed to get the green light, he decided to mine the sordid showbiz scuttlebutt surrounding some of Hollywood's biggest stars during its golden age, and pieced together the titillating compendium *Hollywood Babylon* – a title partly inspired by Cameron and dedicated to her inside as "The Scarlet Woman." Anger hoped the book would help dig him out of his pit of penury, and in the years ahead it would, becoming a sequel-spawning bestseller, as much of a calling card for him as his films.

In the meantime, however, the filmmaker was down on his uppers, and after suffering an emotional breakdown, he wound up convalescing in a Parisian asylum. From there, he wrote to Cameron relaying his predicament, but though she desperately wanted to go to him, she could not afford to travel. Writing back, Cameron reflected on how she could have avoided so much confusion and suffering over the years if only she'd joined him in Europe in the period before Crystal was born. She then revealed that her daughter was conceived in the same bedroom Anger slept in when he lodged at Samson De Brier's house. Cameron pictured them spending their lives together but was reluctant to leave Los Angeles because her Great Work was focused there.

Metaphysically, she had recently arrived at Binah on the Kabbalistic Tree Of Life, the sephirot identified with Babalon, which signalled her attainment of rational understanding and the power of love. Cameron felt it was very rare for a woman to reach such a status, and admitted she may have hit a barrier in herself, and doubted she was able to progress further. She was currently conducting peyote rituals out in the desert with her two latest disciples, a male who went by the name of Ankh, and Lisa Webster, a young, kohl-eyed clothes designer with an interest in Egyptology. Cameron was still harbingering Jack and Crowley's post-Christian Armageddon and envisioned LA as the epicentre for where it would all go down.

Beseeching Anger to come home to her, she sent him an ink drawing of a black-winged mask hovering over the mouth of a chasm and, the following month, two prose poems she'd been working on, both seemingly dedicated to departed loves. The first was written in honour of her spiritual godmother Jane Wolfe. The second was an ode to Jack called 'The Knowledge of Him Torments Me.' The title said it all.

Eleven months later, in January 1962, after eight years working in exile in Europe, Kenneth Anger returned to America. Cameron was thrilled at the prospect of his homecoming and was there to greet him at the airport, almost unrecognisable to him, having lopped her hair off again. Anger was promptly whisked back to the Wavecrest apartment, which he duly dubbed "The Witches Cove."

Once he'd acclimatised, the filmmaker was dismayed to discover the full extent of how many of Jack's precious possessions had been mislaid and destroyed over the years. Like a good archivist, he began making an inventory of the surviving items, relieved that some of Jack's ritual accoutrements, such as his magick wand and dagger, were still extant. Jack's library, however, was now reduced to less than a dozen books and, in time, Anger would fork out a pretty penny rescuing some of the missing titles from the city's bookstores. Cameron's amulet was also missing, and when Anger visited Samson De Brier at his home, he learned how she'd torn up manuscripts and letters, some of which Samson retrieved from the trash behind her back. Regrettably, other papers were lost forever, burnt to ashes in his fireplace.

On the upside, Jack's *Songs for the Witch Woman* poems were still intact, and Cameron shared them and her accompanying drawings with Anger. She'd shown them to the poet Robinson Jeffers, too, who singled out the poem 'Merlin' as a particularly fine work. Approaching the tenth anniversary of his death, Jack was still a constant presence in Cameron's life, and Anger was wowed by one of her most recent works, *Dark Angel*, a magnificent portrait of a brooding Belarion, bewinged with billowing hair.

However, Cameron was now indulging in some startling revisionism regarding her relationship with her first husband, which she shared with

Anger during a marathon heart-to-heart session that ran on into the wee small hours. Having reiterated her conviction that Jack magically created her, she now added a fresh spin: that he ultimately wanted to destroy his creation by burning her alive.[3] Anger was well aware of Cameron's Joan of Arc complex, and her belief that in a past life she'd been burnt as a witch in Spain, but what he was hearing now cut him to the quick. At first, he suspected she was engaging in one of her death wish fantasies; however, after reading allusions to such a thing in Jack's poem 'Desire,' he wondered. (A sense of ritual immolation seemed to vibrate from Cameron's being, and John Gilmore talks of how she reminded him of one of the "victims" in French playwright Antonin Artaud's quote: "…burning at the stake, signalling through the flames.")

Cameron went on to explain how she felt a similar peril of being destroyed by fire when she and Jack stayed in a mountain village in San Miguel de Allende, four months before his death. There, she described a cross on a hilltop where the locals had once burnt witches and recounted how villagers began making the sign of the cross whenever she appeared in the street, even pelting her with stones. Cameron may well have been conflating this with an even more outrageous anecdote, which was widely circulated by her friends over the years, concerning the time she aped Lady Godiva and rode naked into a San Miguel church on the back of a white charger, while a service was in progress, in what one can only assume was a daring act of pagan provocation. Needless to say, all hell broke loose and the police were called, and Cameron was reprimanded by the local authorities and told she was no longer welcome in town. Nevertheless, she remained proud of such escapades and boasted how they all helped create her legend down there.

Later, Anger turned the conversation around to Cameron's wanton acts of destruction, particularly in regard to Jack's magical papers and her own artwork. Here again, she displayed a real ambivalence in her feelings towards her late husband: love and respect for him one moment and a very real sense of fear and hatred the next. Concerning a photographic portrait of Jack, for instance, Cameron confessed how, after his death, she found herself spending many hypnotic hours staring at the image until Jack's voice repeatedly commanded her to burn it. Anger still took her to task for destroying her own paintings, calling her actions criminal, but Cameron batted it back, nonchalantly, admitting she was guilty of all the crimes. Justifying her deeds, she argued that her artworks were sacred talismans, existing for all eternity on the astral plane for those who could reach them. Anger countered that it was still a selfish act and accused her of depriving him and others of their beauty and instruction. At this, Cameron seemed to dislocate and drift off, explaining that it was that other person who burned them – Hilarion, her magical alter ego.

Considering Cameron and Anger were both emotionally volatile artists, their life together was blissful for a few months. Alienated from their respective families, they found solace in one another until unresolved sexual tensions began to rear its ugly head. It was becoming clear that Cameron was falling in love with Anger and had designs on a romantic relationship. You would have thought that she'd have learned from the example of Renate Druks and Paul Mathison, that there were only diminishing returns getting hung up on a gay guy, and such a notion was doomed to failure.

At any rate, things came to a head one night when Anger picked up a pretty blonde boy on the streets of Venice and brought him home. The nineteen-year-old, who went by the name of Prince Little, hunted scorpions and embedded them in amber, which he then sold as key rings. With his epicene features and freckles, he bore an uncanny resemblance to Cameron. Anger claimed he magically conjured this adolescent elemental and marvelled at the synchronicity between the boy's name and the fact that he'd bought a copy of Antoine de Saint Exupery's mystical fairytale *The Little Prince* for Crystal earlier that day.

Greeted by the sight of the two of them together, Cameron flew into a jealous rage and attacked Anger, tearing at his clothes. Collecting his stuff, Anger left with the boy and caught a bus out to the desert where they engaged in a sex magick ritual hailed as *The Mars Working*, whose climax Anger linked to a dazzling meteor shower that rained down on New Mexico. On his return to town, Anger moved into an address just down the street from Samson's place on Barton Avenue.

In April of 1962, the covey of Crowleyites in California were abuzz at the arrival of The Great Beast's son, Aleister Atatürk (aka Randall Gair). Despite being a 26-year-old man, Crowley's heir was still struggling to find his way in life and was prone to immature and delinquent behaviour. He spent some time staying with former Agape Lodge members, such as Reea Leffingwell, but he threw tantrums, wrecked a mine she owned and damaged the caravan she lived in and soon outstayed his welcome.

During his visit to L.A., Cameron introduced him to some of her friends who were part of the Semina scene. Though in no way Thelemites, many dug his father's novel *The Diary of a Drug Fiend*, a thinly-disguised dramatisation drawn from Crowley's use of narcotics, which described how addiction could be overcome, ultimately, by divining one's true will under the Law of Thelema. Atatürk attempted to style himself as his father's successor, but his efforts to attract a new following proved fruitless, and he ended up being deported back to England for failure to pay a medical debt.[4]

In the wake of his departure, Cameron left Venice and took a six-month sabbatical to the desert. By the spring of 1963, she was living temporarily at her parents' new home in Sierra Madre. Her mother was still mourning the passing of Hill, who died the previous November, a veteran employee of JPL which had since been subsumed by NASA.

Karl Germer also passed away that autumn, leaving behind his third wife Sascha. The following May, Cameron wrote to his widow, asking if she could bury Jack's ashes in the grounds of the Germer's home in West Point, Northern California. There, she hoped they could rest alongside those of Sascha's husband, Jane Wolfe and Crowley himself, unaware that *his* ashes were actually buried beneath "The Aleister Tree" in the garden of Germer's former residence in Hampton, New Jersey. Cameron's request was duly noted, but it never came to pass, and she eventually scattered Jack's cremains in the Mojave Desert.

After years spent hearing about her through third parties like Karl Germer and Kenneth Anger, Crowley's archivist Gerald Yorke finally established a personal correspondence with Cameron. Though Thelema had long ceased to be his chosen path, he was interested in getting her take on the Babalon Working and wondered if she still believed that Babalon was manifest within her. Cameron's response was gnomic in parts, but in charting the arc that her magickal life had taken, she admitted to initially resisting the path for which she had been destined and claimed that she was instrumental in Jack's separation from the Agape Lodge due to her mistrust of all religions.

Still, she admitted that through Jack's magical instruction, over the course of their marriage, she began showing signs that she was due to manifest the Babalon prophesy, and had reached the point where she was presently in no doubt as to her position in the Thelemic hierarchy. To illustrate her point, she invoked the ancient, Kabbalistic name of God, Yahweh, and assigned each of the four letters of the Tetragrammaton (YHVH) in the following way: Crowley represented Yod, the father. Leah Hirsig, He, the mother. Jack signified Vau, the son. While she, herself, symbolised the final He, the daughter.

By the summer, Cameron had made amends with Anger and was asking him to help facilitate an earlier plan they'd had: to exhibit her work in Paris and London. She was absorbed in painting again and, working all through the night, she'd hit a purple patch. *The Black Egg* was a wonderfully witchy self-portrait, in which Cameron, dressed in white robes, held a black egg like the Eucharist in her hands. Her blacked-out eyes added an extra spooky touch but were only painted in as an afterthought because Crystal coloured the original eyes with lipstick. The image seemed steeped in symbolism: In tantra, for instance, the fifth element, the Akasha or spirit, is symbolised by a black ovoid which represents the darkness from which all creation is conceived. While in Ancient Egypt, the egg features in the hieroglyphic block of the Egyptian goddess Isis. But there were also a couple of artistic precedents, too, that she was doubtless familiar with. *Guardian of the Black Egg*, a painting by Leonor Fini, from 1955, is a serene portrait of a cloaked female figure with a black egg resting on her lap. While *The Giantess* (*The Guardian of the Egg*), arguably Leonora Carrington's most famous work, which she created in 1947, depicts the caped female of the title clutching a spotted egg.

One composition, *Demonic Vision*, featured a tiger's head emerging out of an ink spill, its nose morphing into the long neck of a black-eyed voodoo priestess. While another self-portrait revealed Cameron as earth mother, suckling baby Crystal, which was ironic considering she never breastfed. Cameron experimented with collage, too, and gifted one untitled piece to Joan Martin, consisting of a fragment of a skeletal hand from a larger painting, pasted onto an abstract background daubed with gold and silver foil.

When *Semina 8* was released that year, it featured a Cameron poem and an ink drawing of a sphinx, which may have been the same one she gave to Ned Wynn: "It was of a sphinx-like creature called *Her* or *She* or something like that. It was fabulous." Even when they were out of her own possession, and had been gifted to other people, Cameron's artworks still had a strange habit of disappearing or being destroyed, and it happened once again with the piece she presented to her nephew-in-law.

Cameron's work also continued to inspire those around her, and when Bob Alexander started his own publishing imprint, contrarily dubbed Press Baza, one of his first releases was an anthology by Aya, entitled *Marks of Asha*, that included the poem 'Notes Between Worlds,' dedicated to her friend:

> *"A witch bewitched, this life stalks itself.*
> *Watching from the corners of her own mad eyes."*[5]

Alexander, now known as Reverend Bob, had recently founded the Temple of Man, a non-sectarian sanctuary, where poetry met music met spirituality met art. Along with many of her friends, Cameron was ordained into the Temple, and, as became custom, dedicated some of her pictures to it.[6]

As previously stated, Aya's husband Elias Romero, was one of the early progenitors of liquid light shows. He deployed his "protoplasmic projections" at Club Renaissance on the Sunset Strip, sometimes in conjunction with his cohort, the musician Christopher Tree, who ran his own "Lite Show" there, as well as at venues like the Gas House and Cheetah club in Venice. It was a multimedia experience made up of stroboscopic lights, liquid projection, spontaneous live music and dancers. "I never played any other way than spontaneously. I never desired to play a song or the same thing twice," Tree explains.

It was through Elias and Aya that Tree came to meet Cameron: "I thought she was a technically excellent artist, but I didn't like her art or the message of her art; it didn't sit well with me, but it was good. Elias greatly appreciated Cameron's art but he thought it was a little dark also. He was influenced by her but was not into the black stuff. She was always dark. She was into Crowley and that wasn't my cup of tea at all, but I respected her ability, just not the feeling it conjured. She was a very conflicted person and I related to her as a tragic figure. I always had mixed feelings about her. I certainly wasn't interested in any romance with her, but we had discussions – not that we agreed on much. I didnt approve of much of her thinking or the way she handled her daughter. I have a very strong relationship with children and have worked with them with music. I liked Crystal and got along with her okay, but I would discipline her – not hit her – but made damn sure she would stop being aggressive or dumb or nasty with others. I would hold her arms as she'd try to hit me, and Cameron would never say anything. Crystal needed someone to tell her what not to do. Children want to know boundaries, and Cameron didn't do right by her. She went with Crowley's 'Do What Thou Wilt' and she let Crystal do whatever she wanted. It wasn't healthy. I mean, Cameron gave her peyote when she was six!"

One night, however, Tree took a peyote-enhanced moonlit walk with Cameron along Venice Beach, and, as they talked, he saw a softer side to her: "She described going to a bullfight in Mexico and how the matador was gored in the groin by the bull, and I was impressed with her sympathetic identity with the incident and the bullfighter. I felt it affected her very strongly. Her response was not dark, and I liked that because she didn't extend much sympathy."

That last sentiment was evidenced in Cameron's adverse attitude towards Tree and his light show. "I think she was my enemy, in a way, because at the time I was doing the music light show and I think she wanted to destroy it out of artistic jealousy. I had a silent confrontation with her at one point. She had hooked up with a musician I played with, a Greek trombone player named Nick Ivases, and I'd come down on the weekend from Big Sur, where I lived, to pick him up to do the light show on the Strip. He was staying at a place north of Santa Barbara, that friends of mine were renting. It had once been a motel bar and restaurant and it even had a dance floor. It was at the junction of Highway 101 and Highway 1, near Gaviota Pass. And when I got there I was surprised to find he was with Cameron, as I'd been there a week before and she wasn't here. And he said, 'We just bought a side of beef' – and he was vegetarian! I couldn't believe any of it. The next thing I knew, us three, and the two people who had the place, were sitting around the kitchen and Nick said he wasn't going to do the light show, and then Cameron and I were staring at each other and we got into a psychic conflict for several minutes. No one said anything until she got up and left the room and Nick said, 'Let's go,' and they were never together again. It lasted a week and she was out. It was an extraordinary experience, very strong. It was out of jealousy. Maybe she thought the light show was usurping her powers and she wanted to stop it. She was a ritualistic person and the ritual of the light show was non-ritual. I wrote a poem – she never saw it: 'The new ritual is unknown until performed and gone after it's ended.' It's not about the light show, it's about spontaneous presentation; ritual in a sense of consciousness, not attachment to anything. The philosophy was in direct contrast to hers. Cameron could be intimidating and she was on a power trip in a certain way. She had illusions of grandeur that's for sure, but it depended on the situation. Other ways she could be down-to-earth."

That winter, Cameron agreed to participate in a TV news interview on the topic of witchcraft, but the conversation went south when the interviewer began mocking the subject. In hindsight, she blamed herself for the negative experience and put it down to her own naiveté.[7] That same week, *Time* magazine ran an article under their Religion section on LSD, profiling two dissident Harvard Professors, Timothy Leary and Richard Alpert, whose experiments with psilocybin mushrooms and LSD on their student volunteers brought them censure from the faculty. Alpert was subsequently fired and Leary quit to further pursue this exciting, new discovery. Having turned on all the major Beat visionaries, Leary moved his base of operations to Zihuatanejo, Mexico in the summer of 1963. As it turned out, Cameron had been in the area on a Mexican trip during the same period and regretted not connecting with Leary while she was down there. Her boyfriend Burt had rhapsodised about his ecstatic experiences with LSD, now Cameron couldn't wait to get her hands on the wonder drug that promised to reveal the terra incognita of the psyche.

However, the reality was she couldn't even afford pot. Cameron had long prescribed to Joseph Campbell's dictum that: "…the person who takes a job in order to live – that is to say, for the money – has turned himself into a slave," and she hadn't held down a job since leaving the navy. Living on welfare provided unfettered freedom, but the money didn't stretch far and she was forced to sell the Celtic harp she'd been learning to play. To get the electricity put back on, she scored a Christmas gig arranging the window display at Bullock's department store, doing the same kind of work she'd once done as a teenager back in Davenport. The drastic change was such a shock to her system she came down with a bout of flu!

In the New Year, Cameron and Crystal left Venice and moved across town into Anger's second-floor apartment on Silverlake Boulevard. According to Joan Martin, their symbiotic relationship reached surreal new heights when they began experimenting with hormone tablets: Cameron ingesting male hormone tablets and Anger female ones in an aberrant attempt to become each other. Inspired by this, and their new living arrangement, they reportedly consummated their relationship. If Cameron had her druthers, Anger would've become husband number three, and the union would've doubtlessly ended as disastrously as her previous marriages. As it was, any romantic notions were quickly extinguished, when Anger moved out soon afterwards and left for New York, leaving Cameron behind consoling herself by wearing his black leather pants.

Karl Germer's death left a power vacuum in the upper echelon of the O.T.O. and, with no immediate successor, Crowley's American order was left to languish in leaderless limbo for years to come. In the meantime, Cameron and Anger continued to carry the Thelemic creed forward, disseminating Crowley's ideas through their lives and work. Anger's latest offering, *Scorpio Rising*, wickedly juxtaposed the rituals of a bunch of Coney Island bikers with a sassy pop soundtrack that ironically undercut their machismo. Conceived by Anger as "a Thelemic hymn to freedom," it would become his closest thing to a breakout film.[8] The lacklustre response to his work from some of Crowley's ageing adepts, whose approval he sought most, left him disillusioned, however, and, at the end of his tether, he pronounced them all traitors to Thelema. Now back in LA, he called for their demise, demanding they make way for Young Turks like himself to blaze a trail.

On the very day Anger made this proclamation, October 3, 1964, a benefit for Cameron was held at the 500-seater Cinema Theater on the corner of Western Avenue and Santa Monica Boulevard. Titled The Transcendental Art of Cameron, it was part of the theatre's Movies Round Midnight screenings, which had been running for a year now under the auspices of Cameron's friend John Fles and his creative partner, Michael Getz.

The Cinema Theatre specialised in screenings of non-mainstream film fare such as Tod Browning's *Freaks*, French New Wave offerings from Truffaut and Goddard, European masterpieces by Fellini and Bergman, and fresh, underground features like Jack Smith's *Flaming Creatures* and Kenneth Anger's newie *Scorpio Rising*.[9] On sale in the lobby were copies of Cameron's latest artistic offering, an illustrated chapbook titled *Black Pilgrimage*, that had been published by Press Baza. The title of her gothic poem had, once again, been drawn from her late husband's writings, this time from part two of Jack's The Book of Antichrist, which recounted the impact Babalon had wrought upon his life. The booklet boasted a colour cover of a frayed, tattered wing, while inside its ink-splattered pages were littered with Halloween motifs, such as a dark Angel of Death, a spikily drawn cat, a crucified witch and vampire bats.[10]

Commencing, fittingly enough, at the witching hour, the event began with the sound of Cameron's amplified voice reciting verses from her magical diaries as she sat in the projection booth, while 35mm slides of her artworks were projected onto the screen. Although the display worked visually, Cameron's overly dramatic delivery elicited chuckles from some in the audience. After an intermission, Cameron's film appearances were shown, kicking off with Ed Silverstone Taylor's *Street Fair San Francisco*, followed by *The Wormwood Star* and clips of her performance in *Night Tide*. A full screening of *Inauguration of the Pleasure Dome* was meant to bring the event to a finale, but what promised to be an enchanting evening turned ugly when Anger showed up in a combative mood, flanked by two goons, and demanded a halt be brought to the proceedings.

"Paul Mathison had a copy of the film; I don't know how he obtained it, and they wanted to do an evening and show *Pleasure Dome* in honour of Cameron," Curtis Harrington explains. "Kenneth was in his usual state of hysteria and claimed that Paul had stolen the print and had no right to show the film, but it was for Cameron, y'know. It wasn't for Paul; it wasn't for me."

(Documents confirm that one-third of the film was owned by *Pleasure Dome* co-star Katy Kadell, so it's possible Mathison may have asked her permission to borrow the print.) Harrington recounts what happened next: "Cameron was up in the projection booth in the theatre, and Kenneth arrived with a couple of toughs and stormed the booth. They had knives and they were holding a knife to Cameron's throat. It was a terrible scene and then somebody called the police. I happened to be there with a couple of friends of mine from Iowa who were football players, and the last thing in the world I expected was to ask them, but I said, 'Listen, guys, you better go up there and straighten this thing out!'[11] I mean, they were really big, tough guys, and the next thing I knew, they had brought down one of Kenneth's guys bleeding and his hair all dishevelled and they were holding him. Oh, it was the most terrible incident, but that's the sort of thing Kenneth did."

John Fles remembers the evening slightly differently: "We did the benefit for Cameron and gave her the money. Anger would always show *Pleasure Dome*, so long as he could be in the projection booth and introduce it himself. He didn't want to let the film out of his physical grasp. I said, 'No problem.' So he came and did the intro, but then he accused Cameron of killing Jack and other men in her life and he then said, 'Since all you people are here to honour Cameron, I'm gonna drop some hydrochloric acid!' And he did drop something, but the crowd just thought it was far-out theatre. No one left. Their response was 'Let's have more action!' I said to Kenneth: 'We're locking ourselves in the booth till everyone leaves the theatre!' Our shy projectionist was caught in the middle. It all started with a deck of Crowley's tarot cards that Anger claimed Cameron had borrowed from him and not given back. You could feel the tension."

Mike Getz had seen Anger outside the theatre, shortly before the show started: "There was a long line of people waiting to get in. Anger was carrying a briefcase under his arm and sticking out from it was a long, curved dagger. There was controversy over who owned the print of *Pleasure Dome*. John had arranged to get a print from Curtis and immediately Anger got upset because he said it was his print. But because we'd already publicised the event, we played the film and figured we'd worry about who owned it afterwards. People had no idea what was going on. We realised Kenneth was with some of his motorcycle friends, dressed in biker garb, and they were there to take the print when it was done. Curtis' team were dressed in suits and ties and looked like a bunch of accountants who worked out. Cameron was in the projection booth doing some tarot cards and Kenneth managed to break in, and he grabbed the cards and he threw them out of the projection window. I don't recall the hydrochloric acid but he could've done; he was an eccentric fellow. The crowd was pleased with the extra added attraction and, at the end, when the movie finished, the booth was rushed by two factions, three in each group. The print came off the projector and they began fighting with each other over it. I was at the bottom of the stairs but I heard all the ruckus. Later, my assistant manager, Stu Fox, found the print under a couch in the foyer and secured it in our office. They all fought, tumbling down the stairwell, as 500 people left the theatre, and continued out into the street and disappeared into the dark of night."

Although Anger and his crew left empty-handed, he allegedly vented his fury by calling in bomb threats to the theatre. And then, for days afterwards, he launched a one-man picket outside the venue. A photograph taken by Charles Brittin captured the stern, suited Anger brandishing a placard, blaming the Cinema Theatre management for not respecting the rights of filmmakers. "I think my wife Barbara and I were the only two people who honoured the picket line," Brittin recounts. "We stayed there and he was kinda touched when he saw that photograph. He'd been filming a lot of heavy leather and chains and stuff but he was always dressing as a very dignified personality. He was unpredictable. He's a little more irascible now, but he had a pretty straightforward, upright, puritanical image for himself then. A number of people had prints of his and no one had lawyers or signed contracts. I do remember someone telling me that, at one point, he went down in front of the screen and appealed to the audience and someone said he tried to get an attorney. He was being a businessman: art vs. business. He didn't appeal to his artist friends to protest. He did it in a very individualistic way."

According to Shirley Berman, Cameron and Anger were also at loggerheads over the ownership of some Crowley manuscripts that had once belonged to Jack. Anger was holding on to the papers, fearing they'd perish sooner or later in Cameron's hands. "What I gathered from Cameron was that it was over the Crowley manuscripts," Berman contends. "Anger said that they were his, not hers. I couldn't figure out why he thought they belonged to him, but if there was something that she was doing that was publicised, he would show up with banners and picket [laughs]. There was so much stuff happening. I remember Cameron was scared and Kenneth is crazy – he's a sweetheart but crazy!"

Writing to him from England, Gerald Yorke bolstered Anger's position, exclaiming: "I think you are well-advised to break with Cameron. She is too crazy and unstable ever to get anywhere really worth going to. How you must be enjoying your magical war; fun but dangerous. Those who live too much by magic are inclined to die by magic."[12]

His embitterment unsated, Anger instigated a poster campaign against Cameron, dubbed The Cameron File, in which he denounced his former soulmate as the "Typhoid Mary of the Occult World." For $15 a pop, Anger promised documented proof that would be a "clinical inspection of the remains of the late witch… and a counting of the dead souls who fell by the way." The poster was signed using Anger's new sobriquet, Father Allahabad, and bore a horned devil as his Puck Press logo, as well as his current whereabouts… San Francisco.

Cameron's apartment at 49 Wavecrest Avenue, Venice, as it looks today. (Photograph taken by the author.)

Artist Possessed

Cameron (Marjorie Parsons) is an artist possessed. With a peculiar mystique and an outstanding skill of draftsmanship, she presents us with a fantasy world filled with horrors and ecstasies. In spirit, though not in style, this contemporary Los Angeles artist recalls Bosch and late Goya. Her varied exhibit, including some fine nude drawings, will be shown through September at the Paull-Five Gallery on Larchmont Ave.

H. J. S.

Cameron's show at the Paull-Five Gallery reviewed by Henry J. Seldis.

The *LA Examiner* newspaper article chronicling Sherry's suicide attempt.

Sherry under arrest following his suicide attempt. *LA Mirror*.

1431 Silverlake Boulevard: the apartment building where Cameron and Kenneth Anger shared a flat for a short spell. Their apartment is on the top floor on the left, partially obscured by the tree branches. (Photograph taken by the author.)

Cameron's friends, Joan and Don Martin. "Cameron considered Don one of her teachers." (Courtesy of Joan Martin.)

Cameron with disciple Lisa Webster (left) and person unknown. Hollywood, circa 1961. (Courtesy of Joan Whitney.)

Cameron with Crystal and the wife of a Venice artist/poet. (Courtesy of Joan Whitney.)

12 - Exorcising Ghosts

> "What the caterpillar calls the end of the world, the master calls a butterfly." Richard Bach, *Illusions: The Adventures of a Reluctant Messiah*.

It has long been alleged that the decisive factor that helped get President John F. Kennedy elected in 1960, by the then narrowest margin in American political history, was the Machiavellian moves his father Joe Kennedy made, leaning on his son's playboy pal, Frank Sinatra, to pull strings with his Chicago mob connections, to help get the vote out in the critical swing states of Illinois and West Virginia.

The scion of an ambitious and wealthy patriarch, JFK came equipped with movie star looks, a fashion plate wife and fresh ideas, including an audacious dream of putting a man on the Moon before the decade was out. Though he'd never live to see it accomplished, the relatively youthful president seemed in step with his times, as a young, new generation, reared on rock 'n' roll, Beat literature and the Hollywood antiheroes of the 1950s, began to make itself felt.

Many stargazers believed the changing times were set in motion by the turning of an astrological cycle that marked the end of the Piscean Age, an era symbolised by Christ, suffering, self-sacrifice and guilt, and the advent of the liberational Age of Aquarius. Superficially, Cameron and Kenneth Anger also shared this view, but they further believed this new constellation was conjoined with Crowley's Aeon of Horus, a period that promised radical regime change.

In Britain, the Babalonian power of female sexuality, embodied by a pair of good-time girls, Christine Keeler and Mandy Rice-Davis, helped topple the Conservative government, and in the fallout from the Profumo sex scandal, a hoary hierarchy of ruling class fossils were consigned to the dustbin of history. A working-class cultural revolution was underway, personified by four likely lads from Liverpool, whose infectious, upbeat pop and scouse wit was about to turn the whole world giddy. Leading the British musical invasion of America, The Beatles helped raise the sagging spirits of a country still mourning the shocking death of its slain president. Taking a lead from Bob Dylan, whose switched-on songs seemed to drop like manna from heaven into his head, Lennon and McCartney journeyed deeper into their own lives for material, which yielded a bounty of consciousness-raising records that helped define the era, and became a soul-stirring soundtrack to some far-reaching social reforms.

The Civil Rights Act, which was soon to be signed into law, meant that Black Americans could no longer be *legally* treated as second-class citizens. Homosexuality would soon be decriminalised; abortion and divorce laws loosened and the contraceptive pill promised sex for pleasure (theoretically) free of procreation. Reflecting these new social mores, the decade would see the repeal of artistic censorship across the board.

Cultural outlaws like Cameron and Kenneth Anger had lived outside such legal boundaries for years, anyway, but the artistic underground that they had played such a significant part in, was about to go overground in a very big way.

Like Herb Cohen, many of Cameron's contemporaries view her as one of the seminal figures who helped usher it all in. "Cameron was very advanced in terms of racial attitudes," Charles Brittin asserts, "and she certainly dealt with gay culture very intimately. She was on the edge of the sexual changes and in breaking down most of the traditional behaviour patterns through the use of drugs, which was a major part of challenging the establishment and conformity. That *was* political. But it didn't move or merge into organised political action."

For Brittin it did, as he and his wife Barbara redirected their lives, retreating from the *Semina* scene to become full-time civil rights campaigners. Dennis Hopper heeded the calling too, and joined Martin Luther King, Jr. on his famous march from Selma to Montgomery,

Alabama. Ostensibly, Cameron remained apolitical, although Brittin contends she was concerned by the events of the day: "She *was* concerned, and actually a few other people of that art world were, but never to the point of taking any action. There was psychological distress and horror at what was happening. When Barbara and I became very active there was sympathy and appreciation but no direct participation. They were already alienated, and I understand exactly because I was that way, too. Doing things that moved them into the world of politics was not going to happen. They were artists, and artists are dedicated to beauty and insights and deeper things than world events. It was very hard for them to grasp the facts or to move over that line to something where they could put that aside for a while. Cameron was sympathetic, but practically none of that group did anything more than that."

By the mid-60s, Renate Druks had become an admired painter in her own right, and several of her canvases reflected a Babalonian theme, depicting nude women draped languorously over wild beasts. In direct contrast to Cameron, Druks earned a reputation for white witchcraft and was sometimes called upon to perform exorcisms at the homes of her rich, glamorous friends.

After divorcing Paul Mathison, she found love in the resolutely heterosexual arms of ex-Chicago Bear footballer Ronnie Knox, or so it seemed. "Ronnie was a rather *sensitive* young man," Curtis Harrington teases. "He was interested in poetry and everything, which is unusual for a football player."[1] But Druks' romantic idyll was rocked when her son Peter, who played Ganymede in *Pleasure Dome*, committed suicide aged just 19 years old. The shocking loss devastated the artist and she never fully recovered. In her despair, she searched for explanations and began to blame herself for exposing her son to what she now regarded as malignant forces in Anger's film, believing it had cursed him. She also pointed an accusatory finger at Cameron for, allegedly, introducing her boy to soft drugs that acted as a gateway to the harder stuff.

Months later, at a star-studded party thrown by her friends, the actor Jack Larson and the film director James Bridges, Druks met the young actor Allen Midgette who was staying at the hosts' Brentwood home. Having amassed some impressive acting credits to his name, working for such heavyweight Italian film directors as Bernardo Bertolucci and Pier Paolo Pasolini, Midgette was now making the rounds in Hollywood, under Larson's and Bridges' guidance. One role he was being touted for was *Reflections in a Golden Eye*, the new pet project of director John Houston, but the actor was already becoming disillusioned with Hollywood, even before he got started. "Films in Europe could be a testy, bitter experience, but I accepted it," Midgette explains. "But the whole acting thing was in and out for me. If it was good, it's good; if it was bad, it's bad. But Hollywood was too weird for me and I had to eject quickly. I couldn't handle it. I'm a wild person, gentle, but not civilised."

A good example of this is given by Jack Larson, who recounts Midgette's memorable contribution to the party: "There were lots of our friends there like Leslie Caron, Warren Beatty, Cecil Beaton, Christopher Isherwood, Gavin Lambert and Candice Bergen. The next thing, Allen takes centre stage and proceeds to tell Beatty and the others how superficial they are, and what impoverished actors they were, and how they had nothing to give, whereas he was real and had done films in Italy. I didn't know what to do. It was just dumbfounding. The only one who enjoyed it was Gavin Lambert – he was aglow with enjoyment at this diatribe. It was not good for Allen's health or state of mind, so the next day we went out to find him another place to live."

In a separate incident, Renate Druks caused a bit of a scene, too. During a demonstration of her psychic prowess, she asked Warren Beatty if she could read his palm and, on inspection, told the film star: "Only murderers have that line." After weathering both barrels from Midgette, this was all too much for Beatty, and he and Leslie Caron left in a huff. "Leslie later thought that what Renate saw was Beatty playing Clyde Barrow from the forthcoming *Bonnie and Clyde* movie," Larson explains. "Warren is not a murderer – except romantically."

Midgette picks up the story: "So I dropped out and moved to West Hollywood with my friend Larry Hall, whom I'd met in Rome. Larry was an actor too, and was trying to work in films, but was unsuccessful. He did sculpture and was a philosopher and really into the occult. He introduced me to Cameron in the street one day. Cameron looked at me and said, 'How are you?' And I said, 'Well, actually, I've been crying for the last three weeks,' and she gave me an understanding look and seemed to take it in. I told her about the problems I'd had with directors and she understood."

The actor also related the whole Druks-Beatty incident: "Cameron was amazed we'd met. She and Renate weren't friends at all by that point. Also, I told her I had Cherokee blood, and Larry was part Indian too, and Cameron said she'd had a vision that two Indians would come into her life. She later did a painting of me and a Native American friend. She recognised that in me. She was intrigued by everyone's past; she wanted to know about your family and things in your life. She was interested in hearing about my experiences with Japanese culture and working with Bertolucci. She wasn't aware of Pasolini, but she really liked Bertolucci's films and was also interested in Elsa Morante, the Italian novelist, who was a friend of mine. They were both very independent women who didn't seek the spotlight but were great artists."

At the time Cameron was living in a pad on Larrabee Street, just down from the Sunset Strip. Needing a room, Midgette stayed there off and on, couch surfing. "I could hear her doing rituals and incantations in the room next door. They were affirmations to the universe. But she wasn't witchy at all, but very self-contained and aware of what was going on. She was tough with a soft side. I could make her laugh a lot, but she was basically strangely pragmatic. She did things she had to do without complaining."

Another new face entering Cameron's life was Charm, a childhood friend of Aya's. A former concert pianist, Charm had gone on to marry Aya's first husband, only to leave him, just as Aya had, to pursue an artistic life: "He wanted me to wear low-cut dresses and be a trophy wife." Instead, she took up spray painting, and her dreamlike depictions of spirit guides caught Cameron's eye. "I remember Cameron saying, 'Are you trying to copy me?' It was an oblique compliment, said with a little smile. It was an acknowledgement of her gift. I was young and inexperienced and she allowed me to be an initiate. I was her neophyte; she was the master. That was the order, as it should be. She was familiar to me as a teacher and a dear friend. I felt I'd known her in a previous lifetime. My experiences were not as exotic as hers, and she thought of me as a sweet girl, y'know, pat on head. 'She might be okay as an artist' – that was her feeling. She was this very magical, striking, charismatic woman. Her image was the Goddess and she reminded me of the Empress tarot card, and I would see her as an eagle – which has the link to Crowley's Horus. She would recommend his books and his tarot deck, which she was very good at. She had this vibration that she'd been in places no one dared to look."

Moved around from pillar to post all her life, Crystal never got beyond a fourth-grade education, and her lack of schooling was becoming a major concern for Cameron's friends who tackled her on the subject. "We had arguments because I thought Crystal should go to school and Cameron didn't want her to," Marsha Getzler recounts. "Cameron believed it was all in there. But I said, 'Yes, but she's got to learn how to get it out.'"

"I think Crystal was an undiagnosed dyslexic but they didn't understand that back then," Charm asserts. "She always wanted money, and she'd earn some pushing people's shopping carts around the market. She was good at counting money. She'd say, 'I got four quarters – that's a dollar!' But there were behavioural problems, too."

"When she was about nine years old, Crystal began pulling her bank robbery stunts," Joan Martin recollects. "At first the banks thought it was cute, but when it kept happening the bank manager called Cameron in and demanded she do something. Crystal didn't go to school and I felt bad for her. She might have done well in a Waldorf school, where they allow them to be individuals and use art as a teaching tool. But Cameron was not a great mother. She didn't know how to take care of a child. I'm not a great mother either, but Cameron was too caught up in her own world."

Charm believes Crystal's increasingly delinquent behaviour was the price her mother paid to live a free-wheeling lifestyle: "Cameron had her own agenda. She wasn't going to follow a strict regime because she would've lost a lot of freedom to move around. Cameron wanted freedom and felt she should let Crystal go and be free and everything will work out. I wish I could have done more and taught Crystal how to read and write. Then she got into men when she got older."

During this new era, fresh ideas on child-rearing were being touted, including the notion that parents should allow their child to grow, uninhibited by any strictures or discipline. It was a theory born in reaction to the repressive, Victorian model that Cameron's generation was raised in and, for someone who felt ill-equipped to deal with a child sometimes, such an ethos provided a convenient justification to give Crystal a free rein. However, Charles Brittin disregards the notion that Cameron's parenting was part of any such theories: "As I perceive those people, they weren't thinking on that level at all. Nowadays younger people approach having a child almost like having a career and you study, you research into how you do it. I don't think they even thought about that back then. Children just came accidentally, they weren't planned like that. I see it now in a lot of my friend's children, who were born back then, who say to me: 'What were you people thinking about? What were any of you people doing?' In some ways, Wally and Shirley seem to be the one couple that got it right – Tosh is charming. If they were reasonably sound, stable people, they did alright and, if they weren't, their children suffered. Parenting was one of the things we got wrong."

Some of Crystal's learning and behavioural difficulties may have had genetic roots also. As already stated, there had been no prenatal care on Cameron's behalf, at a time when her use of peyote and other potent substances was routine. But even if Crystal hadn't been born with any hallucinogenic toxins swirling around in her system, Cameron had since remedied that by administering the "devil's root" to her anyway. She then followed that up by making the most controversial of all her choices relating to her nine-year-old daughter: dosing her with LSD.

Through her artistic contacts, Cameron eventually got her hands on the hot new kick everyone was raving about. Sold on its beneficial properties, she initiated Crystal too, at an acid party she threw one night at her crib. "Everything was electric in LA," asserts Allen Midgette, who was also present. "Everyone was taking LSD and peyote. Cameron gave me my psychedelic experience for the first time. She was a great person to get high with. She was full of stories." Unfortunately, for those revellers that evening, the LSD party came to a premature halt when gunshots were fired off outside, which was enough to give anyone a bum trip.

Maybe Jack's chemistry expertise had rubbed off on Cameron because when she couldn't score LSD, she brewed up a batch of her own, made up of God knows what! "Making LSD – I think she played a game about making potions," argues Charles Brittin. "What she was actually making I'm not sure. I don't think she was making anything from raw materials. I think she got prepared ingredients from whatever the market was, but she did have her own mixes for different things at different periods of her life. In the early 60s, when LSD was still legal, and Timothy Leary came to Hollywood and brought a lot of good stuff with him, I shared what was available."

Dr. Leary was falling in love with his new-found celebrity, especially knowing how his "Turn on, tune in, drop out" mantra was being heeded by a growing segment of the public. Some, however, found the frivolity of his message, and his cult of personality, off-putting. Cameron's co-star, Linda Lawson, was also discovering herself through LSD, in the radical drug-induced therapy sessions she attended with her movie producer husband, John Foreman. The sessions were conducted in a controlled environment by the psychiatrists Arthur Chandler and Mortimer Hartman, who treated other movie stars, most famously Cary Grant.

Lawson remains furious at the way the use of LSD became hijacked and cheapened by its Pied Piper: "I think LSD could have been an extraordinary psychiatric tool, but I blame Timothy Leary. I was at a party once and he was there, and I said, 'He better not come near me because I will stick a fork in his head!' Because he turned LSD into a high or a kick, instead of what it really was. I remember watching a TV programme, years ago, about a man who had been in a concentration camp, and whatever he went through there had made him completely catatonic. He could not speak, and they tried everything they could do, and they finally gave him LSD and it opened him up, and you saw this man begin to sob and cry and finally he began to talk, and I thought this ass Timothy Leary turned it into a joke and a street drug. I blame him because he was a respected professor at Harvard, so who wouldn't think that he knew everything? But he was nothing but a fool!"

Over the winter of 1964, the author Ken Kesey and his band of Merry Pranksters drove their multicoloured school bus coast-to-coast, turning people on to the joys of LSD, like psychedelic Johnny Appleseeds. Kesey had previously volunteered as a guinea pig for mescaline and psilocybin experiments, conducted at the Menlo VA Hospital near San Francisco, and poured his experiences of working as a night attendant on the psych ward there into his debut novel *One Flew Over the Cuckoo's Nest*. Sherry was an early fan of the book and somehow got it into his head that Kesey had based his charismatic lead character, R.P. McMurphy, on himself – a doubtful proposition. Kesey did admit many of the book's characters were composites of real-life patients, but McMurphy was, according to Kesey's widow Faye, "The one thing that was missing from the hospital – the one thing needed. It is the absence of such a character to save them. Many people have claimed it was based on them."

It was a kind of fabulous thinking that Cameron also indulged in. For example, she had begun to believe that Bob Dylan's elegiac ballad 'Sad Eyed Lady of the Lowlands,' was written with her in mind. "She listened to Dylan and all that sixties, from the heart, Americana music that was part of that scene," Allen Midgette attests. Another later rock song that especially resonated with her was the Crosby, Stills, Nash and Young number 'Almost Cut My Hair,' which fed into Cameron's lifelong fetish about her locks. Hair length had always been a hot-button issue for her.

As a bridge from the 1940s bohemian period, through the Beat era and to the hippie movement, Cameron, unsurprisingly, fit snugly into this countercultural context. Dressed in simple Mexican dresses, sitting around smoking pot and listening to sitar music, she looked like an older hippie woman. She even knocked up a leather miniskirt for herself and a matching pair of hot pants for Crystal. Cameron had dropped out of mainstream society yonks ago and, according to Midgette, she saw this as the greatest act of revolution. "Her attitude was you use the government but don't work for them."[2]

Meanwhile, back in Belle Plaine, Betty Rusk was organising the 25-year high school reunion do. She'd sent a mail-out about it to Cameron in California, which somehow, miraculously, reached her, but the reply that came back left her and her old classmates scratching their heads. "She was talking to outer space. I thought it's got to be LSD," recounts Dorothy Miller. "From someone with her talent, it seemed like kind of a waste."

"It was a way-out reply, and contained a picture of herself out in the desert of California," Betty Rusk recalls. "She was one of the flower children."

One thing Cameron *was* particularly interested in responding to, albeit briefly, at the time, was a mutually appreciative correspondence with Joseph Campbell. After years of admiring the mythologist's work from afar, she sent him some slides of her paintings and, in response, Campbell wrote back marvelling at "…the little shock of enchantment each one emitted, each time."[3]

As precious as they were, Cameron was not in the least bit proprietary when it came to her artwork. She could be extremely generous when it came to sharing it, not just with lofty figures like Campbell or her intimate circle of friends, but even complete strangers who showed an appreciation. One day, she left her *The Beast/The Vampyre Woman* canvas sitting outside her pad and ended up giving it to a passerby who'd taken a shine to it. As Charm explains: "Cameron felt it was vanity and ego to keep it. It was not essential. It was already there. There was a record of it on the astral plane."

Not long after Allen Midgette left Los Angeles, to work with Bernardo Bertolucci in Rome, the Larrabee scene broke up. For a spell, Cameron moved around the corner to a house on Keith Avenue, a place she'd initially found for Don and Joan Martin, but they had since vacated the residence to move up into the mountains of Santa Cruz. This temporary shelter was then swapped for a cottage at 5927

Willoughby Avenue, back over in Samson De Brier's neck of the woods. Charm recollects the huge trunk Cameron kept at the end of her bed there, and the secrets it contained: "My daughter was convinced it was full of magick tools, but it actually held her personal items, like her military photos. I remember Cameron gave a small laugh and said, 'Do you wanna see something?' And she whipped out a photo of herself in her Navy uniform and said, 'Actually, my real name's Marjorie,' and she gave a little smirk. And I said, 'You gotta be kidding!'"

In April of that year, Cameron heard through the grapevine that Sherry had died in Florida. According to his family, he suffered a brain haemorrhage while sat up reading a newspaper in bed, although his nephew Ned suspected that it was more likely an OD or suicide. Looking back, Ned feels Sherry was ill-equipped to deal with Cameron, and life in general, and understandably takes his uncle's side when reviewing their relationship. "He was an extremely sensitive guy and I think the situation with Cameron just destroyed whatever was left of him. She cut his heart out. He was no match for her, and I wish they'd never met." Sherry's legacy, his writings, which he bequeathed to his nephew, were all later destroyed in a fire. But for all their tempestuousness, it says something that, rather than renouncing it, Cameron retained the Kimmel surname for the rest of her life.

Towards the end of the year, Cameron, along with Anaïs Nin and Samson De Brier, was invited to participate in Curtis Harrington's new film project for Universal Pictures, *Games*. Co-written and directed by Harrington himself, the film starred Simone Signoret as a mysterious older woman who inveigles her way into the lives of two young newlyweds, an art collector played by James Caan, and his rich, beautiful wife portrayed by Katherine Ross. As the story unfolds, Signoret's character instigates a series of mind games with the couple, with murderous consequences, but all is not as it seems. With eccentric characters and occult chills, the picture was imbued with many of

Harrington's hallmarks but, in the end, neither Cameron, Samson or Nin made it into the film. In lieu of their appearance, the director borrowed Samson's triptych mirror from *Pleasure Dome* for a scene and also hung one of Cameron's abstract paintings on the wall of the couple's apartment.

Another picture utilizing Cameron's work was *Blues for Benny*, a short film made by John Gilmore about the adventures of a runaway black kid. "Curtis loaned me a couple of Cameron's pieces: a female face and a small one of a figure wrapped in vines that had appeared in *The Wormwood Star*. The pictures decorated the walls of a subterranean bar featured in the film. The film ended up in flames when the producer burnt the print to collect on some insurance money."

Cameron's role in Harrington's film may not have panned out, but the director did introduce her to a young actor he was mentoring, Robert Aiken: "Both Cameron and I would become quiet in each other's presence. She was not conducive to chitchat, but she could say the most mundane thing and it would be meaningful. A passing remark about someone would be substantive and a great insight. She was very perspicacious and had an acuteness of the mind. She was very centred, very quiet and still, and a good listener. She was always willing to be helpful to my personal life."

Cameron was finding some long-overdue answers to her own life, too, this time in the pages of *The Heretic of Soana*, a novella by the German dramatist Gerhart Hauptmann. In it, the author recounts his meeting with a mystical, old goatherder named Ludovico, a man whom locals believe has sold his soul to the Devil. Vowing to uncover the backstory of his life, the author wins his confidence, and the goatherd relates the tale of a parish priest named Francesco, who once practised in Soana, a Swiss hamlet overlooking the Lake of Lugano. The priest is told about a brother and sister who live high up in the Alps, ostracised by the villagers for their heathen ways and alleged incestuous union, so he sets out to convert them and bring their seven illegitimate children into his flock. He treks up the mountain to their hovel where the sister insists she's innocent of all allegations and explains her offspring were fathered, not by her sibling, but by passing tourists. She maintains she only lives with her brother because he cannot fend for himself, and agrees that her brood will start attending mass at the church on the summit.

While there, the priest becomes captivated by her enchantress of a daughter, Agata, and on his way back down the mountain he is unable to banish the image of her from his mind. His heart expands as, for the first time in his life, he begins to notice the wonder and beauty of nature. He is struck by an epiphany that makes him question the dogma of the Church. Instead, he now sees God reflected in the natural world, radiating its universal life force around him.

Back at his rectory, the priest suspects that witchcraft is being used on him and, enraptured by Agata, he asks God to deliver him from her spell. He discovers the outcast family engages in priapic worship and spies Agata riding on a goat leading a bacchantes procession. Tortured by his crisis of faith, he consults the burgomaster and the old pastor who initiated him, for he now laughs whenever he sees a crucifix in church. When Agata comes into town for confession, the villagers try to stone her to death, but she finds refuge under the desirous priest's roof, who, unable to contain himself any longer, falls from grace and kisses her. He later escorts her home but, en route, they fall onto the grass and he experiences the transcendental wonder of sacred sexuality. The priest feasts upon this "fruit of paradise" and the scales fall from his eyes as he realises just how dead and empty his life has been. When his heretical behaviour is exposed, the priest is attacked and driven out by the appalled villagers. He is then excommunicated by the Pope for showing no remorse. There the story seems to end, but as the author leaves the goatherder's cabin, he passes his wife coming up the path and is overcome by the radiance of her beauty and realises she is Agata.

With the book's basic theme, the renouncing of Christianity for a more life-affirming, pagan existence, it was obvious why the story resonated so personally with Cameron. It mirrored her own transition away from the organised religion that had once been foisted upon her, to the pagan path she was now on. A subconscious realisation that first revealed itself all those years ago in that emotional freak-out in Lugano, where the story was set. It also helped explain the mental duelling on the Paris-bound train, between her heathen self and the priest, as they each battled for possession of her conflicted soul.

Aya was also living on Willoughby Avenue, while Cameron was there, and during that period she remembers how her friend became increasingly paranoid, rounding on her and others when a thief stole her magical tools and tarot cards from her car: "I guess she was smoking a lot of pot because she was turning on people, saying, 'Did you take it?'" Cameron's neurotic state reached a crescendo one day when Wallace and Shirley Berman received a disturbing phone call from her, and they immediately made it over to her place. What they found there unnerved them. "Cameron was just sitting in the middle of a room and wouldn't talk, just wouldn't do anything," Shirley Berman recollects. "We actually thought that we were going to have to take her to a hospital until she finally said, 'I'm glad you're here. I think my life is going to start all over, beginning today.' Wallace asked her what happened, and she took him away into another room, and when he came back he said, 'Oh, God! Oh, God! She just threw it all away – all the paintings!' She had an incinerator in the backyard, and she burned all her paintings in the incinerator. I couldn't believe it. It was unbelievable. They were such beautiful pieces. Some of them were pieces from Curtis' *Wormwood Star* film, but what mainly were lost were the large paintings – the portraits.

They looked like door frames, the shape of them. They were magical. They were so gorgeous."

Some of the paintings dated back to the Pasadena period, and it seemed as if, in destroying them, Cameron had crossed a threshold and was exorcising the ghost of Jack. She was consigning that period of her life to the past, giving herself a chance to finally move on. "I think she felt very bad about it after she did it, but that's what it was all about," Shirley Berman confirms. "Cameron was an extremely sensitive and vulnerable person, and I'd say that three-quarters of the time that I saw her, she was totally depressed. She grieved for many, many years. I don't know how obvious that was to other people, but it was certainly obvious to my husband and I. Anytime Cameron called us we would go; anytime she wanted to stay at our house she was welcome. I think Jack was her life. He was the strong one in their relationship because he taught her how to live and she was very comfortable with him. She grieved for a helluva long time over him, and doing what she did kind of ended it for her and turned things around. After that, her personality and mood changed."

Once she was feeling a bit better about things, Cameron visited the Bermans at their Topanga Canyon home and dug the hideaway nature of life there; so much so, she ended up staying on. At first, she moved into a property belonging to a married Native American guy named Hank. "Hank had animals and was a very religious man. He was involved with shamans coming through town," explains Shirley Berman. "His religious use of peyote was one of the test cases that made it legal, although they did bust him for having eagle feathers. If he'd been on a reservation he'd have been fine."

Another mutual friend of the Bermans, living in Topanga Canyon at the time, was the movie star Russ Tamblyn: "People say Wallace had these followers, but he didn't – he wasn't a leader. He wanted people to find their own selves. I was the only follower. Wally was my mentor and

I followed him everywhere. He took me to hundreds of exhibitions, and when I met him we started growing our hair long. Wally was *Semina*'s key spiritual figure, like a Krishnamurti. He had this enigmatic aura, and I never met anyone like him – and I was a movie star! He had that kind of spiritual aura and personality."

But Tamblyn was left puzzled when the Bermans introduced him to Cameron – not least by her sexual orientation. "She had this very witchy aura, and I was never sure whether she was straight or gay. She made this strange scene with these gay guys. I knew about that scene, and that she was respected as a really good artist who went to deep places. She certainly had a uniqueness about her. She looked mysterious and had a sexual vibe. She was into the occult – that was her big thing. It was a little spooky, and I was a little spooked by it, and Wally would say, 'Look out! Sometimes the black arts can backfire and go crazy in your life, and you must treat it with great respect.' So I became familiar with her strangeness. We never spoke about art, it was about personal things. To have an understanding was the best compliment you could give someone, like the way you look at something and see it. Like how a tree grows or a flower." Cameron gifted Tamblyn two ink drawings, but they met the same fate as many of her other artistic offerings: they were destroyed in a fire at the actor's home.

Topanga was fast becoming a cool haven for rock musicians to live, a scene that was based around the Topanga Corral honky-tonk. Tamblyn and Berman introduced The Rolling Stones to the joint when they blew through town, and Tamblyn remembers Crystal hanging out at the Corral too, engaging in a not-very-appropriate relationship with a much older guy connected to the place. It doesn't take more than a dime-store psychologist to realize that Crystal was desperate for the platonic love and attention of a stable father in her life and, in its absence, she looked to other older men to fill that void. Depressingly, there were several creeps around who were only too willing to respond to her sexual coquettishness and, as a consequence, as Tamblyn recalls, "Crystal was always getting into trouble. It was a very seedy scene."

After Cameron left Hank's place she stayed on in Topanga, shacking up with an old girlfriend, Judy Chester, whom she'd known off and on since the mid-50s. "When I first saw Cameron, she was performing at a poetry reading at a studio belonging to my boyfriend, the artist John Altoon. Crystal was still a babe in arms at the time, and she'd be holding her while doing her poetry readings. Her presence was extraordinary, very striking. She had this mane of wild red hair that framed her face like a halo. She was always wearing far-out clothes. They were unusual and had her own stamp. People were of two minds about her. Some were frightened to know her because she was a witch; witchcraft stories went around about her, so people thought terrible things. During that period, she came and stayed at my home on Belden Drive in Beachwood Canyon. I was good friends with David Meltzer, too, and he would come over and stay the night with his friend Bob Collins. I thought Bob was the cat pyjamas. He wasn't very tall, but he was blonde and his features were all perfect, so cute. But before I could do anything, Cameron jumped on him! Then, all of a sudden, he was not on the scene anymore. I thought maybe Cameron devoured him! We then lived on Ogden Drive together, not far from Santa Monica Boulevard, in these tiny little cottages with courtyards. She had this ability to find these wonderful, out-of-the-way hideaways in the city. We were girly girls; we'd go thrift shopping and antiquing. One day I found this old Rococo frame that was long and narrow and she did a portrait of me, emerging like a butterfly from a cocoon with wild dark hair, and she gave it to me as a gift. Her life was pretty bare. There weren't many possessions at all. Her drawings went with her but not massive pieces, sketches. I believe she was drawing welfare – we were all broke. I got her a job as a waitress in a diner on Santa Monica. I even chose the uniforms, but she hated it. It's hard to imagine her working for anyone."

Other mutual male friends included Wallace Berman, Burt Shonberg, and Art Grady, "The Peyote King," who left free samples of the cacti, in pill form, on tables at the Renaissance Club and other hangouts on the Sunset Strip. "I had lived with Art. He felt peyote was sacred, and he would grind the buttons up and put the powder in gelatin capsules and put them on the tables of the Renaissance Club where I worked as a waitress. He felt if a patron took one then they deserved 11 more, and I left them out on the table for them. Lord Buckley played there and became a pal of mine, and we did peyote together.

Although Chester had enjoyed romantic flings with Dennis Hopper and Dean Stockwell, Cameron never spoke about their shared conquests. "She was private about her friends and never encouraged overlapping cliques. My relationship with Cameron was the same as the one she had with Charles Brittin and his wife. It was very down-to-earth and non-esoteric. We'd sit around the kitchen table at my home on Bonnell Drive, and discuss recipes for apple pies. Alcohol was not in with our scene, but we smoked a lot of pot, and we tripped together out in the desert. We'd go walking around ghost towns with our children with us. There was nothing said about her past; she kept it to herself. There was no talk about the tarot or Crowley; she never spoke about her family or Jack Parsons or Sherry; she didn't share that part of her world. As tight as we were, there were things that were just off-limits. Our relationship was 'in the now.' Cameron compartmentalised parts of her life."

One case in point was the character actor Linden Chiles, who lived in a little compound not far from Chester's place. "Cameron knew him before she came up to live with me, but never once brought him over or took me to his house. She was very precious about her friends, especially men friends, and she didn't introduce girlfriends to the men in her life. She kept them apart. I knew she had affairs, one-night stands, but there was never anybody steady."

A few years earlier, Chester had opened a popular women's boutique on the Strip called Pleasure Dome, of all things. "My partner chose that name. It was named after the poem, not the film. Although I never met him, I heard Kenneth Anger was very angry that we used that name." The success of the store meant that Chester could afford to have a swimming pool built at her home, which became a popular hangout for lots of little kids in the neighbourhood. But a problem soon arose: "Crystal was very sexually precocious and played sex games with the kids, and the parents forbade their children from coming to my home. So, sadly, I had to find them another place to live."

Charm was dropping in and out of the Topanga scene, too, and one night Cameron showed up and asked her to take care of Crystal because she was leaving town. "She'd heard L. Ron Hubbard was in Panama and she wanted to track him down. She was after his blood and out for vengeance. She blamed L. Ron for stealing Jack's ideas and was convinced he had something to do with his death. She did not think Jack's death was an accident. I couldn't take Crystal because I had a niece who was not in good shape, and I adopted her boy who was a drug baby."

To Cameron's consternation, Hubbard's Church of Scientology had flourished over the years, but success brought suspicion and, off the back of some negative press exposés, Hubbard was becoming increasingly despotic and elusive.[4] Commodore to his own fleet of ships, with a cadre of disciples at his beck and call, he was sailing around the world trying to flee investigations into his organization. Hubbard hoped that by staying on the high seas, he could continue to operate his empire outside of any governmental jurisdictions. Although Cameron's mission to wreak revenge fizzled out to nothing, it demonstrated just how strongly she still felt about Jack's mistreatment at the hands of his former friend. Allen Midgette recollects that she even participated in a local TV programme against Hubbard: "She was very down on Scientology, but she wouldn't say Hubbard was an idiot. She respected intelligence in any form."

To her friends it was obvious why Cameron felt so passionately: "Jack was the most important man and influence in her life," asserts Joan Martin. "It was stormy, but after he died she wanted to honour his memory and he became more precious to her then. She was carrying on Jack's occult work and she took on that image. Cameron said when she first met Jack, he wore robes and had long fingernails and she was not at all like that, but after he died she took on his role. She had theories on his death. She went out to put gas in the car and when she came back he was dead. If she'd have been home she would have died too, so she intimated that there was a survivor's guilt at work."

After a two-year cooling-off period, following the violent dust-up at the Cinema Theatre, Cameron decided to patch things up with Kenneth Anger and wrote to him trying to broker a reconciliation. Her letters seemed to do the trick, and a rapprochement of sorts took place when Anger visited Los Angeles and introduced Cameron to his new protégé, Bobby Beausoleil, a young rock musician he was grooming to play the lead part in his new film *Lucifer Rising*. One great anecdote, that Cameron enjoyed telling for years afterwards, revolved around a visit the three of them made to The Hollywood Cemetery. This was a favourite haunt of Cameron and Anger, who made a perennial pilgrimage to the crypt of his hero Rudolph Valentino, while she sat at the grave of Evie Abbott's ex Tyrone Power, who had more than a dash of the Jack Parsons about him. On this particular occasion the cemetery's cantankerous owner, Jules Roth, was in the process of locking the place up, and when he saw the trio loitering around he pulled up in his car and barked, "You've got 60 seconds to get out of here." Bristling at this, Anger puffed himself up to his fullest pomp and retorted: "I don't believe you know whom you are talking to! *This* is the famous artist

Cameron, and *this* is the famous musician Bobby Beausoleil, and *I* am the famous filmmaker Kenneth Anger!" To which Roth deadpanned, "OK, 30 seconds!"

With their relationship on a much better footing, Midgette joined Cameron and flew up to San Francisco to meet Anger, who was living in the former Russian Embassy on Fulton Street, a grand but dilapidated Victorian mansion, whose front door was inscribed with Crowley's 'Do what thou wilt' maxim, spelt out in blood-red paint.

While in town, Anger reportedly introduced Cameron to Anton LaVey, the "Black Pope" of the newly consecrated Church of Satan, whose congregation celebrated man's carnal instincts and Darwinian nature. LaVey was an aficionado of film noir, and *Night Tide*'s moody atmospherics appealed to him strongly, so he was delighted to meet its shadowy star. He would later cite the film in his list of all-time great satanic movies.

In his soon-to-be-released book *Les Américains*, the French author Roger Peyrefitte falsely claimed that Allen Midgette was a warlock in Kenneth Anger's coven but, on the contrary, the actor did not find the filmmaker at all to his taste: "I met Anger and found him hostile and vulgar. He was the antithesis of what I read in Crowley. I'd read Crowley's books and liked them, but I didn't wanna belong to any societies, but I could use it in life." On the other hand, Midgette found Bobby Beausoleil, "A nice, sweet, young man, very gentle and poetic, who just sat there playing the lute, barefoot. I remember Anger knocked on Bobby's door looking for him and said, 'Bobby, if you're in there, you'd better come out or you'll be excommunicated from the temple!' They were living that high-intensity energy thing where people get it without speaking. Whereas, when Cameron and Anger met, I walked out 'cause I couldn't handle the tension. Cameron liked Anger but knew he could be a horror. He would be charming with her one minute and then change. He knew how to get to her." Proof of this came when Anger began to engage in a series of mind games with Cameron – allegedly after they consumed some punch laced with LSD – and they quickly parted again on bad terms.

Following his breakup with Beausoleil, Anger escaped to swinging London, where, his dark reputation preceding him, he was welcomed into the inner court of The Rolling Stones. The filmmaker would later take credit for helping to paint the group's music black, by inspiring their flirtation with the infernal forces on their diabolic groove 'Sympathy for the Devil.'[5] Cameron, meanwhile, left California and relocated to the pueblos of Santa Fe, New Mexico.

Charm, Cameron's friend and fellow artist. "Cameron had been in places no one dared to look." (Photo taken by Aya.)

Judy Chester around the time she was living with Cameron.
(Photo courtesy of Judy Chester.)

Cameron joins the swinging sixties wearing a miniskirt and top she stitched together herself and carrying a bag made out of eagle feathers. Photograph was taken during a visit to Don and Joan Martin's place in Santa Cruz. Late 60s. (Courtesy of Joan Martin.)

13 - Thumbsuck

"Every revolution evaporates and leaves behind only the slime of a new bureaucracy." – Franz Kafka, *Conversations with Kafka*, by Gustav Janouch.

The winter of 1967 found the actress Pat Quinn house-sitting for friends in Santa Fe and nursing her new son, Caleb: "I was getting back to nature, baking bread, meditating and doing the whole organic thing. There were people in the Dome Wilderness there, tuning in and dropping out."

Early one morning, she was awoken by an intruder coming through her bedroom window: "All of a sudden this twelve-year-old nymph walked through the window and that was Crystal. Although I was living in an upscale neighbourhood, it transpired Crystal wasn't at school and was living with her mother down in a charming little adobe, getting by on her small veteran's pension and welfare."

At the time, Santa Fe was a mountain village of mud and straw and, by all accounts, Cameron led a pretty primitive life down there, with Crystal forced to bathe at times in irrigation ditches. In an echo of the Highland Park incidents, they were targeted by local elements, and more than once Cameron returned home to find their place broken into and her jewellery stolen.

Uprooted and with an absence of friends her own age, babies were one thing that Crystal could shower some love on, and she took to Quinn's newborn, instantly. "Crystal loved babies," Quinn recounts, "and, through her, I met her mother. She brought her over and she pursued a friendship. When Cameron got fascinated with someone she zeroed in. I was polar opposite. She was fascinated by dark and I was fascinated by light. She was a lesbian, but she never tried anything on with me – it would've been the end of the early, budding relationship. But she would be very coquettish with me. I was there for six months, and then I got a call to test for the film *Alice's Restaurant*."

Crystal knew the area where Pat Quinn lived well because she'd visited the residence next door belonging to the sculptor John Chamberlain. He and Cameron had been brought together by Allen Midgette, who was also checking out the Santa Fe scene. Having completed work on two Andy Warhol-Paul Morrissey flicks, *Nude Restaurant* and *Lonesome Cowboys*, Midgette embarked on a successful lecture tour of American campuses, impersonating the "King of Pop Art." He was so convincing in the role, that both faculty and students were taken in and believed they were getting the real thing. The jape was only uncovered when one of the Warhol crowd spilt the beans. "I'd gotten tired of working with Warhol and had to get out of New York," Midgette explains. "I knew Cameron was going to Santa Fe and I wanted to go, too. Santa Fe had Indians and beauty and Cameron loved the desert. I spoke with Chamberlain at Max's Kansas City bar in New York, and he told me to give him a call when I got there because he had a wife and kids down there. His wife and Cameron became good friends. It was a magical tour. I stayed with Cameron and Crystal for a week, then got my own place."

Though he was best known for the distinctive sculptures he welded together from battered automobile parts, Chamberlain, like Warhol, was also exploring the artistic possibilities of experimental film, although, as he candidly admits, there was an earthier motive behind this move: "Why did I get into film? Why the hell does anyone get involved in films? I wanted to get laid!" While he was in Santa Fe, Chamberlain conceived *Thumbsuck*, a film study on how children act around their parents. "A parent's role is to steer children to adulthood, but I couldn't get that thought across to anybody because they didn't have any idea what parenting was about. The children were terrific but the adults were somewhere else."

The entire film was recorded over two weeks in December 1968, and Cameron's section was shot at a house in Arroyo Hondo, just outside of Santa Fe. She was filmed applying white kabuki-style make-up while Crystal, and Chamberlain's two sons, Jesse and Duncan, watched her and lolled around on a giant inner tube from a tractor tyre that was being used as a couch. Cameron completes the job by painting a red triangle on her forehead (the alchemical symbol of fire), decorative dots above her eyebrows, and is captured in a close-up toking on a spliff.

Plans were afoot to travel to Greece to shoot more scenes on location, but Cameron refused to go without Crystal, and the project was shelved. Today, Chamberlain dismisses the unreleased film out of hand: "*Thumbsuck* is a children's movie, and there were principles I wanted to inscribe. The footage of the children worked but *Thumbsuck* was a refuge. The only thing good about it is the title."

The title derived from Duncan Chamberlain, who was eight at the time, and still in the habit of sucking his thumb. Today he's a 64-year-old professional sculptor in his own right, who doesn't recall his co-star with much fondness: "Cameron came to the house and took over. She wasn't a very good houseguest; she was kinda diva-ish… interrupted my routine." His father is even more disparaging, and claims he only used Cameron in the film because "she was in the vicinity and liked to be photographed." Other than that, he didn't dig her looks, or rate her art, and regarded the occult "as about as useful as tits on a nun!"

Rebutting the criticism, Allen Midgette pooh-poohs Chamberlain's motives and concept. "Chamberlain sucks you in and puts you down. It's all about him. But he uses interesting people to make it look like he's interesting. Pop Art isn't very interested in anything but Pop Art. It's not that deep. You only have to look at his sculptures to see that. If he wasn't making money, he wouldn't do it. I wasn't around when they made that film but I saw it later and Cameron's part is very beautiful. It was just like the way she performed in life."

New Mexico's majestic landscape had drawn other chums of Cameron into the region, including Dennis Hopper, who'd upped sticks and moved to nearby Taos. His wild, pharmacological ride through the decade of excess was about to reach its zenith with the era-defining *Easy Rider*, which would turn him into an icon and teach Hollywood how to capture the counterculture on celluloid.

Today the actor has, understandably, hazy recollections of Cameron and Chamberlain visiting his notorious party house there: "Oh my, a lot of people passed through that house. It had thirteen separate bedrooms with entrances from the outside and there were constantly people staying there. It was like a zoo! So to precisely know who was in the house [laughs], at one point or another was like… absurd."

Cameron was familiar with the area, having stayed on an American Indian reservation there for a spell back when Crystal was a baby. Now, mother and daughter settled on a commune of a quite different tribe: Wavy Gravy's Hog Farm, leaving just before they decamped and moved on to Woodstock in time for the music festival of peace and love.

On the 20th of July, a month before the hippie hootenanny, an even more momentous event occurred when astronaut Neil Armstrong disembarked from the Apollo Lunar Module and stepped onto the surface of the Moon. Launched and powered, in part, by the rocket propulsion technology that Jack Parsons helped formulate, the Moonshot was an eternal testament to man's ingenuity and creative imagination, and you can imagine how cock-a-hoop Jack would've felt at this technological triumph.

Far-reaching aeronautical technology had finally caught up with the flights of imagination projected by science fiction writers and, by the end of the '60s, one such scribe, Jack and Cameron's old crony Robert Heinlein, was savouring the success of his novel *Stranger in a Strange Land*. Its story entered on a suprahuman raised on Mars who is transported to Earth where, in a thinly veiled allusion to the Agape

Lodge and *The Book of the Law*, he becomes a famous guru of his own neopagan religion, though he ultimately meets a sticky end. With its themes of space travel, group sex, mind control, religious cults and the corruption of power, the book found a receptive counterculture audience who *grokked* it in all fullness.

Due to the popularity of the novel, Heinlein was invited to join television anchorman Walter Cronkite as a guest commentator during the historic Apollo 11 broadcast. Like so many, Heinlein held out great hopes for the future of space exploration but became disillusioned by the unimaginative vision of bureaucratic boffins, who would in time reduce the lunar landscape into just another strip of land to hoof a golf ball around.

Aleister Crowley's slow-burning influence arrived with full force in the late 1960s, eclipsing that of other fashionable gurus, like his contemporaries Gurdjieff and Ouspensky. Evidence of his permissive power over the age came when his bald, baleful visage graced the cover of The Beatles' *Sgt. Pepper's Lonely Hearts Club Band* album, arguably the most celebrated artefact of the time.[1]

The previous year, the most outspoken Beatle, John Lennon, inflamed the religious right in America by issuing the matter-of-fact statement that his band was now more popular with kids in England than Jesus. This comment, and his suggestion that rock 'n' roll would outlive Christianity, almost derailed The Fab Four's musical juggernaut Stateside. Bonfires were made out of their records, and radio stations across the Bible Belt refused to spin their disks. There were even threats of violence from the Protestant terrorist group, the Ku Klux Klan.

That same year, the underground newspaper *International Times* was founded in London, partly funded by a donation from Paul McCartney. Its January 1969 issue featured an illustrated article on Crowleyan sex magick, penned by Kenneth Grant, who continued to help spread the word of Thelema when he coedited (with John Symonds) the widely-read *The Confessions of Aleister Crowley: An Autohagiography*, published several months later.

Viewed as a darkly glamorous cult hero, Crowley's use of sex and drugs hit home with many leading counterculturalists, planting him centre stage of an occult revival just as the London pop scene was undergoing a retro Edwardian and Victorian fashion craze. Both John Lennon and Timothy Leary publicly parroted Crowley's "Do what thou wilt" dictum, but despite such celebrity endorsements, many who name-checked The Great Beast did not dedicate themselves to the serious study of Thelema but used it as a superficial swan dive into hedonism. Certainly, as the decade progressed, sex lost its sacred dimension and was reduced to just "balling," while drugs were increasingly taken less as a transcendental sacrament and more as an easy way to anaesthetise oneself.

Earlier in the decade, America's Cold War chess game for global supremacy against International Communism led to its further military incursions into Vietnam. Its indiscriminate terror bombing of impoverished civilians behind the Bamboo Curtain split generations and polarised countries, inciting a violent blowback at home and abroad. As race riots and anti-war demonstrations raged on American streets, Kenneth Anger envisaged a parallel war of Miltonic proportions being waged simultaneously on the astral plane, with Lucifer and his fallen angels fighting on the side of the love generation against the oppressive forces of the status quo.

Progressive politics were dealt one fatal blow after another with the shocking assassinations of Malcolm X, Martin Luther King and Bobby Kennedy. And while the "Peace and Love" Pollyannas wrestled with the "Kill Your Parents/Smash the State" radicals for the soul of the counterculture movement, and the Democratic Party disintegrated into internecine conflict over its stance on the Vietnam War, the silent majority of the American electorate propelled presidential hopeful

Richard Nixon into power on the promise of restoring social order back to the country.

In his essay Freedom is a Two-Edged Sword, Jack Parsons pointed out that the other side of the blade, responsibility, was every bit as important as the liberty he upheld. It was a crucial caveat desperately lacking in the sixties generation, and one that carried with it some quite dreadful consequences. After The Summer of Love raged, the hangover kicked in, and when moon-eyed kids continued to migrate from all over the country to join the Haight-Ashbury party that had already wound down, "heavies" moved in to hoover up the rich pickings and easy prey.

On August 6, 1969, Kenneth Anger's erstwhile muse, Bobby Beausoleil, was arrested in L.A. for killing Gary Hinman, a mantra-humming music teacher, over a mescaline deal gone awry.[2] It was the first in a series of sadistic, drug-related homicides that culminated in the gruesome Tate-Labianca murders. In the trials that followed, Beausoleil and his accomplice Charles Manson – the Judas goat who directed murderer Charles "Tex" Watson and his female accomplices to the Tate-Labianca slaughterhouses – were all tried and sentenced to death, subsequently commuted to life imprisonment with eligibility for parole.

The maleficent forces unleashed by those shocking killings seemed to hang like a pall over the ill-fated Rolling Stones' free concert held at the Altamont Speedway in Northern California that December. As the evening wore on, the violent conduct of some belligerent members of the Hell's Angels Motorcycle Club, who had been recruited to provide "security" for the event – a great example of the woolly-headed logic of the times – escalated into the horrendous stabbing of a pistol-wielding audience member, Meredith Hunter. The savagery was caught on camera by film documentarians the Maysles Brothers, and as their chilling concert footage made it plain to see, the countercultures' much-vaunted utopian dream was descending into barbarity and chaos. Pondering this, in retrospect, it's worth repeating what Anaïs Nin wrote regarding the climax of *The Inauguration of the Pleasure Dome*: "Love became hatred, ecstasy became a nightmare. Those who began with a sensual attraction, ended by devouring each other." She could easily have been prophesying the rise and fall of the 1960s.[3]

For Aya, however, the sixties can be explained in straightforward astrological terms: "We had Pluto in Cancer and they, the hippies, had Pluto in Leo, which is all about self-expression: 'Let's wear our hair long and be who we are.' They just wanted to boogie. It's not just the time you're born in, it's the time you're growing up in. Cameron was born just prior to the group karma of the Great Depression, so it was different for her. Everything is placed in history. Each cultural paradigm has its astrological assignment; it burns the old and makes way for the new. Cameron's generation was looking for vision and a voice. It was about opening up the prison of domesticity and the enslavement of the female. The lesson of the sixties was about allowing our subdued inner child out to play. The one after was about getting back to a new Virgo kind of order."

It was through Aya, and her new husband, William Royere, that Cameron was eventually spirited back to California from New Mexico, via magical means. "I had sent her a talisman and William was a practitioner of ceremonial masonic magic, so he ritually summoned her. Having heard all the sensationalistic stories about the enigma that was Cameron, William was frothing at the bit and couldn't wait to bring her back and meet her in person and share in all this magick. He knew she was a powerful magickian and he wanted to talk to her about working in the undercurrent, dark kind of things."

Initially, Cameron was far from impressed: "For years she never forgave me for splitting up with Elias, and when she finally met William they had a face-off.[4] She rounded on him and said, 'I could kill you for bringing me here!' But, eventually, they became close. They would duel on a magick level; it was all very Scorpio. Those two certainly had that in common, and they would get into some fierce word things. She had a million stories to tell us. She was very into *The Morning of The Magicians* book and told William to read it. I think she missed male energy in her life."

Authored by Louis Pauwels and Jacques Bergier, *The Morning of the Magicians* lifted the veil on an array of arcane subjects, ranging from the architectural use of masonic symbolism, and the occult roots of Nazism, to Crowley's tenure with The Golden Dawn. Some of that book's most fanciful theories, relating to extraterrestrials, found a welcome home in Erich von Däniken's hugely popular (but totally discredited) hypothesis *Chariots of the Gods?*, which argued that ancient astronauts were responsible for fashioning some of the planet's most famous architectural anomalies, such as Stonehenge, the Pyramids of Egypt and the Moai on Easter Island.

Cameron's own obsession with UFOs was rekindled when she and Crystal repaired to a section of Joshua Tree named Pioneertown, where they were joined by Norman Rose, Larry Hall and Allen Midgette. "We were all into UFOs," Midgette recounts. "While in the army, Larry had worked at the Roswell base in New Mexico where that famous incident involving the UFO crash allegedly happened back in 1947, and he spoke about seeing a hot dog-shaped UFO there. I had seen one, too. We would all go out to the Devil's Punchbowl, scanning the skies for them. Cameron did a ritual out there and we celebrated with champagne." As a result, Midgette began to understand how UFOs provided Cameron with a transdimensional link with Jack.

As the name suggests, Pioneertown originated as a 1940s Hollywood Western movie set, complete with functioning living quarters for the use of the actors and film crew. But it had since been abandoned by the film industry, so it provided a free place to live for a spell, and Cameron commandeered the post office building as her private roosting place.

When the weekend cowboys rode into town to use the scenery for a spot of roleplaying, Cameron joined them for a round of pistol shooting. But the fun and games were eventually brought to a halt when Crystal began carrying on with an older dude out there, which brought the law down on them all and, like a good outlaw, Cameron was forced to sneak her daughter out of town under the nose of the local sheriff.

Shots of Cameron in the John Chamberlain film *Thumbsuck*. (Courtesy of the John Chamberlain Estate.)

14 - Seasons of the Witch

> "The primordial deity for our ancestors was female... A self-generating Goddess... Giver-of-life, Wielder-of-death and Regeneratrix." - Marija Gimbutas, *The Civilization of the Goddess*.

Those who lived on the frontline of the sixties, and managed to survive it, seemed to stagger into the early seventies like shell-shocked beasts. As social pluralism continued apace, experimentation with lifestyle became ever more widespread. Behaviour that was once seen as the sole preserve of the hippies and the heads, soon became mainstream, with drug use as common among pill-popping housewives as it was with zonked-out rock stars. The sexual revolution spread to suburbia, in the guise of wife-swapping parties, enabling the parents of the love generation to get in on some of the debaucheries they'd been left out of. While the latest vogue for witchcraft and the paranormal brought the occult sciences out of the shadows and into the full spotlight of the mass media.

It was a decade that would see the loss of some major presences in Cameron's life and a host of new personal issues to overcome. It began with the death of her mother in September 1970, which brought a closure of sorts. For years mother and daughter had lived in different worlds, and their relationship had been a difficult, lifelong struggle. "There was something about her mother," Charm explains. "She was a mundane woman, and Cameron would say about her, 'You know how it is in Iowa.' It was like a woman-to-woman thing."

Cameron's own deteriorating health was becoming a serious concern, too. While living in New Mexico, she'd been hospitalised and treated for a collapsed lung and, since then, her respiratory condition had only worsened. She was suffering from bouts of chronic bronchitis and emphysema, hastened by her 50-a-day smoking habit. This, along with the recurrent tremor in her hands, meant she'd been unable to paint for four years, so her work was reduced to sketchbook drawings.

Some of the nudes Cameron conceived to complement Jack's *Songs for the Witch Woman* poems featured in the debut issue of *Matrix: For She of the New Aeon*, a literary anthology celebrating the sacred feminine, edited and co-published by Aya and Charm. The accompanying photograph of Cameron, snapped by Aya, revealed her increasingly weathered appearance.

By the early '70s, Pat Quinn was living back in West Hollywood, on North Genesee Avenue off Santa Monica Boulevard. In the previous decade, it had been considered a smart neighbourhood, home to grips, carpenters, scenery painters and camera operators from the movie studios. In more recent times, however, the area had taken a serious downturn and was far from the "beautiful valley" its Italian name described. "There were a bunch of addicts up and down that road," Quinn confirms, "and the further south you travelled along the avenue the increasingly funkier it became."

Cameron was aware that Quinn had been the former lover of her current obsession Marlon Brando, and when they reunited in L.A., she held out hopes that her friend might introduce her to him, but the actress had no intention of facilitating that: "Marlon would not have appreciated it. He would have been very annoyed."[1]

According to Allen Midgette, Cameron viewed Brando as a Nietzschean Übermensch, something Pat Quinn confirms: "Cameron saw Marlon as an Antichrist because he was an atheist but, there again, maybe she just wanted to fuck him. Maybe it went beyond that to iconic hero worship." When Cameron told Quinn they were both fighting for Brando's soul, the actress had no idea what she meant: "I just laughed. I'm not that complicated." Like her fabulous belief that she had somehow inspired Dylan's 'Sad Eyed Lady of the Lowlands,' Cameron now claimed that Brando's latest picture, *Last Tango in Paris*, was also about her on some level. "Actually, the truth is that most of the dialogue in that film was based on my dialogue with Marlon," Quinn states, "except the bit with the butter! The film is about Marlon's relationship with his mother and family and the women in his past."

When Brando made a rare guest appearance on the Dick Cavett TV show, Cameron and Midgette popped round to Quinn's house to watch it as neither owned a television set. During the interview, the actor steered the conservation away from his film career, especially the controversy surrounding *Last Tango in Paris*, to discuss the rights and issues of Native Americans, and deferred to members from the Indian tribal councils who he'd invited to join him on the show. This was a subject close to Cameron's heart, too, but her dreams of meeting *The Godfather* star never panned out.

However, Cameron did get the chance to meet Bob Dylan when the singer comped Quinn tickets for his Valentine's Day gig at the LA Forum, a series of concerts that were captured on his live album *Before the Flood*. "After the show, we went to the Beverly Wiltshire Hotel and I introduced her to Bob," Quinn recollects. "He and I were old lovers, old friends. Cameron was trying to be very mysterious, but he didn't pay much attention. I introduced her to Jack Nicholson, too. She would light up when she was near somebody famous. She was a small-town girl when it came to that."

By the early 70s, rock music had usurped theatre, literature, cinema and the fine arts to become the pre-eminent medium in which an artist both reflected and shaped the spirit of the times, and Crowley's influence during this period became even more keenly felt. In London, Kenneth Anger had a propitious meeting of minds with Led Zeppelin's guitar god Jimmy Page, when the two Crowley devotees met at an auction of The Great Beast's memorabilia. Despite successfully outbidding the filmmaker, the two became fast friends and, seizing the moment, Anger invited the guitarist to score and play a cameo role in his latest film project *Lucifer Rising*, his visual celebration of Crowley's Aeon of Horus.

In the film's most eye-catching sequence, a fleet of flying saucers hover over the Temple of Luxor, beckoned by the Egyptian Gods Osiris and Isis, to signal the arrival of the Crowned and Conquering Child. (In the famous legend, Horus flies to the sun on a great winged disk of many colours). This scenario correlated with Anger's and Cameron's current belief that UFOs emanated from the fourth dimension, not from outer space, and could be contacted and manipulated by magickians via the astral planes.

Unfortunately, Anger's history of falling out with people wound up repeating itself and the collaboration was shelved. The breakup sent the self-styled film sorcerer reeling back into the arms of his incarcerated, former apprentice Bobby Beausoleil, who replaced Page's Eastern, trance-like drone with a shimmering rock ambiance that complimented the film beautifully. It remains to date, the only film soundtrack ever recorded from behind bars.

With his otherworldly persona and spellbinding stage performances, another Crowley-referencing, British rock musician, David Bowie, emerged to become the most visionary artist of the era. His thematic use of outer space to convey a sense of personal alienation, dovetailed nicely with Cameron's own poetic preoccupation, while his public declaration of bisexuality helped make that particular orientation, which Cameron also shared, chic.[2]

In 1972, on the back of his breakthrough success with his alter ego Ziggy Stardust, he became the premier rock star of the Space Age, and, that same year, Jack Parsons secured his own special place in the cosmos when the International Astronomical Union named a moon crater after him (on the dark side of the moon), in honour of his contribution to rocket technology. In the immediate aftermath of his violent death, Cameron had been quoted by the *Daily News* as saying that many of her husband's friends had tried to confer academic titles upon him, while he was alive, but he flatly refused. Twenty years later, this accolade was brought about through the auspices of his old friend and colleague at JPL, Frank Malina.

When Pat Quinn vacated her pad on the corner of Genesee, Crystal and her husband and their young son took it over and, shortly thereafter, Cameron moved into a residence close by. The area was pockmarked with sex shops and porno theatres and, in one sense, it seemed fitting that this triple X-rated backdrop was Cameron's new stomping ground. Although there was little sacred in the sexuality on display, she'd certainly done her bit to help light the touchpaper of the sexual revolution, which reached its climax in 1973 with the grubby porn flick *Deep Throat*. (The film's revelatory scenes of fellatio became a cause célèbre and brought hardcore pornography into the mainstream. Ironically, its title provided the name of the anonymous whistleblower in the Watergate scandal, that helped bring down a Nixon administration that had launched a moral crusade against what they saw as the rising tide of smut.)

Aya, for one, couldn't believe where Cameron was living: "She was living right in the middle of the sex stores and porn theatres, for God's sake! I would go crazy where she lived. She was a ritual magickian on the side almost. Can you imagine knowing all that and living that day-to-day life? It's strange. She liked to be invisible in the middle of everything."

Aya and her husband had recently established The Ayara Foundation, a non-profit healing arts centre based in their Laurel Canyon home, which provided tutelage in astrology. Weirdly, when Cameron performed an invocation there, she left the couple outside the magic circle, unprotected, something that still baffles Aya to this day.

One of Aya's astrology students was the photographer Andee Nathanson who met Cameron at the Laurel Canyon house, though she was unnerved at first when she found herself on the receiving end of Cameron's flirtatiousness: "Cameron studied me and scared me, but

Aya said, 'No, no, no, it's okay.' She had these unflinching eyes that looked right through you and I wasn't sure if she was attracted to me or not. It was challenging but I didn't know what she was challenging me about." Despite her initial misgivings, she also became fascinated: "Cameron was like a blonde medicine woman. She looked like a woman of the desert. This woman understood silence, like a desert fox. She'd go on walkabouts. She was hardcore in many ways. She was an Aries Moon, which is a very masculine moon. To be beautiful and have those qualities is pretty far-out, especially for those times. She was early to the table."

As it turned out, Andee Nathanson's future husband, the film producer Rick Nathanson, had also encountered Cameron, independently of each other, while he was living as a tenant in Samson De Brier's duplex. "I lived in the front house on the bottom floor, and I would talk to her when she'd come visit," Nathanson recollects. "She'd sit on the porch steps outside and rock back and forth and tell pieces of stories."

Cameron was now in her 50s, but she still enjoyed her macabre conceits: "At the time she was carrying around a velvet bag in which she claimed she kept the head of her husband, Jack Parsons. She would allude to Jack and say, 'Those bastards!' – referring to L. Ron Hubbard and the Scientologists. She had long, yellow-white hair, thin lids on her eyes and a fair complexion. She was enigmatic. I considered her one of those Hollywood icons. I grew to like and admire her."

On February 17, 1976, Wallace Berman was killed whilst driving through Topanga Canyon late in the evening, when his car was broadsided by a young truck driver high on Quaaludes and alcohol. Although he was brought back to life and transported to a hospital, he died from his injuries in the early hours of the next morning, 50 years from the exact day he was born, an event he'd long predicted. The much-loved artist had been a dear friend to Cameron and an early champion of her work, and his galvanizing spirit created a wealth of artistic possibilities that touched the lives of numerous individuals. Proof of this came at his funeral when, what was intended to be a private family affair, turned into a full-blown celebration, as 500 people showed up at the Berman's house. The scene brought Shirley Berman some much-needed levity on a sorrowful day: "My husband was Jewish and this poor rabbi, that no one knew, was outside doing the ceremony, and he kept on seeing these cars show up and people walking up and he just freaked out completely. It was absolutely hysterical."

A few months before he died, Cameron joined the Bermans for a memorable dinner at their Topanga Canyon home, where they engaged in some badinage straight out of *The Wizard of Oz*. "Oh, it was so funny," Shirley Berman recalls. "At one point Wallace said to her: 'Well, I know you're a witch, but do you practice white magic or black magic now?' And Cameron started to laugh hysterically and said, 'Wallace asked if I was a good witch or a bad witch.' It was really funny."

Following her husband's death, Cameron became quite an inspiration to Shirley Berman, particularly in the way she had lived her life, persevering through good times and bad. "After Wallace died I thought a lot about Cameron. I didn't want to live like her, but I wanted to take some of the lessons from her life and the way she lived it."

Just a year later, another important man in Cameron's life, Burt Shonberg, passed away at the pitifully young age of 44. In the intervening years, the muralist's life had taken an even stranger turn, and by the mid-70s he was no longer Burt Shonberg at all but Jack Bond, an intergalactic agent from Time Coast, a cosmic space located somewhere in the fourth dimension.

Shonberg's paintings were now prized possessions, and his artwork graced several notable album covers, including *Out Here* by the psychedelic rock band Love. Most recently he'd contributed the patriotic cover art to the album *Spirit of '76* by the rock band Spirit.[3] Though his creativity never diminished, Shonberg's behaviour had become increasingly paranoiac over the years, to the point where even his sidekick Ledru was perplexed by it: "We'd go to Schwab's drugstore every day for coffee and cigarettes and he would doodle on the napkins, then get paranoid and say people were watching him while he was making notes. They were these fabulous drawings and he'd throw them in the wastebasket and go outside and watch as people rummaged through the trash retrieving them. He thought they were spying on him, trying to find out what he'd been writing. He was convinced he was being followed by government agents. It was all about the crimes of industry, the crimes of business, and corruption in government. He felt government people were after him and said someone had actually shot at him. But he'd say cosmic forces like The Mysterians protected him because he was lawful, in relation to Love Law and in a karmic sense. The Mysterians were forces in higher, lighter astral planes."

On the evening of September 16, Ledru returned home to the apartment they shared in Seal Beach and found his flatmate lying dead on the couch, with one eye open and one eye closed, having suffered a massive heart attack. "Burt's death was not a surprise to him. He knew where he was going. He'd found answers to the existential questions and he'd completed what he'd come here for. His works were in the world so he was ready to go. He'd scoff when I'd say he should protect these paintings. He said, 'I'll try and have my body disappear when I leave.' He had a way of lightening up a situation."

That same year Cameron was introduced to the experimental filmmaker Chick Strand, who was interested in using her in a forthcoming project. Cameron initially demurred, saying she no longer wished to be photographed as she was self-conscious of her wrinkles, which she blamed on the harsh climate and living conditions in Santa Fe. Instead, she narrated a story revolving around the death of Jeanne Spalding, her

Rainbow Girlfriend who'd committed suicide all those years ago, an event that obviously still haunted her. This time, however, she added a new twist to the story and related how the boyfriend who died continued to visit Jeanne from beyond the grave, transferring his consciousness into her mind via the bureau mirror in her bedroom. "Cameron talks about how a doctor attempted to exorcise this girl by putting a cold steel clamp in her vagina, and somehow this reminds Cameron of her friend's death," Strand recollects. "The story was very, very important to her, and the images in the film, during her part, relate to her story quite literally… well, almost."

Cameron's tale became a vital part of Strand's film *Loose Ends*, which wove a non-linear narrative using unsettling found film footage from the past, including images of a horse being butchered in a slaughterhouse and scenes of starvation from the Warsaw ghetto and the death camps. "The film she's in is not the film I originally intended," Strand explains. "I had wanted her for *Soft Fiction*, a film in which several of my friends tell me stories about themselves, but I preferred to have most of them told on camera. But I was editing *Loose Ends*, amongst others, at around the same time, and found that Cameron's story would be perfect for it."

Strand taped Cameron's voice as they sat in her backyard smoking pot. Cameron was growing her own at the time but would soon be busted for "cultivation." Strand's cigarettes were out of the question, however, as Cameron had quit the Marlboros and embarked on a health kick, which included trying, unsuccessfully, to switch the whole family on to macrobiotic food.

It's not unreasonable to assume that, had Jack Parsons been alive to hear Johnny Rotten's punk protestations of being an "Antichrist" and an "anarchist," it might have brought a wry smile to his face. Although a subcultural phenomenon in Britain, the punk movement failed to catch the wider imagination in the States, with its influence limited to the underground music scenes of the country's two major metropolises, New York and Los Angeles.

For a couple of years, Crystal's next-door neighbour was Exene Cervenka, the frontwoman of LA's premier punk outfit X. "We lived there between 1979-80 and the neighbourhood was on the slide," the singer reminisces. "It was a sleazy time. You would find gay men having sex in your backyard and there were street hustlers outside the house."

The unseemliness of the surroundings mirrored Crystal's own sexual proclivities, which were becoming increasingly risqué following the meltdown of her marriage. One night, Cervenka came home to find her neighbour skyclad in the middle of the street. "Cameron came out and walked her back home but she still didn't clothe her. They were pagan in that way." The incident later inspired the last line of the X song 'In This House That I Call Home':

> "*I finally look in your sweet eyes and somebody comes with a bottle of beer; after he leaves I turn for a kiss and see the lady next door, she's naked in the street.*"[4]

Cameron's modest abode on N. Genesee was tucked behind two other properties and accessed via a narrow pathway. It was partially obscured by the branches of a towering pine tree that grew by the side of the house, and once Cameron allowed the bamboo cane to grow wild in the front garden, it provided extra privacy. For some who visited, it was a mysterious grotto in a dark pocket of West Hollywood.

Allen Midgette paid a call to his old friend there and became one of the few people to experience the rare opportunity of watching her at work. He observed as Cameron "channelled" a sequence of automatic drawings that became known as *Pluto Transiting the Twelfth House*, an astrological meditation on the mystery of death, revealed in a series of delicate spirographs whose cosmic vibrations seemed to resonate off the page. "She had such a soft touch," Midgette attests. "She was into being directed from the universe. She used to make telescopes out of card and then fix coloured paper to the end of it, like a makeshift kaleidoscope, and look inside and paint a landscape from it. She would use indirect methods like that to get to something."

1984-1995

A sense that the decadent, Dionysian climate of the previous two decades had flamed out seemed vindicated with the landslide re-elections of arch-conservatives Ronald Reagan and Margaret Thatcher. The political pendulum may have swung right, but even Reagan's folksy presidency was not immune to ideas that digressed from traditional values or conventional thinking. This became evident when stories began leaking out from the White House suggesting the President's schedule was often divined by an astrologer who had the ear of the First Lady. In the media furore that broke out following this exposé, a beleaguered administration began taking flak from all sides. A delegation from the Federation of American Scientists wrote to the president grousing how they were gravely disturbed that he indulged in "such evident fantasies," while the religious right denounced the White House for engaging in "occult practices." Though Joan Quigley was eventually unmasked as Nancy Reagan's trusted astrologer, Carroll Righter was also named as part of a cabal of stargazers whom the family sought guidance from over the years, a man whose house Cameron had often visited for astrological studies. With all the controversy, it was as if the sixties had never happened.

In 1973, Dr. Marshall Ho'o introduced the ancient martial art of T'ai Chi Ch'uan to a new TV audience, via his television show on the local public network KCET. As part of his mind-body-spirit approach to health, the doctor helped legitimise acupuncture and the use of holistic medicine in California. In the mid-80s, with her health a persistent worry,

Cameron took up the discipline and participated in group sessions on Saturday mornings in Bronson Canyon in Griffith Park, under the tutelage of the master himself. She also enjoyed the 45-minute lecture that followed, in which the doctor often spoke on the benefits of Chinese herbal medicine.

The practice seemed to ground her. It was a good way of keeping her mind agile and her body supple, and she became proficient in using the sword and the stick. Cameron also took a serious interest in her teacher's relationship with his partner/assistant Strawberry Gatts, a pioneer in the field of holography, who had previously worked with the eminent mystic and philosopher, Manly P. Hall. "Cameron respected Marshall very much and she talked to me about my relationship with him," Gatts elucidates. "She became very focused on us and talked about what she had dreamt about us. With her background, she had developed an expertise in areas like shared intuition."

When Gatts visited Cameron at her home on Genesee the surroundings did not disappoint: "Cameron had a three-pronged iron cauldron outside, which she said she used for ceremonies, and inside I remember she had these incredible drawings of angels on three, black-framed panels that stood side-by-side. They were four to five feet high and a few feet wide, and she told me they had been commissioned years ago by a major church in L.A. to become stained glass windows. But she took it all very lightly at the time and went away on a trip to Mexico and was late with her commission. When she returned to the church with them she said the vicar berated her and chucked her out, and she said it was an important turning point in her career because after that she went on to lead this vagabond lifestyle." (The story Cameron recounted most likely dated back to the Mexican trip she made with John Muir in the summer before Crystal was born.)

When the subject of Jack Parsons was brought up in conversation, it appeared Cameron was still querying the official version of events regarding his death, and toying with new storylines surrounding the circumstances. "She talked about how she felt Jack perhaps did not die in the explosion. In fact, she said the government had invited him down to work in a little house outside Los Alamos and there was a fire and an explosion there, and she felt his death could've been a cover-up – that he was still alive when they whisked him away. Maybe she couldn't handle his death, so she was creating this other image."

While the veracity of that scenario was certainly questionable, Gatts was left in no doubt as to Cameron's supernatural essence: "She really was an elemental. I could see that in her and in her granddaughter Iris, too, who had that same physiology. Whereas, with Crystal, I detected that there was some kind of physical and psychological disturbance with her that had something to do with the way Cameron was working with energies. Cameron was part of a larger realm. She was a fire-type elemental and, to that end, I remember she'd been invited to give a talk to a group of people and something caught fire there and they blamed her for it and she said, 'But it wasn't my fault.'"

Through the mid-to-late '80s, Cameron was dedicating much of her time to the stewardship of her grandchildren. Predictably, given the upbringing she'd had, Crystal found it difficult to keep a disciplined grip on her rambunctious offspring and Cameron was, to a greater degree, left in loco parentis. Regret may not have been part of her make-up, but some friends felt Cameron was making up for her own parental dereliction and the lack of boundaries she'd given Crystal, although this was rather undermined by her continued practice of turning younger members of her family onto pot at very tender ages. She hoped it might expand their minds, but with one grandson, whom Cameron rechristened Silver, it did nothing to curtail his juvenile delinquent behaviour, which included taking his grandmother's jeep for joyrides, destroying one of her harps, and pawning Jack Parsons' treasured scarab ring.

"Almost all the time I knew Cameron then, she was battling the courts and fighting the school system in regards to her grandchildren and getting constantly enraged by it," Aya recalls. "She was a proud lioness fighting for her pride. Her Sun sign, her nature, was very down-to-earth, very much the earth mother, not the wild nature she displayed. She was a pioneer in the way she thought and had a very fiery side to her that was warrior and militant in a lot of ways, and she would be in confrontations of various kinds. One was by being in the military, but the other was when anybody threatened her children, forget it, she was Martian!"

One person who took time out to offer Silver some guidance was Genesis P-Orridge, co-founder of the British cult bands Throbbing Gristle and Psychic TV, who was infamous for marrying industrial music with performance Shock Art.[5] Cameron's introduction to the more outré side of British pop culture came courtesy of William Breeze, an erudite musician with a background in the New York art world, who would soon rise to become the new all-seeing eye of the rejuvenated O.T.O. Breeze made a point of re-establishing contact with Cameron and bringing her back into the fold, expanding her social activities in the process. Through Breeze, Cameron met a younger generation of O.T.O. initiates like Sallie Ann Glassman, who was naturally excited to meet the living embodiment of Babalon – an archetype that she, herself, was working with at the time. But instead of being greeted with sisterly solidarity, the young priestess was treated to a frosty reception and the high-handed side of Cameron's personality, who prejudged her unexpected guest as an inexperienced young pup. "Cameron was a great artist but she was mean to me," Glassman recounts. "She made it clear that she didn't like me visiting with Bill, probably because she wasn't expecting me to be there, and she wouldn't let me in. She left me outside with the dog. I was going to leave, but the dog was wonderful, a real noble creature. Eventually, I showed her my Enochian Tarot deck illustrations and she said, 'You just did someone else's work!' and threw it on the ground. She had a lot of fascinating and exotic stories to tell, and I said it ought to be written down as a legacy, not to be lost, and she gave me a withering look and said, 'Who would you suggest – *you*!?' And I said, 'Well... yes... maybe.' The other time we met I was giving a lecture in L.A. to an O.T.O. gathering and in the car, en route to the venue, she said, 'You're not the sort of person who should offer up an opinion; you should wait until you are asked. You're not an original thinker.' But I gave the lecture and that shut her up. It was as though she felt I was an obnoxious upstart that needed to be put in her place. I took it as a challenge."

On May 10th, 1987, Cameron appeared with Crystal and her granddaughter Iris in the women's section of the *Chicago Tribune*, for a feature about mothers and daughters. The article was part of an ongoing project by the photo-essayist Carla Weber, whose pictures saluted timeless maternal bonds, using several familial set-ups as examples. Weber originally shot the session with Cameron and her offspring back in 1981 and was forced to reschedule the shoot three times because Cameron didn't feel the astrological conditions were right. When Weber did eventually show up at Cameron's house, it was a curious experience indeed: "I didn't know Cameron prior to taking the photos, but I knew I would appreciate the unconventional qualities that she possessed. I ended up falling asleep in her living room, and I slept for many hours, and I remember being freaked out when I woke up. I awoke with a huge headache; it wasn't like me to fall asleep in a stranger's house, and I felt rather strange and drugged. I then came back two weeks later and worked with Cameron, as well as Crystal and her daughter, Iris. Crystal was pregnant and seemed challenged, but it was difficult to ascertain what exactly the issue was. She never looked at me or the camera directly. Her daughter Iris, although young at the time, had quite a spark. I remember thinking that she could turn out to be quite the beauty."

That August, Cameron was featured in the BBC Radio 4 documentary *Ruthless Adventure: The Lives of L. Ron Hubbard*. The programme, which took a great deal of Hubbard's officially sanctioned life story at face value, was researched and narrated by Margaret Percy, who interviewed Cameron earlier that year at her home. Kenneth Anger also contributed to the documentary and, for a while at any rate, the two appeared to have settled into a brother-sister type of relationship, with all the ensuing ups and downs. They were even talking about collaborating on another film together.

It was Anger who put the BBC researcher in contact with Cameron, and when Percy sat down with her host at her home on Genesse, she could still detect a vestige of beauty in her, despite the wrinkles and ravages of age: "I thought she must've been stunning when she was younger," Percy attests. One standout memory from their meeting came when Percy asked a couple of questions that seemed to make Cameron uncomfortable and, on both times as if on cue, her dove Pax began cooing in the background. "It was an eerie experience," Percy recalls.

Back in 1969, the British *Sunday Times* ran an exposé on Hubbard's participation with Jack in the Babalon Working and cited Aleister Crowley as a catalytic influence on Hubbard's teachings. To counter this claim, Hubbard issued a cover story in which he painted himself as a cloak-and-dagger intelligence agent, sent into the Fleming mansion on South Orange Grove to rescue his future wife Betty from the evil clutches of Jack Parsons' black magic ring. This dubious scenario played hard and fast with the facts, yet in the subsequent radio broadcast Cameron, surprisingly, gave credence to this line, musing how Hubbard "may have been an agent – as he claims."[6]

During this period, friends mention how Cameron sometimes suspected her home was being surveilled by the FBI and, in discussions with William Breeze, she also suggested how invisible government agencies might have been responsible for her own initial involvement with Jack: "She would space-out and say, 'Maybe I was sent in there' (to Jack's house on Orange Grove). 'Maybe I *was* an intelligence drone.'" Whatever the origin story, Breeze maintained that Jack really hadn't prepared her well to live the life of a practising magickian. He could also see that over recent years there'd been a sea change in Cameron's view of Hubbard: "She may have reached some sort of accord with the Scientologists. She was approached by them and knew some people in L.A. – that's how she got Jack's FBI file. She wasn't down on them and she wasn't down on Hubbard any more. She actually liked Ron; she thought he was charming."

Over the decades, The Church of Scientology had grown into a multimillion-dollar empire, boasting movie star converts, but one person whose low opinion of Hubbard had decidedly not wavered, and had only grown more virulent over time, was Kenneth Anger. To a perennial Hollywood-watcher like him, Scientology's foothold in Tinseltown only added fuel to his ire, and during his own interview for the same radio documentary he made his feelings abundantly clear, describing Hubbard as an "elemental demon."[7]

Even though she'd never been a member of either organization, Cameron believed that, due to her rich history, she'd earned a rightful place in the highest echelons of both the O.T.O. and Scientology. But there was a new metaphysical system that she'd recently discovered, which added yet another dimension to her spiritual life.

Thanks to Pat Quinn, Cameron was hipped to José Argüelles' book *The Mayan Factor*. "Cameron wanted to go to Isla Mujeres with me to make the Mayan women's once-in-a-lifetime homage to the priestesses. She was beginning to put up icons like Chinese Goddesses; she was still searching. She then turned onto *The Lion Path* and she and Larry Hall were deeply involved in that."

Like Crowley's *Book of the Law*, the Lion Path was rooted in Ancient Egypt, but that's where the similarities ended. Originated by the philosopher and physicist Charles Muses, a friend and collaborator of Joseph Campbell, this shamanic system blended ancient mysticism, fringe science, self-transformation and the transmigration of the soul. It centred on the three divergent paths the soul takes after death, each one symbolised by the three couches found in the anteroom of Tutankhamen's tomb. The central lion couch led to regeneration and a voyage to a new dimension. The hippopotamus couch signified reincarnation back on Earth, while the cow couch left the soul loitering like a ghost in the afterworld if its mission in life was unfulfilled. Muses taught that during a meditative state, an individual could align themselves, at specific time intervals, with the energy harnessed from the womb of the Goddess Isis, which was emitted via the rays of her star, Sirius.

As well as generating new perceptions and a higher state of consciousness, the results promised to restore the vital forces and metamorphose the cells in the body, enabling the soul to emerge like a butterfly from a chrysalis into an immortal body of light. Although she'd ultimately have a falling out with Muses, Cameron became a vocal advocate of his teachings and urged friends and others to "get on the Path," boasting to Aya, "Ever since I read this, this happened."

Inspired by this new system she committed to paper a series of singular coloured shapes, charting her personal progress. One integral aspect of *The Lion Path* was the process of reincarnation, a prevailing concern of Cameron's, particularly in regards to the possibility of Jack returning to her. "I'm sure she was using this energy for something, and I think what she sought most of all was to find Jack again," Aya asserts. "Find him in any of the forms she could. And that was the search as long as I knew her. God! I hope they're together now."

One possible route back was that Jack might reincarnate in the guise of one of Cameron's grandkids, and particular hopes centred on her granddaughter, Iris. Although it soon became clear that such an incarnation had failed to materialise, two of the grandchildren were given the Parsons surname and, following Cameron's request, they were all invited on a guided tour of JPL, the billion-dollar funded space research and development complex that their namesake co-created from scratch all those years ago.

To her neighbours, Cameron brought some much-needed character to the community. One of them, Harry Blease, would often spot her practising T'ai Chi in the garden. "She had all the hippie trinkets, like peace signs, hanging from the tree. You could walk up that tree and there's an area where you could sit and hang out and smoke a joint. Everything was trippy, like the hippie days, like another world. Everyone called her the witch, not because she was mean, but because she had long, grey hair."

Cameron's latest dog, Sheba, another Alsatian cross, became a local fixture too, as she would lie in the middle of the street, immovable, forcing cars to drive around her. Cameron would take her along on trips to the desert, the Mojave or Joshua Tree, and they'd sleep in the jeep together. "She mainly kept herself to herself," Blease recollects, "but you would see her walking the dog, sometimes with a big joint in her mouth. She walked about as fast as the dog did… very slow."

As well as T'ai Chi, Cameron would often practice her Celtic harp while sitting outside in her garden. "She played harp beautifully," Aya attests. "She had beautiful hands. It was kind of a meditation for her and she liked Celtic sounds and folk songs. She felt that was her roots." One of Cameron's favourite resources for Celtic music was Saint Paul Sunday, a classical and folk music show on public radio. Tuning in, one Sunday morning, Cameron discovered the ethereal, medieval music of Hildegard von Bingen, the 12th-century, German abbess. The rapturous sound, she later told William Breeze, was "riveting. I couldn't turn my attention away from it. I sat there just paralysed listening to it because it sounded very much like the way I sing when I'm by myself."[8]

Cameron endeavoured to find out more about this multitalented woman, who had counted Popes and royal heads of state of Europe amongst her friends. "She was a poet, she was a musician, she was a painter. She was everything that I am," she told Breeze and, straight off the bat, Cameron drew parallels with the synchronicity in her name, connecting Hildegard to both her magical moniker, Hilarion, as well as her father's first name, Hill.

More significantly, Cameron came to realize that the Benedictine abbess was the missing piece of the Lugano puzzle that had eluded her over the decades. Believing Saint Hildegard was one of her previous incarnations, she extrapolated that the reason she travelled to Lugano all those years ago and stayed next to that convent was because she was subliminally trying to reconnect with her former cloistered life. This revelation was imbued with additional meaning when she discovered the abbess corresponded with Eleanor of Aquitaine, the royal consort and religious crusader. For Cameron had an Irish friend called Moya, a woman whom she'd been playing the harp with over the past ten years, who believed that she'd been Eleanor in a previous life.[9]

From Joan of Arc to Hildegard von Bingen, the mystical side of Christianity continued to exert its pull on Cameron. "It would be normal for Cameron to see the divine in the Christian or anti-Christian, which is Crowley," explains Aya. "One way or the other, you're still using the Bible upside down or sideways. That's her transcendental self and that's in her art."

Towards the end of the '80s, Cameron wrote to her old friend Charm, admitting that she was tired of life in Los Angeles and was considering a move to Mount Shasta in Northern California, where Charm resided. It was an area of outstanding natural beauty, rich in Native American lore and, according to New Age belief, served as a vortex for the Great White Brotherhood, an enlightened body of ascended masters whose healing energy was said to radiate from their mountain lair.

"She'd done an astrological chart to divine if such a move was in the stars," Charm explains. Apparently, it wasn't, but their last visit together brought their friendship to a new plateau. "The last time we met she was so sweet and had mellowed out and was so into her grandchildren. I had evolved and she was in a different place. We were equals, both grandmas, and when I left we embraced and she said, 'You've healed me.' It felt so good, as though we were seeing each other without the veils."

Tosh Berman would bump into Cameron now and again as she made her way to the local grocery store. She seemed an incongruous presence amid the sea of faces, like the poodle-haired rockers making their way to the nearby Guitar Centre. "Her face was old and wrinkled, but she had a peachy clean complexion and an inviting Irish smile."

At a retrospective of Tosh's father's artwork, held in January 1988 at the L.A. Louver gallery in Venice, Cameron enjoyed a moving reunion with David Meltzer after a 20-year absence: "She'd become the white witch, the Wiccan," Meltzer recounts. "She was all dressed up in white, with a big explosion of totally white hair, tipped in red. Cameron asked: 'Is David Meltzer here?' And I was standing right in front of her. We'd both changed quite a lot and we just laughed. It had been a fascinating journey. I cherish that memory. So much melted away in laughter. For a moment you were selfless."

As well as receiving old thespian flames, like the ever eccentric John Drew Barrymore, and her former beau Linden Chiles – a coupling that humorously reminded Crystal of the *American Gothic* duo mentioned earlier – Cameron also reconnected with another blast from the past… George Frey. "I had gone to see the Dalai Lama speak about world peace at the Shrine Auditorium in 1989 and, as I was leaving, someone called my name and I turned around and it was Cameron." Frey returned to the house on Genesee and stayed for a couple of hours. "Cameron wasn't very interested in the Dalai Lama, she wasn't too impressed. Y'see, with the Dalai Lama, there's nothing mystical about him."

When Robert Aiken visited his old friend, around the same time, he took a series of photographic portraits of her: "She reeked with spirituality. I think she was perhaps going blind, but she was aware of how extraordinary the portraits were. I was very interested in taking the photos because of her presence and demeanour and soulful quality."

Through Aya, Cameron discovered the text Woman and Superwoman by Dr. A.S. Raleigh, who billed himself as The Official Scribe of the Hermetic Brotherhood and Hierophant of the Mysteries of Isis. Raleigh's Edwardian-era treatises ran the gamut of esoteric subjects such as magic, metaphysics, alchemy, Atlantis and spiritualism. Published in 1916, Woman and Superwoman focused on "feminism viewed from a hermetic standpoint," and charted the evolution of aeons during which the masculine and feminine took turns as the dominant power principle, in accordance with the cycles of the zodiac. (In the Thelemic calendar such cycles began with the Aeon of Isis, a prehistorical period when the Great Mother Goddess was venerated, followed by the Aeon of Osiris, an era symbolised by the self-sacrifice, death and resurrection of the Patriarch, superseded, in 1904, by the Aeon of Horus.)

Cameron taped herself reading from the book at home, and the resultant recording was broadcast on local public radio. Delivered in her husky voice, you can just make out the noise of workmen hammering in the background and kids running in and out of the house. Prior to its airing, she forgot to credit the source, so many assumed the tract was written by Cameron herself. She sent copies of the tapes to friends, including Linda Macfarlane, a Canadian Thelemite, who'd contacted her having grown disenchanted with the way she felt women were being marginalised by some occult groups.

"Cameron was a larger-than-life icon whom I admired from afar, and I wanted to speak to like-minded women, but the Superwoman tapes made me uncomfortable. They were not my cup of tea. She referred to Raleigh's script in our correspondence and said I was free to distribute it; that was her crusade. She was devoted and dedicated. Her main focus was the theory of women's evolution from prehistoric times. She was reading Marija Gimbutas and was interested in the archaeological digs in old Europe. It was groundbreaking, consciousness-raising stuff."

Such a subject raises the still open question as to how much Cameron considered herself a feminist. Some feel that as a rarefied artist, she was above such politicking. Though she had certainly begun to question notions of patriarchy, by the 1980s, the once inclusive feminist movement – exemplified by Aya and Charm's *Matrix* journal, which featured poets and thinkers of both genders – had degenerated into a puritanical subsect that denied women's sexual power and espoused a victim-centred, misandrous dogma based on labyrinthine logic which turned off both sexes. However, in other ways, Aya is adamant that Cameron was most definitely a feminist, aggressively so: "She didn't believe in husbands as mates. 'Get rid of 'em, they're only good to bring babies' – that was her belief. One part of her nature was different from the other part. One was rather destructive and Martian, and the other was serene and conservative. She was always both seeking and fighting the male, like the power struggles with Germer and Anger. Yet, she was still somewhat indoctrinated by Crowley. I always resisted that and told her, 'But he doesn't like the power of women.' But she didn't see it like that."

Linda Macfarlane elaborates: "Although Cameron complained about being treated badly by the Germers in the old days, Crowley was still important to her. Crowley had jewels, but also a weight of burden with his misogyny, but she implied, through her ordeals, that she loved him immeasurably. He was a father figure to her who had revealed so much."

In the spring of 1989, after a 30-year absence, another long-overdue reunion took place when Helen Parsons Smith visited Cameron at her home. Both ladies had been widowed for decades (Wilfred Talbot Smith died five years after Jack in 1957), but during the meeting, Helen brought up some housewifely questions, like whatever happened to Ruth Parsons' trunk of clothes and Jack's Italian mahogany bed. To this, Cameron gave a fanciful tale about how she'd carried the bed across the desert and left it under a palm tree, despite the fact that it weighed a ton. Though she was left bemused by some of their conversations, Helen was inclined to leave Cameron some money before she left until she noticed the high quality of combs and hairbrushes in her bathroom.

While she was in town, Helen was one of many old friends and acquaintances who attended *The Pearl of Reprisal*, a retrospective of Cameron's art held at the Municipal Art Gallery in Barnsdall Art Park. Works included the most recent series *Pluto Transiting the Twelfth House*, as well as old favourites like *Peyote Vision*, whose mysterious penetrator Cameron now identified as a solar God. Another celestial being that arrested visitors attention was *The Flashing Figure of Adonai ha-Aretz*, Cameron's colourised, bare-breasted version of a monochrome drawing depicting the ruler of Malkuth in the Kabbalistic Tree of Life, found in Volume 1. No. IV (The Temple of Solomon the King IV section) of *The Equinox*, the official organ of Crowley's Argenteum Astrum's (Silver Star) order.[10]

There were screenings of *The Wormwood Star* and *Inauguration of the Pleasure Dome*, and Cameron also read some of her poetry, making her entrance on a dark stage, carrying a solitary candle that lit her wan, wizened face. On the day Helen Parsons Smith visited the exhibit, patrons were treated to the sight of Cameron wearing shorts, prompting Helen to say, "I wish she'd put those chicken legs away." There was further levity on the day a now elderly Samson De Brier attended. As he sat listening to Cameron reading, the PA kept cutting out, making her inaudible. Samson grew exasperated by this and began complaining so vociferously that the director of the gallery exclaimed: "Get that old hairdresser out of here!"

Despite this incident, it was a show for which Cameron was inordinately proud. "Cameron came to a point late in life where she had definite pride in herself and pride in her position, which she understood to be a spiritual one," explains William Breeze. "She characterised it as being sort of underground, in a sense that when Crowley writes about how spiritual revolutionaries frequently work on the inner planes, and to outward appearances you wouldn't realise who they are or what they do, but they have this tremendous effect on society. She felt that she was sort of a feminine spiritual leader and believed she was responsible for much of the women's movement. But she could also be – and I think it's probably either a family or an Iowan trait – very wry and self-deprecating. It's almost English, but not quite, it's a bit different."

That year, in conjunction with Breeze, Cameron helped edit some of Jack's libertarian tracts that were turned into the book *Freedom Is a Two-Edged Sword*. The front cover pictured Jack standing in the doorway of their Manhattan Beach house, shirtless with a pipe in hand.

Cameron capped off an eventful year when she was interviewed for a Japanese documentary on UFOs. She related her account of the craft she spotted back in 1946, one of the first civilian sightings ever recorded. Considering how she always believed the sighting was Jack's celestial confirmation that she was the chosen vehicle for Babalon, her unique view on UFOs was that they were not high-tech at all but functioned to re-establish paradise on Earth by restoring "elemental powers that are available to the matriarchy."[11]

The new decade brought close encounters of a not dissimilar kind in the guise of the author Peter Moon, an ex-Scientologist fixated with

Jack and Hubbard's Babalon Working. As an upshot of their meeting, Cameron was woven into the time-travelling tapestry of the Montauk mythos, Moon's series of books investigating alleged mind control experiments conducted at an Air Force base in Montauk, Long Island. Cameron initially enjoyed the attention Moon's way-out theories gave her, as they only added to her legacy and legend, but, according to William Breeze, who introduced the two of them, the meeting of minds was a short-lived thing: "Cameron eventually wrote back to say he was too extreme for her. She was willing to entertain some pretty loopy notions, but I think she had a good sincerity sensor and I'm not entirely convinced of his sincerity. You can always find data that looks good when forced together to support a thesis, but it's very poor logic, very poor research. That's not the scientific method. That's not magick. Crowley says right out there: 'Magick is the art of causing change in accordance with the will.' It is science pure and simple. So why would we want to indulge in these sorts of retrospective mediaevalism? It's the reason they didn't have an enlightenment until we had a scientific enlightenment. It's because they were incapable of reasoning outside of these boxes. If you've already got in mind the results you want, you're not going to do the science. So deciding this is what you want to believe, and then looking in the past for plausible evidence that you can sort of tweak to connect up, is the easiest thing in the world. All the paranoiac conspiracy people do that."

Moon's slant on Cameron was later documented in his book *Synchronicity and the Seventh Seal*, which, amongst other things, made much out of the fact that the Wilson family name appeared in both Cameron's and L. Ron Hubbard's family tree and that the Cameron surname was also shared by other shady protagonists involved in this fantasy. Moon also roped Crowley into the mind-warping mix, claiming that when The Great Beast visited Montauk, back in 1918, he created a space-time portal through which the USS *Eldridge* destroyer was catapulted during the infamous Philadelphia Experiment.

One fateful day, in 1994, as she went to open the front door, Cameron tripped over her cat Firestone and damaged her leg in the tumble. It turned out to be a fortuitous fall that inadvertently prolonged her life because when she was given a CT scan at the hospital, the doctors discovered she was suffering from a brain tumour.

As a consequence, Cameron underwent radiation treatment, which resulted in the loss of her hair. At the same time, she sought out alternative, homoeopathic treatments and began experimenting with various herbs and teas, even drinking small amounts of her own urine, like some yogis teach, to help reprogramme the body. Joan Martin had taken up beekeeping and, along with the jars of honey she sent Cameron, she also included some Propolis, the secretion bees use to seal their hives, a substance high in protein that contained medicinal properties. Cameron told Martin about her great-grandfather, Thomas Brentlinger, who had been the town's beekeeper in Belle Plaine and shared her belief that bees were carriers of magic. Cameron hoped the bee glue would help her failing eyesight also, and yet, ironically, as she confirmed to Strawberry Gatts, her gradual loss of vision only seemed to sharpen her ability to perceive the Elemental Kingdom: "She said that elementals and visions from that realm were becoming clearer. She could shift her vision and see those worlds better."

To her closest friends like Aya, Cameron confided that she was only staying alive for the sake of her grandkids: "She was very uncomfortable and miserable and still running her family. She was worried about her grandchildren's welfare. What was gonna happen when she was not there? There were no males around or father figures. This was a no-man family; it was very strange. Poor Iris was rebelling, and it seemed like they were fighting, but they were really close."

Cameron was about to become a great-grandmother, but what should've been a cause for celebration turned into a worrying ordeal, when the pregnant Iris began having problems eating. At her wit's end, Cameron turned to her T'ai Chi master, as Strawberry Gatts recalls: "Marshall said, 'Bring her to my house and we'll get her health and energies back to normal.' Everyone felt he helped save her life. He helped her understand the different procedures of pregnancy."

On April Fools' Day, 1995, Samson De Brier, Cameron's friend for over 40 years, passed away at the Hollywood Presbyterian Hospital. According to his close friend Wendy Hyland, Samson had become quite the curmudgeon in his dotage, prone to bouts of embarrassing behaviour. He pointedly double-checked his till receipt with the cashier to make sure it was accurate, while customers huffed and puffed in the queue behind him, and he made scenes in restaurants over their no-smoking policy or lack of heat. He even acquired a peculiar phobia about apples, fearing their ageing effect, but did not mourn the passing of his libido, opining with a Wildean flourish: "Imagine yourself in a mirror displaying such outrageous positions, looking so foolish. If one could see oneself during such things, one would refrain from participating in such activities." [12]

Samson preferred the haven of his home and did his best to inure himself from the ugly world outside. After he died, Hyland noticed, with a mixture of melancholy and wonderment, how the lemon tree in his garden failed to bear fruit that year. A memorial was held for him at the art centre Beyond Baroque in Venice, a venue housed in the very same building Curtis Harrington once used to represent the police station at the end of *Night Tide*. Paul Mathison, Harrington's friend and colleague from that film, showed up to pay his respects, despite now being wheelchair-bound. Photographs were taken from Samson's house and exhibited upstairs, and both *Inauguration of the Pleasure Dome* and *Salome* were played for the mourners.

According to mutual friends, the relationship between Cameron and Samson had broken down in recent years because he felt she was too impossible to deal with. But death can often heal old rifts and wounds and Jack Larson, who sat near Cameron at the memorial, recalls how "she looked tragic and was very saddened at Samson's death." Shirley Berman was also present, and although they'd spoken to each other on the telephone in the intervening years, this was the first time she'd seen Cameron in the flesh for ages. She was relieved to find that time had not withered her dry sense of humour. "It was just before Cameron died and her hair was just growing out and she said, 'I've spent all my life covering my ears and I had to lose my goddamned hair!' It was so funny. She was wearing a bandanna beneath a cowboy hat; she was cute."

By the time Aya visited her, a month before her death, Cameron was accepting her fate with gallows humour. "She was very morbid by then. One of the last things she said was, 'The dog's dying. The car's dying. I'm dying. We're *all* dying!'" By that stage, Cameron's cancerous brain tumour had metastasised to her lungs. Although she would've preferred to die at home, she spent her final days at the VA Medical Center, with the final curtain falling that July. Curtis Harrington visited her there and recalls how Cameron accepted her looming death "with complete serenity." A high priestess in the O.T.O. was called upon to perform the last rites, and Cameron eventually died in the arms of her granddaughter, Iris. Around her deathbed were pictures, including an old photograph of her with Jack staring adoringly into each other's eyes. Following her cremation, her ashes were scattered across the Mojave Desert, just as his once were.

As with Samson De Brier, a memorial for Cameron was held at Beyond Baroque that August, with some of her most admired paintings on show, including her portrait of Jack, *Dark Angel*. Curtis Harrington's heartfelt homage *The Wormwood Star* was projected, and one of his personal favourite paintings by Cameron, *The Black Egg*, formed the centrepiece of a makeshift altar.

Pat Quinn was asked to read a tribute: "I wrote something about how Cameron was a constellation unto herself," and William Breeze read an unpublished Maya Deren piece, titled *Lilith*, with his girlfriend: "It's almost couched as a dialogue like, 'What is woman?' Which I thought was appropriate. If anyone could get a handle on Cameron, Maya Deren could [laughs]."

Looking back today, some of Cameron's closest friends pay their respects to a woman they knew over a five-decade span. "I loved her dearly. She was a very big part of our life," Shirley Berman acknowledges. "I say, if someone lived most of the time the way they wanted to live, it was Cameron... definitely on her own terms."

"Over a forty-year cycle my view of the deep relationship I had with Cameron changed a lot," muses Aya. "In one sense she was right in-your-face and had no time for artifice and chitchat. All encounters were close – there were no mere acquaintances. Cameron was on a spiritual journey to who she was, a vision quest, working on herself and the laws of magick, art, metaphysics, the principles of the healing arts, shamanic philosophies and the marvels of inner and outer space. She'd been through it all and came out the other side. She was one of a kind."

Charles Brittin concludes: "I think of Cameron as an enormously talented person who made so many bad moves in her life, out of which she did something transformative. She produced something from things, that I think were really damaging to her, but she survived them all. I can't say her talents were frustrated or damaged, I think they were enhanced by the suffering and the illusions and the delusions. Great art is often delusional. But that she survived as long as she did amazes me. She survived long enough to be sort of the simple, nice, sweet person towards the end whom I got to know. I think of her as having an enormous life strength and life force. Despite everything that happened to her and everything that fell apart, she turned it into something creative."

Cameron's secluded home on 1149 ¼ N. Genesse Ave, West Hollywood, as it looks today. (Photograph taken by the author.)

Cameron, Crystal and Cameron's granddaughter, Iris. 1981.
(Courtesy of Carla Weber.)

Cameron and Crystal, 1981. The photographer recounts that Cameron rescheduled the shoot three times for astrological reasons. (Courtesy of Carla Weber.)

Cameron attending Aya's 50th birthday celebration at Loreon Vigne's Temple of Isis in Geyserville, California, in 1982. (Photo courtesy of Aya.)

Cameron (wearing hat) performing group T'ai Chi Ch'uan in Bronson Canyon in Griffith Park. (Photograph courtesy of Dorothy A. Odsen.)

Cameron and a friend. (Courtesy of Aya.)

Cameron hugging the tree in front of her house on Genesse Ave. "She reeked with spirituality." 1987. (Courtesy of Robert Aiken.)

Portrait of Cameron by Linda Macfarlane.

15 - Epilogue

As is often the case with artists who have recently passed away, Cameron's artwork attained new critical heights of interest and appreciation at a level that eluded her during her lifetime. It began the very year she died when her erotic drawing, *Peyote Vision*, was included in the *Beat Culture and the New America* retrospective held at the Whitney Museum in New York. Kenneth Grant objected to her inclusion in the show, believing it an insult to link such an avatar with what he considered lowbrow culture. In his book *Hecate's Fountain*, published three years earlier, Grant cited Cameron's momentous incarnation of Babalon as a catalyst for the formulation of his own New Isis Lodge. Even though they never met or communicated with each other, his psychic connection to her remained strong, as he confided to a friend: "Cameron is more real to me than the people who brush past me on the London underground."

Cameron and the ghost of Jack Parsons were just some of the many multidimensional inhabitants floating in and out of Grant's fictional "Mauve Zone," but, in 2000, Belarion was given his own starring role when Adam Parfrey's Feral House published *Sex and Rockets*, the first proper biography dedicated to him. Although the book certainly helped introduce Parsons' extraordinary story to a wider audience, the inclusion of an unsubstantiated sensationalist rumour, that smeared Jack as a sexual deviant, pissed off those who knew him and his admirers alike. Hot on its heels, came the publication of *Strange Angel: The Otherworldly Life of Rocket Scientist John Whiteside Parsons*, a far weightier and more authoritative take on Parsons' abbreviated life, authored by George Pendle.

The film rights to the former biography were snapped up by Hollywood producer Don Murphy, a man responsible for *Natural Born Killers* and Johnny Depp's Jack the Ripper romp *From Hell*. When Murphy met with Jack's first wife to discuss the project, Helen Parsons Smith delivered an arch, opening gambit: "So, Mr. Murphy, are you interested in sex or in rockets?" In subsequent interviews, Kenneth Anger began to tout himself as the director for the forthcoming *Sex and Rockets* feature, and Murphy's admiration for the sometimes prickly filmmaker extended to naming his own production company, Angry Films, after him, as a mark of respect. Since then, the project has remained languishing in development hell.

On the flip side, on June 14, 2018, *Strange Angel* debuted on the CBS All Access channel. Sadly, the TV series was a highly fictionalised and dragged-out adaptation of George Pendle's biography, containing the kind of sexed-up and sensationalised scenes that are typical of so many Hollywood productions. Despite the fact that many of the original Agape Lodge members were retirees – and *Republicans*! – on the screen, they were replaced by thrusting nubile voluptuaries with tattoos and stripper tits beneath their satanic hooded robes. Even more predictably, there was a sinister underscore whenever the Agape Lodge's headquarters hove into view. Despite some spirited acting, the show failed to hold people's attention and, as a consequence, it was cancelled prematurely after two seasons before Cameron's character even made an entrance.

In 2001, having spent much of his middle age as a director for hire, helming camp TV confection like *Dynasty* and *Charlie's Angels*, Curtis Harrington's career came full circle and he ended where he began, remaking his early Edgar Allan Poe short *Usher*. In it, Harrington cast himself as the ageing poet Roderick Usher and also dragged up to portray the poet's twin sister Madeline. His old friend Renate Druks made a cameo appearance in the film but was unable to attend its première due to ill health. Shortly afterwards, she abruptly left her Hollywood apartment and checked into a retirement home, refusing to see any visitors. "I have not heard from her since," Harrington sighs, mournfully. "I've tried, but she won't accept any calls. It's like she decided that she's going to die and it's all over."

That same year, some of Cameron's most cherished works were included in *Reflections of a New Aeon*, an artistic celebration of Aleister Crowley held at the Eleven Seven Gallery in Long Beach, California. Featuring artistic offerings from Crowley's votaries, as well as The Great Beast himself, Cameron's contribution included the simply stunning *Fossil Angel*, one of a series of drawings dating back to the late 50s, that included the undisplayed *Fossil Bat* and *Fossil Unicorn*. The application of white ink on dark blue paper lent these images a ghostly, translucent quality, reminiscent of an X-ray radiograph. The deftness of touch on *Fossil Angel*, in particular, made it appear as if the angelic apparition had materialised out of wisps of smoke, recalling Buddy Anderson's comment on how Cameron's artwork looked "like smoke moving about." Lesser-known pieces were also on display. *Horned God* was an almost Christmassy illustration of a stag-headed man in tights, while *Man with Sphere* depicted a bearded, bedraggled beggar carrying a red orb in his hands. One of Cameron's more whimsical offerings, dating back to the mid-50s, was a gouache drawing of two dancing harlequin figures with lion manes and rattails. Its title, *Hekas Hskin Etoz Beahi* (aka *Dancing Pair*), may either have been misspelt or misread, as in all likelihood its proper wording should've been *Hekas Hekas Este Bebeloi*, a phrase that roughly translates as "Far, far, from here be the profane," a warning for the profane to depart before being forcibly banished, that is used in the rituals of The Golden Dawn.

One perennial favourite was the sublime rendering of Cameron's daughter *Crystal*, who, in the wake of her mother's death, left Genesee Avenue with her youngest children and relocated to a residential desert town outside of L.A., where she still lives today.

As the noughties progressed, Cameron's presence began making itself felt in cyberspace, with some wags even going so far as to set up social media accounts for her from beyond the grave. The fantasy of her magically mating with Jack while L. Ron Hubbard scried the astral plane during the Babalon Working was regurgitated ad nauseam online, and was then given a theatrical spin in 2004 when Maureen Fitzgerald's play *Moonchild* was performed at The Access Theatre on Broadway as part of the New York International Fringe Festival. In what seems to have been a 1940s version of *Rosemary's Baby*, the play received mixed reviews, although some Thelemites in attendance were pleasantly surprised by the treatment, despite it taking liberties with one particular scene which had Crowley flying to America in his own private aeroplane. The production was at least bolstered by a professional cast, with Cameron's part played by the actress Heather Tom, best known for her role in the American soap opera *The Young and the Restless*.

The same scenario was given a more experimental twist just a year later, when Alison Rockbrand's Canadian Travesty Theatre group performed Paul Andrew Green's radio play *Babalon* at the Gielgud Studio Theatre in London. Played by an unknown cast, the show was welcomed as a novel addition to the West End stage.

The following year, Cameron was featured in the critically lauded *Semina Culture*, a bicoastal exhibition that gave some long-overdue recognition to Wallace Berman and the amazing confluence of artists, poets and movie stars who featured in his folio. By the time it reached the Grey Gallery in early 2007, for the New York leg of its run, Cameron already had her own exhibition running simultaneously at the Nicole Klagsbrun Gallery in the Chelsea art district. The well-received show featured many unseen drawings culled from the pages of her sketchbooks, including a sequence of prostrate nudes entitled *Slaves: Dedicated to John Fles*, together with the aforementioned *Pluto Transiting the Twelfth House* and *Fossil* series of pictures.

On hearing of the show's positive reception, Curtis Harrington became tearful and reflected on his friend's posthumous recognition: "I considered it a terrible injustice that, in an American context, her work was not fashionable. They couldn't see it, and that made me very angry.

Some people considered her to be nobody, a nothing, and I knew I was working with a major artist. So after all these years, it's a real reward for me. I'm so glad she's getting the recognition she deserves."

Four months later, on the 6th of May, Curtis Harrington passed away at his home, aged 80 years old, having enjoyed a dinner party the night before. Unfortunately, his open-casket funeral service at the Hollywood Forever cemetery was upstaged when Kenneth Anger gatecrashed the event and, in a premeditated move that was meant to create a spectacle, he kissed the corpse of his estranged friend on the lips, making sure his attendant cameraman captured the moment. He then proceeded to interrupt Jack Larson's eulogy with some colourful running commentary, blaming Howard Hughes for masterminding Jack Parsons' death, and sharing how he'd once held the tentacled hand of a homunculus magically conjured by Paul Mathison.. Then, before he left, he theatrically announced that his own funeral would take place at the same spot on Halloween 2008, before adding, archly, that it would be "invitation only."

Unlike others gathered, who were offended by the rude behaviour, Larson was a good sport and took Anger's outbursts in his stride: "It was an amazing occasion. People were beautifully dressed and any one of them could've been standing up there instead of me, so I just tried diligently to do a good job. I didn't take offence at Anger or regard it as heckling. He just wanted to create a scandal."

So there wouldn't be a repeat performance of Anger's antics, the filmmaker was told the wrong date for the memorial held in Harrington's honour at the Pickford Center for Motion Picture Study, days later. The congregation included old friends like John Gilmore and Dennis Hopper, whose soliloquy contained several references to Cameron.

Seven months later, Harrington's absent friend Renate Druks passed away at her retirement home aged 86 years old.

The fascination of Cameron amongst experimental filmmakers continued apace in April 2008, when Craig Baldwin released his latest work *Mock Up on Mu* at the San Francisco Film Festival. Featuring his signature "mashup" style, which mixed together found footage with scenes shot at the Salton Sea (unbeknownst to him, the area was one of Cameron's favourite old haunts. Back in the early '60s, she would often take moonlit mineral baths there), Baldwin crafted a science fictional saga built around the axis of Jack, Cameron and L. Ron Hubbard. In his own words, the film collage charted "the simultaneous rise and convergence of New Age religious cults, the military/aerospace industrial complex and modern-day myths from Disney to certain sci-fi overlords."

A fortnight later, the curator David Hollander presented an evening of films dedicated to Cameron (including *Pleasure Dome*, *The Wormwood Star* and Chick Strand's *Loose Ends*), at the Marfa Film Festival in Texas. That same month, Cameron joined an illustrious list of 20th-century artists for *Traces Du Sacré* (Traces of the Sacred), a group show held at the Pompidou in Paris. Billed as an exploration of spirituality in Western art in a post-Nietzschean world, Cameron's contribution, her portrait *Dark Angel*, appeared alongside canvases by Crowley and his devotees, Harry Smith and Lady Frieda Harris. Also on show were works by her old collaborators Wallace Berman and Kenneth Anger.

In the summer of 2010, a selection of Cameron's watercolours from her *Lion Path* series was included in the *Endless Bummer/Surf Elsewhere* group show at the Blum and Poe gallery in Los Angeles. At the same time, a rarely-seen portrait of her former lover, Ted Jacobi, could be found hanging next to an absinthe-infused portrait of William Burroughs by Marilyn Manson at *The Alchemy of Things Unknown* exhibition at L.A.'s Khatsoo Gallery. The show was dedicated to mystical and devotional work and included art by William Blake, Crowley and Austin Osman Spare.

The following year, a selection of Cameron's artwork was lent out to the *Pacific Standard Time: Crosscurrents in L.A. Painting and Sculpture 1950-1970* show held at the Getty Museum in Los Angeles. And, in 2012, *Dark Angel* and *Peyote Vision* were featured in *L.A. Raw: Abject Expressionism in Los Angeles, 1945-1980* held at the Pasadena Museum of Californian Art.

However, in October 2014, Cameron was granted sole spotlight when a new retrospective of her work was held at the MOCA Pacific Design Center in Los Angeles. The three-month run, entitled *Cameron: Songs for the Witch Woman*, was well publicised and attended, and a handsomely produced book of the same name finally married Cameron's Beaumont-era ink drawings to Jack's unpublished anthology. Cameron's self-portrait *The Black Egg* made the front cover of *LA Weekly* and, in the accompanying feature, Crystal gave a rare interview in which she reproached her mother, with good reason: "I think she could have taught me more things than I taught myself. I had to grow up fast. She didn't leave me the tools to sort of get through everything on my own. She let me experience things with her that maybe other mothers would say, 'Why did Cameron do this?'"[1]

A year later, most of the exhibits from the MOCA presentation were transported to Jeffrey Deitch's gallery space in Manhattan for an East Coast version of the show, now titled *Cameron: Cinderella of the Wastelands*. Since then, pieces from her collection have continued to be featured in group shows devoted to occultic or metaphysical themes. Most recently, a selection of her work was spotlighted in *The Lion Path: Art, Astrology, and Magic* exhibition held at the Marc Selwyn Fine Art Gallery between April and May 2023. And, between August and November 2024, she was featured in the *Sci-Fe, Magick, Queer L.A.: Sexual Science and the Imagi-Nation* exposition held at the USC Fisher Museum. Then, in April 2025, a solo exhibition of Cameron's work returned to the Nicole Klagsbrun Gallery for a two-month run.

Postscript: Kenneth Anger's prediction that he would die on Halloween 2008 was only off by fifteen years, and he passed away in 2023 at the impressive age of 96.

APPENDIX

CHAPTER 1 - AMERICAN GOTHIC

1) In November 1942, 15-year-old Mary Lou Cameron created some mini wartime drama of her own when she ran away from home with a school friend, Mary Lou Hatchett. She was picked up by the police three days later in Chicago and returned home, and it remains unclear what prompted it: Teenage kicks? A cry for attention? Or was it a symptom of family disquiet? Cameron also claimed she ran away from home as a 15-year-old teenager, but she travelled even further: all the way to Hollywood! So it's plausible that Mary Lou was simply aping her older sister.

2) *Brother, Can You Spare A Dime?* By E.Y. "Yip" Harburg and Burton Lane. Published by Glocca Morra Music (ASCAP) and Gorney Music (ASCAP) Administered by Next Decade Entertainment, Inc. All Rights Reserved. Used by Permission.

3) Cameron interviewed by Sandra Starr. *Lost and Found in California: Four Decades of Assemblage Art.* James Corcoran Gallery. 1988.

4) In an interesting foreshadowing of Cameron's own story, after Loschs' dance career was derailed by depression, she sought refuge in painting and, mentored by Winston Churchill's nephew John, she revealed a natural talent for art; her canvases evoking the same kind of mystical romanticism as Cameron's. Art critics have referred to Loschs' paintings as "evocative magic" and "a gift of divination."

5) There are currently two drawings in The Art Institute of Chicago collection with titles approximating that name: *Weeping Woman I* (1937) by Picasso, a portrait of his lover Dora Maar, and *Weeping Woman* (1883) by Vincent van Gogh.

CHAPTER 2 - GHOST IN THE MACHINE

1) *WAVES of the Navy* anthem. Words by Betty St. Clair.

2) Also working at the photo lab around the time was Daniel P. Mannix who, after the war, would go on to author a string of books ranging from biographies of Aleister Crowley and *The Hell Fire Club* to a *History of Torture*.

3) Arthur "Art" Napoleon inherited his unusual surname from his father Louis, a collector of Napoleonic coins, who gave it as the family name when he was processed as a Romanian immigrant at Ellis Island. In 1954, Nap married TV writer Jo Freeman and, as a husband and wife screenwriting team, they created the TV series *Whirlybirds* (1957-1960), wrote and produced the beach party flick *Ride the Wild Surf* (1964), and the protest film *The Activist* (1969). After that picture, he quit the entertainment business, moved to Europe, and became a psychotherapist. He died in England in 2003 aged 83.

4-5) Cameron interviewed by William Breeze.

6) The revue was likely *Call Me Mister*, which Douglas produced.

CHAPTER 3 - BELARION ANTICHRIST

1) Cameron later opined to Sandra Starr that the Beat Generation was an outgrowth of the 52-20 club, a benefit where veterans were paid $20 a week for 52 weeks by the government after the Second World War. $20 then approximately works out to £354 per week in today's money, which was enough to get by on while you dedicated your life to artistic pursuits. Cameron recalled how the unemployment offices became a sort of meeting ground where people who felt alienated from mainstream culture could meet and hang out. "As Norman Mailer described us, we were totally disillusioned because the public in general were not as sophisticated about the Second World War as most of the people who had been in it, and coming back we didn't find much sympathy or interest. So we kind of hung together as a group – I'm talking about the veterans. It was from the veterans that the Beat Generation came (into being)."

2) Cameron was particularly taken with the tragicomedy number, 'To Keep My Love Alive,' sung by Queen Morgan Le Fay, the show's "singing sorceress," which details the myriad ways she dispatches each one of the 15 knights she marries to "keep (her) love alive."

3) Cameron interviewed by William Breeze.

4) During her wartime service in Washington, Cameron spent a period of time working at St. Elizabeths Hospital, though it remains unclear in what capacity. Intriguingly, Jack's errant father, Marvel, ended his days at St. Elizabeths, where he was treated as a psychiatric patient, suffering from severe depression and delusions until he died in 1947.

5) Interestingly, just prior to meeting Jack Cameron also briefly flirted with a local Theosophy group when she first settled in Pasadena. This particular sect was dedicated to preserving the work and legacy of one of its leading members, Charles Webster Leadbeater (1854-1934).

6-7) Cameron interviewed by William Breeze.

8) One such example, was the story of a man (his name redacted in Jack's FBI file) who claimed that, in June or July of 1940, he was invited by a bartender at Hiller's Bar in Long Beach to attend a weekend house party at Parsons' residence in Pasadena, which turned out to be the Agape Lodge. At the party he was given a glass of liquor, which he believed was laced as he couldn't remember much of the proceedings save that, during his initiation into the order, members were naked beneath their ceremonial robes. The major problem with this tale is that the O.T.O. shut down private ceremonies between March 1940 to March 1941, and didn't move into their new Pasadena HQ until the summer of 1942.

CHAPTER 4 – OCCAM'S RAZOR

1) According to George Frey, thirty years later, Gowan committed suicide by running a hose from an exhaust pipe into her car.

2) Cameron's FBI report mentions another individual who was tied in with her and Jack's circle at that time, whom the Feds eyed with suspicion: Rodolfo P. Walther. He was described as a "close personal friend and frequent visitor at the Parsons' home between 1947-1948," though his "contact in the past two years has been less frequent." Born in Buenos Aries, Argentina, on August 15, 1906, Walther was 40 years of age, 5 foot 7 inches in height, 130 pounds with dark hair. He had immigrated to the States from Germany in 1928, and worked as a sales representative for the Niro Corporation, based in Westport, Connecticut, selling dental supplies for a living, although he showed little interest in this and seemed far more concerned with taking photographs of railway bridges and "other bridges and large buildings." The Feds noted that the Niro Corporation was associated with "the Krupp Steel Company of Germany, (which) is known to be pro-German throughout the United States."

3) Parker was staying with Julie Macdonald when he received the heart-wrenching news that his three-year-old daughter, Pree, had died in New York.

4) Cameron interviewed by Sandra Starr. *Lost and Found in California: Four Decades of Assemblage Art.* James Corcoran Gallery. 1988.

5) Another local jazz buff who attended Jack and Cameron's parties at the coach house was William Claxton, who would rise to become one of the eminent jazz photographers of the age. Claxton recounted how his father delivered a similar "What will the neighbours say?" sermon when he invited Charlie Parker back to his parents' Pasadena home for breakfast after an all-night gig in town.

6) Cameron may have inspired one of Zorthian's stand-out artworks *Interracial Couple*, a pornographic portrayal of a voluptuous red-headed being fucked from behind by a powerfully built black male.

7) Cameron gave the portrait of Joan of Arc to Ganci, who loaned it to a friend, who then moved away just so he could keep it.

8-9) Sal Ganci interviewed by George Pendle.

10) Aleister Crowley letter to Karl Germer. March 1946.

11) The author James A. Eshelman has noted that the Babalon Working contains some elementary missteps, no pun intended. For example, Jack used the 7th Enochian call to open the 7th Aethyr, instead of the 19th call, which meant he invoked a water-type elemental, rather than a fire-type elemental he believed Cameron to be. And, in his e-book *Kaos*, the author and former occultist Joe Biroco expands on this: "In line 23 Babalon instructs Parsons: 'Also seek me in the Seventh Aire.' (But) Parsons had blundered in his fifth invocation by intoning in Enochian the 7th Angelic Key, which, though the 7th call, it is not the call of the Seventh Aire. He should have substituted DEO for LIL in the 19th Key, the Key of the 30 Aires to access the 7th Æthyr… In addition, the 7th Key that Parsons reproduces is also missing several words and (he) corrupts others."

12) According to Loren Cameron, his father Robert spoke about his own close encounter with a UFO during a trip he made with Cameron and Jack to the Mojave Desert. He described it as a probing light that swooped down and hovered over their heads. The experience had a profound effect on him. Cameron warned him not to mention it at JPL, where he worked as an electrical engineer, but he ignored her caution and blabbed about it and was subsequently fired. His second wife also worked at JPL, as a film editor, and part of her job consisted of removing any evidence of UFOs from the rocket test film footage which, she claimed, were a constant presence during the rocket tests.

13) Sal Ganci interviewed by George Pendle.

14) Part of the attraction of black males, at that time, was their willingness to perform cunnilingus. Such men were known as "fish queens." Endearingly, Cameron had her own idiosyncratic theory behind the origin of this slang phrase, believing that snakes and fishes swim inside the womb, acting as the memory of all evolution.

15) Booth was ironically called "Lucky" by friends, due to his unfortunate run of luck. In March 1952, for instance, he was involved in an automobile accident that caused the death of an 87-year-old Pasadena woman named Frances Gove, who died from her injuries a month later. She had been the passenger in a car that collided with Booth's at the intersection of Cyrpus Ave and Villa Street in Pasadena. It was ruled an accident and no charges were brought.

16) Sal Ganci interviewed by George Pendle. In March 1960, Ganci ran afoul of the law when he was arrested for making "intimate advances" towards a vice squad officer. The case went to court, but the jury returned a split verdict and it was declared a mistrial. Ganci disclosed to this author that he'd once taken artistic nude photographs of Cameron, but their whereabouts remain unknown following his death.

CHAPTER 5 - THE CHILDREN

1) Pulitzer Prize-winning poet Conrad Aiken was heavily influenced by the French Symbolist tradition, and the introspection and self-analysis in his work drew praise from, amongst others, Dr. Sigmund Freud who was interested in personally analysing the poet. In 1952, Aiken released *Ushant*, a memoir that dealt with his own dark pilgrimage, beginning with the childhood trauma of finding the dead bodies of his parents – his father killed his mother before committing suicide – something the poet himself attempted later on in life while struggling with bouts of depression. While teaching in England, Aiken became a mentor to the young English writer Malcolm Lowry whose most celebrated work, *Under the Volcano*, is an account of the two men's adventures in Mexico. Interestingly, Lowry had studied under Crowley's disciple Charles Stansfeld Jones, who ran Agape Lodge No. 1 in Canada.

2) Like his compatriot Aldous Huxley, Gerald Heard became an early convert to the mind-expanding properties of LSD and counted wealthy establishment figures like Henry Luce, publisher of Time-Life, and his

wife, the multi-talented playwright and Republican senator Clare Boothe Luce, as conquests of his LSD crusade.

3) Cameron interviewed by Sandra Starr. *Lost and Found in California: Four Decades of Assemblage Art*. James Corcoran Gallery. 1988.

4) Jo Anne Price would go on to have a relationship with the brilliant but tortured jazz pianist, Bud Powell.

5) Sam Kelinson died in Florida, in 1968, aged 62.

6) Gerald Yorke letter to Karl Germer, 10th July 1953. Reprinted with the kind permission of John Yorke.

7) The ingredients in the Cakes Of Light also equate to the five elements: meal (Earth), honey (Air), olive oil (Water), Oil of Abramelin (Fire), and wine leavings (Spirit).

8) According to Joan Whitney, Cameron made another attempt, at a later date, to dispense with Freya, by abandoning her at the top of Mulholland Drive, but, in the end, she had a change of heart and couldn't go through with it. Freya was later killed when she was struck by a car while crossing a busy highway.

CHAPTER 6 - WELCOME TO THE PLEASURE DOME

1) Excerpted from Marjorie Cameron and the Birth of Babalon article by Brian Butler. 2002.

2) Anger interview: *Anaïs Nin: Spy in the House of Love*. Channel 4 TV documentary. 1998.

3) Anger interviewed by Brian Butler.

4) *The Diary of Anaïs Nin Volume 5*.

5) Mindful of the history of the room, the property's current tenants have thankfully preserved the mural and the gold-painted ceiling.

(6-7) *The Diary of Anaïs Nin Volume 5*.

8) Anger interviewed by Brian Butler.

9) Cameron interviewed by Sandra Starr. *Lost and Found in California: Four Decades of Assemblage Art*. James Corcoran Gallery. 1988.

10) Anger interviewed by Kris Millegan. November 2000.

11) Dehn would later forge a career as a successful screenwriter with credits including the sequels to the *Planet of the Apes* series and the Bond blockbuster *Goldfinger*. As it happens, Bond's creator, Ian Fleming, was a former Naval Intelligence agent who once tried to enlist Crowley's magical services during their interrogation of Rudolf Hess, the Nazi POW, who was himself rumoured to be steeped in occult and astrological practices. Though the military brass balked at the idea, Crowley's personality stuck with Fleming, so much so, that he modelled his baddie Le Chiffre on Crowley in his first James Bond novella *Casino Royale*. Fleming reached back even further into occult lore borrowing Bond's code name 007 from the secret signature used by the Elizabethan magi John Dee. After his specialist services were rejected, Crowley consoled himself by taking credit for inspiring Churchill's V-sign for victory. Crowley claimed he created this occult power symbol to counteract and defeat the psychic power of the Nazi Swastika, a symbol which, he also believed, Hitler had stolen from him.

12) Louis Wilkinson to Gerald Yorke letter, 1955. Used with the permission of the Estate of Louis Wilkinson and Pollinger Ltd.

CHAPTER 7 - SHERRY

1-3) *We Will Always Live in Beverly Hills* by Ned Wynn.

4) A letter Cameron wrote around this time strongly infers that she caught Sherry in a compromising position with Curtis Harrington. When the author brought up the subject of Sherry to Curtis, he shut it down quite forcibly and uncharacteristically.

5) John Muir (1918-1977) was distantly related to John Muir (1838-1914), the naturalist, who became known as the "Father of the National Parks." Muir shared many of his relative's environmental philosophies and, in the '60s, he dropped out to live the hippie life in Taos, New Mexico (where he may have reconnected with Cameron). He subsequently

became a notable figure in the so-called "bus culture," after publishing *How to Keep Your Volkswagen Alive: A Manual of Step-by-step Procedures for the Compleat Idiot* in 1969, a repair manual that's been reprinted twenty times and has sold over two million copies.

6) Cameron's residence at 1741 North Normandie no longer exists. The Normandie Village now stands in its stead, in what is today known as the Thai Town district.

7) Anger interview from *Reputations: Alfred Kinsey*. BBC. 1996.

8) Jane Wolfe's letter to Karl Germer. February 1955.

CHAPTER 8 - THE WORMWOOD STAR

1) Although long thought to have been destroyed, this painting materialised in 2024.

2) Curtis Harrington took a shine to *Buried Doll*, and Cameron sold it to him after the shoot.

3) *Nice Guys Don't Work in Hollywood* by Curtis Harrington. 2013.

4) Ginsberg's quote from *Whatever Happened to Jack Kerouac?* documentary. 1985.

5) Burroughs' quote from *Whatever Happened to Jack Kerouac?* documentary. 1985.

6) Although Ed Silverstone Taylor's film is titled *Street Fair 1959*, records prove that Cameron was already living back in Los Angeles in 1959, so the footage was probably shot a year earlier and then completed in 1959. It is entirely possible that the filmmaker didn't get around to adding titles to the footage until many years later. When the film was screened for the Cameron benefit held at the Cinema Theatre in 1964, it was billed as *Street Fair San Francisco*. Because of this, and the discrepancy over when the film was actually shot, it is referred to as *Street Fair San Francisco* throughout this book. Also seen briefly in the film are the beat poets Bob Kaufman and Paddy O'Sullivan, who is glimpsed selling copies

of his anthology *Weep My Children*. There is also, perhaps, a blink-and-you'll-miss-him shot of Allen Ginsberg.

7) Over time, that apartment house at 707 Scott Street was not only home to Cameron and the Bermans but also the poets William Margolis and John Wieners, who dedicated his book *The Journal of John Wieners is to be called 707 Scott Street - for Billie Holiday, 1959* to the period of time he spent there.

CHAPTER 9 - ERONBU

1) *A Preamble* by Victor Maymudes. 2001.

2) Cameron became friendly with some of the musicians who played the Cosmo Alley and coffee house scene, including the bongo player Preston Epps, whose infectious hit single 'Bongo Rock,' showcased his mastery of an instrument that would become inextricably linked with Beatnik culture.

3) When his own passion for acting fizzled out, Gilmore turned his creative talents to writing, penning books focusing on the two most infamous murder cases in L.A.'s history: *Severed*, his biography of the ill-fated Black Dahlia, and *Garbage People*, his investigation into the Tate-Labianca killings. He also wrote memoirs of his two most iconic friends, James Dean and Marilyn Monroe.

4) George Clayton Johnson would go on to become one of television's top scriptwriters, his credits including classic shows like *Star Trek* and *The Twilight Zone*. He also wrote the original *Ocean's Eleven* film as well as the sci-fi classic *Logan's Run*.

5) *Out Here: A brief account of how this all began for me* by Burt Shonberg with Ledru Shoopman Baker III Copyright © 2001 Ledru Shoopman Baker III.

6) As cult contemporaries, Crowley and Gurdjieff reportedly crossed paths back in 1926, when The Great Beast visited Gurdjieff's Institute for the Harmonious Development of Man in Fontainebleau-Avon, south

of Paris. What transpired between the two mystics remains hotly disputed on both sides, but one Gurdjieff-slanted account claims Crowley was dismissed from the premises by his host with the kiss-off: "You are dirty inside."

7) It appears the ERONBU ranch still stands today in the shape of Rancho Mojave, although the original quarters are long gone and have been replaced with a Southwest-style casita.

8) Cameron interviewed by Sandra Starr. *Lost and Found in California: Four Decades of Assemblage Art.* James Corcoran Gallery. 1988.

CHAPTER 10. NIGHT TIDE

1) It's been written that Cameron was portraying a "Lovecraftian Deep One" sea creature in *Night Tide*, but Curtis Harrington denies this.

CHAPTER 11. BLACK PILGRIMAGE

1) Quoted from *Out Here* by Burt Shonberg with Ledru Shoopman Baker III. Copyright © 2001 Ledru Shoopman Baker III.

2) In the *LA Times* article, Cameron's address is listed as 6918 Woody Trail, Hollywood. This was most likely a temporary address and/or friend's address, or a false address given so that Sherry could not track her down.

3) According to Helen Parsons Smith, Jack was physically abusive during their marriage and possessed a violent temper; he would smash things around the house during domestic disputes, but it's unknown whether he behaved in this way with Cameron.

4) Aleister Atatürk subsequently dropped the special name his father bestowed on him and, for the rest of his life, reverted back to his birth name Randall Gair and added his mother's maiden name, Doherty. Over the years he found it hard to hold down a job, was plagued by schizophrenia, and, for a period, was even reduced to sleeping rough on park benches in London. Still and all, he shared his father's penchant

for fancy made-up titles and regalia and, in due course, billed himself as Count Charles Edward D'Arquires, the self-styled Adjudicator of the Supreme Council of Great Britain. In 1976, he hired a chauffeur-driven Austin Princess to deliver him to Downing Street where he requested to speak with newly-elected Prime Minister James Callaghan about saving his home in Cornwall and lifting the country out of its doldrums; naturally, he was turned away. He was killed as a result of a car accident in Buckinghamshire, in November 2002, aged 65.

5) Excerpt from *Notes Between Worlds* courtesy of Aya.

6) David Meltzer on the origins of the Temple Of Man: "According to the story, Bob Alexander was walking down Macalister Street in downtown San Francisco, which in the early 60s had a lot of junk shops, and he was walking past one of these junk shops when a black man came out and said, 'You're the one!' Bob kinda stuttered and said, 'Oh yeah?', and the man said, 'Come with me,' and this old black man took him to the back of the shop and apparently he was an ordained minister in the state of California who had nobody to hand over his ministry to. And so he said, 'I see something in you', and Bob would never deny that [laughs]. And this man did indeed turn over the papers and ordained him into this ministry. He gave him the license and so forth, which, as it turned out, were perfectly legal and binding documents of the State of California. And Bob, especially in his manic periods, that's all he needed, and immediately he went out and got himself white pants, a white clerical collar, and he began ministering seriously to people like drug addicts in North Beach, going into the emergency hospitals, really taking the role very seriously. The jazz and cultural critic Ralph Gleason wrote an article about this Reverend Bob hitting the streets and taking care of people, and how he cleansed their being, and Bob was real high on that all his life. Then, gradually, he began ordaining others of us into this: poets, artists and musicians, to do ritual ceremonies like marriages, and to be able to legally bury and counsel and so forth. Then he moved back to

Venice and bought this big house, which became the official Temple of Man, and artists would donate paintings to him. He was a really great organizer, a real powerhouse. He could do it all. It always amazed me. I remember working for him as a book warehouse manager in the house and he had that kind of charisma where everyone wanted to work for him. Bob thought it would be great to have artists and poets ordained like myself, Cameron and Aya."

7) Back in 1955, Cameron turned down an offer to participate in the tabloid TV show *Confidential File* on the subject of witchcraft, hosted by the popular newspaper columnist, Paul Coates.

8) Anger's marriage of pop music and rebel imagery became a major influence on young film students like Martin Scorsese and David Lynch, and would lead the cultural critic Susan Sontag to knight Anger as "The best filmmaker in America, period." The film was subsequently credited for helping to create the pop promo medium, leading Anger to be hailed as a Godfather of MTV.

9) One particular film Cameron enjoyed at the Cinema Theatre was Robert Frank's B&W short *OK End Now*, an intimate, day-in-the-life portrait of a New York couple at the fag-end of their relationship. Cameron may have seen a reflection in the film in her own uneasy, romantic relationships. It starred Martin LaSalle, star of Robert Bresson's masterpiece *Pickpocket*, and Sue Ungaro, who bore more than a passing resemblance to Cameron. Ungaro married the fiery jazz genius Charlie Mingus shortly afterwards.

10) Although it is not possible to feature Cameron's poetry in this book, the author and academic Manon Hedenborg White has broken down 'Black Pilgrimage' thusly: "In Cameron's poem, a scarred and weary traveller in rusted garments journeys, with a fellowship of dead priests, through stellar webs to darker worlds within the Lunar mirrors of Suicide, to the frozen shores of a wintery, Northern sea, scattered with petrified

serpents' eggs that are marked with hieroglyphs. She arrives at a white tomb; the burial place of daughters and kings, and black glass palaces, where she entice[s] the mad one from his throne, adorning him with a glass crown. The narrator cries out, desolately, for a Black stared[sic] love, whose name reverberates and echoes." Manon Hedenborg White, 'From Chorazin to Carcosa: Fiction-Based Esotericism in the Black Pilgrimage of Jack Parsons and Cameron.' lir journal 12, 57f

11) It is almost certain that the "football players" Curtis Harrington refers to, who helped sort out the violence that erupted at The Cinema Theater screening, were Ronnie Knox and his teammates.

12) Excerpt from Gerald Yorke's letter to Kenneth Anger. October 20th, 1964. Reproduced with the kind permission of John Yorke

CHAPTER 12 - EXORCISING GHOSTS

1) Ronnie Knox's own life story was rather intriguing. Prior to meeting Renate Druks, he was a rising football star, but following his explosive allegations on a live TV show, about widespread corruption in the National Football League, he became persona non grata to his profession and dropped out to become a self-confessed "noble savage." After he divorced Druks, his life began to slowly spiral. Increasingly self-destructive, he began hanging out in the Venice drug scene and was allegedly institutionalised for a while. He continued to live a free, peripatetic life as a "wandering poet" until he died in 1992.

2) Cameron left the world owing Uncle Sam $4000 in back payments after they found out she falsely claimed the now-adult Crystal as a dependant in the 1970s.

3) Quotation from letter to Cameron by Joseph Campbell reprinted by permission of Joseph Campbell Foundation (jcf.org).

4) One such exposé of Scientology, A True Life Nightmare by Alan Levy, ran in *Life* Magazine, and amongst the letters responding to it was a personal testimony from Cameron's old Pasadena playmate Julie

Macdonald, who wrote: "I was involved with *Dianetics* back in 1951 in Los Angeles. After I saw trusting, innocent people fall for Hubbard's game, I came home and burned my auditor's diploma. On general principles, I don't object strenuously to conmen, but where other minds and lives are hurt, I must draw the line." *Life* Magazine - December 6th, 1968. Her daughter Judy met Hubbard around the time her mother was studying *Dianetics* and found him to be "a horrible man. He made the hairs stand up on the back of my neck."

5) Returning the favour, Mick Jagger went on to provide a hypnotic Moog synthesizer soundtrack to *Invocation of My Demon Brother*, a film regarded by Anger as his most satanic. It includes scenes of an albino teenager named Skip Tracer peering through a crystal wand; news clips of helicopters descending hot LZs in Vietnam; footage of Anger whizzing around a stage like a whirling dervish during a magick ritual in San Francisco; and shots of The Rolling Stones free concert in London's Hyde Park in honour of Brian Jones. The film also starred Bobby Beausoleil, who today remembers Cameron as "a sweet soul."

CHAPTER 13 - THUMBSUCK

1) Wallace Berman also featured on the iconic cover.

2) Like Cameron, Robert Aiken also knew Bobby Beausoleil, having met on the set of *The Ramrodder*, a nudie Western that featured a couple of girls who later became part of the group who lived with Charles Manson. "Bobby was living along the banks of the river in Topanga with three runaway girls," Aiken recalls. "I told Curtis (Harrington) there was this very interesting, beautiful young man, and he invited us to tea and lunch. Later, when he was accused of murder, I remembered how he used to carry a big knife, and Curtis playfully berated me for bringing a murderer into his house." Coincidently, Curtis was also friendly with Beausoleil's victim Gary Hinman, whom he knew through a Vedanta Buddhist temple. Aiken also starred in a couple of Russ Meyer's

sexploitation films, *Vixen* and *Cherry, Harry and Raquel* and, according to John Gilmore, another girlfriend of Cameron's was the actress Sharon Lee, who appeared in the Russ Meyer flick *Motorpsycho*. Like Cameron, Lee had a wild reputation, as Gilmore fondly remembers: "Sharon Lee had participated in the sex scenes in Pasadena. I saw her a few times when she was living in Santa Monica in a little rundown hotel on the boardwalk opposite the merry-go-round in *Night Tide*. She had a photograph of herself and Cameron in front of a house in Pasadena. The couple of times I spent with Sharon we took pills and smoked opium. While I was living in Louisiana in the late 1980s, I heard she had committed suicide while living in Venice."

3) *The Diary of Anaïs Nin Volume 5*.

4) Cameron created the tattered neon outfits worn by Diane Varsi in Elias Romero's early '70s avant-garde short film *Za*.

CHAPTER 14 - SEASONS OF THE WITCH

1) Pat Quinn did broker a friendship between Cameron and Marlon Brando's sister Jocelyn, and together they attended classes at astrologer Sydney Omarr's home.

2) Cameron's cohorts Dennis Hopper and Dean Stockwell befriended David Bowie and spent the cocaine-fuelled summer of 1975 hanging out at the Thin White Duke's pad in Bel Air. Many unsubstantiated legends have surfaced during this occult period in Bowie's life, including the rumour that he was embroiled in a magical battle of wills with fellow Crowleyite Jimmy Page and that he was kidnapped by a coven of witches, allegedly associated with Kenneth Anger, who wanted to harvest his seed in order to sire the Antichrist.

3) In an example of six degrees of separation, where seemingly everybody in the 1960s knew everyone else, Bobby Beausoleil had once been the guitarist in the rock group Love. Reportedly, Arthur Lee even named the band in honour of Bobby's pet name, Cupid. There's also another

Anger-Cameron-Shonberg connection: in 1975, Burt created the cover artwork for the Spirit album *Spirit of '76*. The rock band was fronted by guitarist Randy California, who, in 1967, composed the instrumental song 'Taurus,' which is said to have inspired Jimmy Page's opening chord sequence to 'Stairway To Heaven.'

4) 'In This House That I Call Home,' written by John Doe and Exene Cervenka. Lyrics reprinted with the kind permission of Exene Cervenka.

5) Perhaps inspired by this visit, Genesis subsequently named one of his daughters Genesse.

6-7) *Ruthless Adventure: The Lives of L. Ron Hubbard*. BBC Radio 4, broadcast August 1987.

8) Cameron interviewed by William Breeze.

9) The significance of Lugano was bolstered further when Cameron discovered that one of her favourite authors Hermann Hesse, moved to Montagnola, a nearby village overlooking Lake Lugano, in 1919, living there until his death in 1962. The local landscape was said to have inspired many paintings in him. Also, from William Breeze, Cameron learned that Lugano had been the Headquarters of the O.T.O. back at the turn of the century, when Heinrich Klein, one of its wealthy founders, developed land around Mount Veritas. By the 1920s, the town had become something of a gateway for the European countercultural movements, a sort of proto-Woodstock, where socialist and artist communes set up shop.

10) This original piece, created by Crowley's disciple J. F. C. Fuller, was also used as a subliminal image by Kenneth Anger in his film *Invocation of My Demon Brother*.

11) Cameron interviewed by William Breeze.

12) *Samson: A Personal Perception* by Wendy Elliott Hyland. 1997.

EPILOGUE

1) The Witch Woman Sings. *LA Weekly*. Oct 10-16, 2014.

The following interview was originally published in the August 2011 issue of the occult periodical *The Cauldron*. It was conducted by Matthew Levi Stevens: author, researcher and publisher at Wholly Books (http://whollybooks.wordpress.com).

Matthew Levi Stevens: Having tried to research Cameron myself, I can imagine there was a considerable limit to what you could discover here in the UK, or just by correspondence; was it inevitable that you would follow the trail to the US, and how did you start? Was there a particular 'turning point' where your research opened up sufficiently that you thought "Yes, I can make a book of this"?

Spencer Kansa: Yes. I knew from the outset that, if I was going to do a proper job, I would have to travel to America to do it. I was pretty much a gumshoe and spent the best part of three years tracking people down, interviewing them, chasing up leads, and compiling information. After Jack's death in 1952, Cameron was a gypsy and led a nomadic life for the next 20 years, and piecing together exactly where she was and what she was doing at any given time during that period, was the biggest puzzle. There wasn't necessarily one turning point, but more a series of them, so her story opened up and revealed itself in a very organic way, over time, with the more people I spoke to who knew her. The final picture emerged when the last piece of the puzzle fell into place. My intention was always to write a book that would be accessible to the general reader, rather than pander to initiates of the occult or the art cognoscenti.

MLS: How accessible or available did people make themselves where Cameron was concerned? Would you say she left behind a fair amount of love/respect/admiration – for all that she may have been at times difficult or perplexing, even troubling, to family & friends? I get the impression that both the late Curtis Harrington and the late Dennis

Hopper were generous with their time and recollections and that there was still a considerable feeling of love for her memory & achievements.

SK: Most of the people I approached, who were friends of Cameron over a span of decades, were immensely generous with their time and recollections, and all were highly admiring of her work and the singular way in which she lived her life: wholly on her own terms. There were a few people who declined to be interviewed, which is, of course, their prerogative, and a couple of individuals who really could have, and should have, contributed more but chose not to do so for their own ignoble reasons. It got a little weird at one point too, when one of Cameron's kookier friends began to put it about that I was an agent for the FBI. At least she could've got my nationality right and said MI5. Now, of course, with the passing of so many people over the last few years, most recently Charles Brittin, but prior to him, Dennis Hopper, Curtis Harrington, the filmmaker Chick Strand, Charm and John Carruthers (who knew Cameron and Jack dating back to the late 1940s), the book has taken on an even greater significance because they all played an important part in Cameron's story, and if I hadn't captured their testimonies, they would have been lost forever.

MLS: Contrary to this, do you feel that Kenneth Anger was 'difficult' or remote? Some have said you should have had more from him, maybe an interview. Were there problems? Did he actually decline to be interviewed, and do you feel that this was perhaps a missed opportunity?

SK: I tried a couple of times to interview Mr. Anger, but he declined, possibly because Cameron's still a touchy subject for him and, unlike most other interviewers, I wasn't interested in asking him about Jimmy Page and Mick Jagger. He's reached the point now where he tends to have a stock answer for most of the questions he's asked – partly due to his age and partly because he gets asked the same questions over and over. By that stage, I already had the inside track on his turbulent and complex relationship with Cameron anyway, so in the end, it didn't really matter.

MLS: The response to your book has been great, but naturally when this happens people want more. Are there other areas you wish you'd covered?

SK: Well, there were a couple of avenues I would have liked to explore further, but there just wasn't enough information to go on. For example, during the war, Cameron spent a period of time assigned to St. Elizabeths Hospital in Washington, D.C. This was the psychiatric hospital where the poet Ezra Pound was incarcerated just after the War, but it's unclear in what capacity she was there. There were a couple of other dark alleys I could've gone down but didn't out of sympathy for people who'd already had a hard enough time of things.

We were refused permission to use any of Cameron's artwork or writings in the book, but a lot of her artwork is available to view online now anyway, and her poetry is so intensely intimate, and relies on its own internal logic, that it would've been impossible and ridiculous to speculate on much of the meaning of it without sitting down and talking to the woman herself. Similarly, her magical diaries were not available to me, so again it was impossible to deduce the full nature of all her magical workings.

MLS: There's not much from current O.T.O. folk – did you ask for their help? How do you feel Cameron's memory/'legacy' is perceived in such circles?

SK: In fact, that's not true, William Breeze, the current head of the O.T.O., was an invaluable contributor to the book and is quoted liberally in the final chapter. Bill was incredibly generous to me with his time, counsel and resources. He had a close friendship with Cameron in the last two decades of her life and expanded her social horizons off the back of it. It's extremely doubtful she would ever have met such a character as Genesis P. Orridge without him. Actually, Bill and Cameron even jammed together; she on harp, he on viola. I would love to hear those recordings but Bill searched and, alas, the tapes have gone missing. That's kinda par for the course with Cameron. One of the minor motifs in the book is the reoccurring way in which items and artefacts relating to her have either gone missing or been destroyed down the years, usually by fire, which seems appropriate as Cameron was perceived as a fire-type elemental by Jack Parsons. It got to the point where I'd be interviewing someone and anticipating hearing that, even before they said it.

MLS: Do you feel that Cameron fits into any kind of lineage or tradition, or is hers a more archetypal case, like the shaman who is called, or the anchorite who retreats to the desert? Do you feel that her greater legacy is as an artist or as an occultist, and do you think that either one has maybe suffered because of the other?

SK: Actually, one of the things I admire most about her is the total blurring of all those distinctions. Her art and spiritual life were one. They were indivisible. Shirley Berman puts it beautifully in the book when she recollects how on entering Cameron's home, Cameron *became* her paintings. Cameron was a practitioner of most of the occult studies: the tarot, the I Ching, The Kabballah and astral projection; not yoga, although she did practice T'ai Chi in her later years. But that said, you can be a total sceptic and atheist or know nothing of her spiritual practice, and still be deeply moved and blown away by her exquisitely rendered and beautifully envisioned drawings and paintings. It's the work that remains. These sublime treasures that she seems to have captured and brought back from a netherworld for us all to view.

MLS: (Would you mind perhaps running this through the filters of: A) 'Feminism', e.g. Cameron as a role model for New Women; B) Thelema – inheritor of the mantle of Crowley, Parsons, et al., either the completion/fulfilment of their efforts – or even perhaps superseding them? + C) The 'New Age' in general (Neo) Paganism, Wicca. I was interested to read of her engagement with The Lion's Path in later years, as well as her long-standing interest in Joseph Campbell.

SK: Feminism! What does that word even mean anymore? Well, of course, Cameron predated the 1960s feminist movement. Her heroines growing up were the headstrong stars of the silver screen such as Bette Davis, Joan Crawford and Katherine Hepburn. After Jack, she pretty much lived an independent life, *her way*, and a lot of her friends found that quite inspirational.

In her later years, she became interested in the writings of Marija Gimbutas, who was taking a woman-centric view of history via archaeology, although I know the veracity of her thesis has been questioned by a number of experts over the years. Cameron also began proselytizing the treatise *Woman and Superwoman*, which was actually written by a *man*, A. S. Raleigh, back in 1916 during the Suffrage movement, but I don't think she had much truck with the feminist establishment as espoused by Gloria Steinem, Andrea Dworkin and NOW (The National Organization for Women). Throughout the 70s, 80s and early 90s, the feminist establishment became increasingly autocratic, espousing dogmatic views that were anti-men, anti-sex, anti-art, anti-porn and pro-censorship. People conveniently forget just how puritan and Stalinist that school of feminism was. It's calmed down a little now because it eventually turned off both men *and* women, but by the 1980s, in America, it was in lockstep with a lot of positions held by the religious right. This was totally antithetical to people like Cameron, who had a pagan view of things. Plus, on a social level, Cameron *adored* men! She *thrived* in their company, be they straight or gay. I think men energize women, and when women remove themselves from them, they go to seed, not just physically, but mentally and spiritually. Whereas, unsurprisingly, when she was younger, women could often be very bitchy and snidey towards her, usually out of jealousy for her prowess with men.

I doubt she ever read her books, but it would've been interesting to hear Cameron's take on Camille Paglia, whose writings not only exposed the Stalinist state of contemporary feminism, but also celebrated the Greco-Roman pagan tradition in art and culture, and toasted women's sexual power: historical truths totally ignored by the feminist establishment. Women's sexual power eclipses all other power. It can bring the most powerful and wealthy men to their knees, quite literally. It can topple governments. Pagans not only acknowledge this, they revere it. It's sacred. This was really all Jack Parsons was doing with the Babalon Working, exalting female sexuality in a poetic, Crowleyan way. One thing I excised from the biog, because I wanted to keep the text as taut as possible, was how an awful lot of illicit sex went on during World War II, and not just servicemen whoring with prostitutes while stationed abroad, but also with men-starved womenfolk back home. The Pandora's Box of the sexual revolution was really opened back then, not in the 60s as is widely believed. Our grandparents were not the sexual innocents they've been painted as. Jack, being such a red-blooded horndog during that time, knew this, and was tapping into the sexually liberated zeitgeist that was about to explode.

There's also a feeling that in common with most artists, Cameron was above politics. It reminds me of that great story of Gloria Steinem making a feminist pilgrimage to visit Georgia O'Keeffe, expecting to be welcomed into her home with open arms in the spirit of sisterhood, and when she finally arrives O'Keeffe opens the door, takes one look at her and tells her to fuck off!

Even having embraced Crowley and the occult sciences, Cameron was still searching, as is evident from her embracing of Charles Muses' Lion Path in the 1980s, which kinda complimented Thelema in a way, as it also had its roots in Ancient Egypt. There were some minor disputes between Cameron and her more Wiccan-orientated and Goddess Movement feminist friends, over her love of Crowley. Of course,

Crowley's creed is ostensibly a masculine, phallocentric one – it's a solar religion as opposed to a lunar one – and yet he does state clearly, and *early*, in one of *The Book of the Law*'s most famous lines: "Every man and every woman is a star." Also, his commentary to *The Book of the Law – The Law is for All*, contains a very strident pro-woman tract that even rivals the manifestos of Mrs. Pankhurst and Susan B. Anthony. In the end, I think Cameron did what a lot of us do, what Crowley did originally, she synthesised her own spiritual system that worked best for her.

MLS: What lesson, be it advice or even warning, do you think can be taken away from an understanding of the life & work of Marjorie Cameron?

SK: I think the one, big negative thing that you can see in Cameron's story, and in the lives of many of her bohemian contemporaries, is how their lifestyle had an adverse impact on their children. I've spoken to many artists, poets and musicians over the years, from both the Beat and 1960s counterculture generation that followed, and in the wee small hours, over a couple of drinks, they often say exactly what Charles Brittin says in the book: "The one thing we got wrong was parenting."

Prior to the 1940s, only the wealthy could really afford to live a bohemian life. Before then, if you were a poor artist or a poet you either sold your work or you died penniless. Thanks to the welfare system, a subculture of the World War II generation, and many of the baby boomers that followed, were able to dedicate themselves, full time, to living a creative, bohemian life, and in their mad rush for self-realization and self-expression, the kids got lost and families were destroyed.

Cameron wasn't alone in this by all means. William Burroughs, by his own admission, was a failure as a father. Kerouac was an absentee parent, and both their offspring had pretty unhappy lives. Actually, there's a long list of artists, poets, musicians and writers for whom you could say the same thing. And these are just the people *we know*! We're not mentioning the thousands of folks who swam in the same waters as them. Actually, there's a great documentary on Anaïs Nin, and towards the end, one of her closest acolytes talks about this. How inspired by Nin's writings, some of her female fans in the 1960s left their children and husbands and middle-class comforts, to live a freewheeling, artistic life, only to end up in the 1970s, alone, busted and full of regrets.

With freedom comes responsibility, but too many of the ME generation conveniently forgot this. This fundamental error is what helped destroy the '60s revolution. And then when you throw drugs into the mix with kids, it's rarely a happy ending. Dosing children with LSD, which really did go on, and was something that Cameron herself was guilty of, was an insane act and a recipe for disaster. I'm a social libertarian and believe if you're not a parent, you can pretty much do whatever you want, so long as it doesn't hurt anybody. But if you're gonna bring a child into the world, your personal behaviour has to be curtailed, you *have* to sacrifice. If you don't want to, then don't have any children, no one's forcing you.

This is really where the roots of family breakdown started, and it's the one big issue that modern conservatives actually have banged to rights. The break-up of the family and the chaos that comes with it has been ruinous for children's lives and *is* responsible for the deterioration of communities that has led to a broken society. The absence of fathers in the lives of their sons and daughters is the root cause of practically every social ill in modern society, from gang violence to teen pregnancy to teen prostitution to violent crime. Boys grow up without guidance and discipline, with no concept of what it means to be a man, and they end up getting their ideas from criminals on the streets, and it's just the blind leading the blind. While girls, who are deprived of the platonic love and affection of a father, often prematurely seek and find older male substitutes for it with disastrous consequences. You can see this in the difficult life that befell Cameron's daughter.

MLS: And what's next for Spencer Kansa?

SK: My debut novel, *Zoning*, is coming out this summer, published by Beatdom Books. It's a magical reality story revolving around the interconnected lives of a teenage occultist and a young, budding porn star. It's full of sex, drugs and black magick. It's a juicy read, I promise you.

Index

A
Aadland, Beverly 196
Abbey of Thelema 46
Abrahadabra 112
Abraxas 171
Académie de la Grande Chaumière 56
Aeon of Horus 279
Aerojet 56
Agape Lodge 94, 214
Aiken, Conrad 326
   Tetelestai 108
Aiken, Robert 251, 326, 335
Aiwass 44
Alexander, Bob (aka Baza) 146, 150, 171, 226, 230, 332
Alices Restaurant 266
Alpert, Richard 228
Altamont 271
Altoon, John 256
Anders, Luana 196, 205
Anderson, Buddy 80, 81, 84, 85, 99, 100, 110, 113, 315
Angelou, Maya 186
Anger, Kenneth 129, 130, 154, 195, 208, 231, 233, 240, 258, 278, 317
   Fireworks 131
   Inauguration of the Pleasure Dome 132, 138, 140, 143, 146, 149, 208, 231, 232, 241, 272, 299, 303, 318
   Lucifer Rising 259, 279
   Reconciliation 259
   Scorpio Rising 230
   The Story of O 218
Argenteum Astrum 108
Armstrong, Neil 268
Artaud, Antonin 211, 221
Atatürk Aleister (aka Randall Gair) 58, 223, 331
Aunt Nell 13, 116, 121
Aya 145, 154, 155, 174, 175, 177, 193, 195, 198, 215, 226, 244, 253, 262, 272, 277, 280, 289, 293, 294, 295, 297, 298, 302, 304, 305, 332, 333

B
Babalon 49, 50, 95, 138, 167
   Working 93, 159
Bach, Richard 239
Baker III, Ledru Shoopman 192, 195, 212, 283
Baldwin, Craig 318
Barrymore, John Drew 152, 296
Baudelaire, Charles 62
Beatles, The 240, 269
Beatnik 175
Beaton, Cecil 242
Beatty, Warren 242
Beaumont 107
Beausoleil, Bobby 259, 260, 261, 271, 279, 335, 336
Belarion. *See* Parsons, Jack
Bergen, Candice 242
Bergman, Ingmar 230
Berman, Eugene 165
Berman, Shirley 84, 98, 107, 129, 145, 149, 153, 157, 160, 166, 170, 177, 233, 253, 254, 282, 304, 305, 341
Berman, Tosh 157, 170, 246, 296
Berman, Wallace 83, 84, 150, 152, 161, 170, 172, 174, 183, 215, 257, 316, 318
   Arrested 171
   Death 281
Bertolucci, Bernardo 242, 243, 249
Besant, Annie 45
Betty 49, 51, 52, 79
Big Bertha 130
Bikel, Theodore 185
Bisexuality 140
Black Egg 226
Black Pilgrimage 230
Blackburn, May Otis 45
Blake, William 173, 174, 176, 318
Blakey, Art 80
Blavatsky, Madame Helena 42, 45,

62
Blease, Harry 294
Blues for Benny 251
Book of Revelation 41
Booth, Leroy 81, 99,
　110, 112, 120,
　122, 326
Boucher, Anthony 48
Bowie, David 279, 336
Boyer, Blanche 75, 76,
　78
Brando, Joselyn 336
Brando, Marlon 128,
　187, 277, 278,
　335
Breeze, William 289,
　292, 295, 300,
　301, 305, 322,
　323, 337, 340
Brentlinger, Thomas 13,
　302
Bridges, James 242
Brittin, Barbara 233,
　240
Brittin, Charles 18, 150,
　151, 170, 171,
　212, 213, 218,
　233, 240, 246,
　305, 339, 344
Browning, Tod 230
Bruce, Lenny 185, 186
Bruito, Eugene 111
Buckley, Lord 257
Burroughs, William 33,
　172, 173, 318,
　329
　Naked Lunch 174
Burton, Sir Richard 41
Byron, Lord 134

C

Caan, James 250
Cabinet of Caligari, 136
California, Randy 337
Callaghan, James 332
Cameron, Donald and
　Joan 11

Cameron 93
Cameron, Alexander 12
Cameron, Carrie 11,
　13, 19, 116,
　160
Cameron, Hill 11, 12,
　14, 22, 223
Cameron, James Russell
　14, 331, 332
Cameron, Loren 325
Cameron, Marjorie
　"Candy"
　Arrest 126
　Joan of Arc 162
Cameron, Marjorie
　"Candy" 53
　Brain tumor 302
　Crystal 315
　Dancing Pair 315
　Death Boat 187
　Flashing Figure of
　　Adonai-ha-Aretz
　　299
　Horned God 315
　Lady of the Lake 187
　Last rites 304
　Man with Sphere 315
　Marriage 53
　Pearl of Reprisal 299
　Peyote Vision 170,
　　299, 313, 319
　Pluto Transiting the
　　Twelfth 299
　Posthumous recogni-
　　tion 316
　The Beast/The
　　Vampyre Woman
　　249
　The Black Egg 224,
　　305
Cameron, Mary Lou 14,
　66, 160, 321
Cameron, Robert 14,
　89, 91, 324
Cameron, William 12
Campbell, Joseph 63,
　176, 229, 249,

293, 334
Camus, Albert 175
Capote, Truman 201
Carrington, Leonora 225
Caron, Leslie 242, 243
Carrington, Leonora 165
Carruthers, John 83,
　85, 98, 339
Celtic harp 294
Cervenka, Exene 337,
　285
Chamberlain, Duncan
　267
Chamberlain, Jesse 267
Chamberlain, John 266,
　267
Chandler, Arthur 247
Charm 244, 245, 249,
　250, 258, 262,
　276, 277, 295,
　339
Chester, Judy 256
Chiles, Linden 296
Christianity 295
Church of Thelema 60
Churchill, Winston 31,
　34, 321, 328
Claxton, William 324
Clift, Montgomery 187
Cocteau, Jean 58, 131,
　150, 154
Cohen, Mickey 201
Cohen, Herb 185, 195,
　240
Coleridge, Samuel Taylor
　134, 169, 176
Collins, Bob 256
Collins, Buddy 81, 100
Communism 270
Connolly, Cyril 41
Copeland, Darryl 191,
　211
Corso, Gregory 174
Corman, Roger 201,
　211
Craine, James F. 59
Crawford, Joan 18

Cronkite, Walter 269
Crosby, Stills, Nash and Young 248
Crowley, Aleister 41, 45, 47, 52, 79, 95, 134, 140, 151, 152, 171, 172, 176, 215, 223, 278, 298, 318
  Abbey of Thelema 141
  Book of the Law 108
  Bornless Ritual 92
  British contingent 141
  Tarot 214
  The Vision and the Voice 92

D

Dalai Lama 296
Dali, Salvador 165
Dark Angel 220, 304, 319
Davis, Bette 18
Davis, Miles 58, 172
De Brier, Samson 127, 129, 130, 134, 151, 154, 187, 219, 220, 223, 250, 281, 303, 304
De Gaulle, General 31
De Saint Exupery, Antoine
  The Little Prince 222, 224
Dean, James 64, 188, 202, 330
Dee, John 49
Dehn, Paul 140
  London News Chronicle 140
DeMille, Cecil B. 157
Demonic Vision 225
Deren, Maya 131, 197, 305
  Ritual in Transfigured Time 133
Dianetics: The Modern Science of Mental Health 78, 79
Dick Cavett TV show, 278
Dick, Phillip K. 72
Dickinson, Emily 15
Dietrich, Marlene 130
Disney, Walt 130, 318
Donnelley, Thorne 31
Doren, Mamie Van 85
Douglas, Melvyn 34
Druks, Renate 72, 85, 98, 110, 116, 127, 134, 136, 152, 222, 241, 242, 314, 317
Dylan, Bob 186, 240, 278
Dyslexia 244

E

Easy Rider 268
Eaton, Marjorie 203, 206
Egypt 135
Einstein, Albert 82
Eleanor of Aquitaine 295
Eliot, T. S. 175
Emanon 81
Ralph Waldo Emerson 42
Emperor Nero 41
ERONBU 193, 198, 199

F

Farr, Florence 43
Faust 111
Fellini, Frederico 230
Feminist 298
Fini, Leonor 167, 225
Fitzgerald, Ella 80
Fles, John 146, 230, 232, 316
Flynn, Errol 196
Foreman, John 247
Forman, Ed 40, 48, 53, 97
Forster, Marco 53
Foshaug, Martin 87, 88, 101
Foxx, Loree 152, 153
Franco, John 196
Frank, Robert 333
Frazer, James George 63
Freeman, Jo 322
Freud, Sigmund 43, 93, 326
Frey, George 54, 55, 73, 78, 85, 87, 89, 90, 92, 296, 323
Freya 74, 98
Froning, Carol 17
Fuller, Margaret 42

G

Ganci, Sal(vatore) 87, 88, 93, 98, 101, 160, 324, 326
Gatts, Strawberry 287, 302
German American Bund 30
Germer, Karl 46, 47, 52, 95, 117, 118, 141, 149, 156, 229, 298, 325, 327
Germer, Sasha 47, 223
Getz, Michael 230, 232
Getzler, Marsha 215, 244
Gide, Andre 187
Gilmore, John 187, 188, 195, 196, 197, 221, 251, 317, 330, 336
Gimbutas, Marija 276, 298, 342

Ginsberg, Allen 173, 177, 186, 329, 330
Glagolitic Mass 134
Glassman, Sallie Ann 289
Goddard, Jon Luc 230
Goldman, Emma 43
Gowan, Gladys 73, 323
Grady, Art 257
Grant, Cary 247
Grant, Kenneth 141, 269
　Mauve Zone 313
　Objections 313
Graves, Robert
　The White Goddess 176
Gray, Wardell 82
Greco, Juliette 58
Great White Brotherhood 296
Green, Paul Andrew
　Babalon 316
Gronquist, Phillip 87, 111, 120
Gurdjieff, George 192, 269, 331

H
Hair length 248
Haley, Andrew 56
Haley, Delphine 56
Hall, Larry 243, 273, 292
Hall, Manly P. 287
Harland, Phillip 166
Harrington, Curtis 129, 131, 133, 136, 139, 152, 165, 170, 187, 197, 201, 231, 232, 241, 250, 303, 304, 314, 316, 317, 328, 329, 331, 338, 339
　Night Tide 201, 207, 208, 211, 303, 336
　Wormwood Star 112, 166, 168, 170, 251, 253, 299, 304, 318
Harris, Lady Frieda 141, 156, 318
Hartman, Mortimer 247
Hauptmann, Gerhart 251
Hayward, Susan 22
Heard, Gerald 114
Heath, Percy 82
Hecate 132, 136
Heinlein, Leslyn 56
Heinlein, Robert 55, 268
Hemingway, Ernest 128, 175
Hepburn, Katharine 29
Heretic of Soana 251
Herms, George 178
Hesse, Herman 84, 150, 175, 337
　Steppenwolf 84
Hilarion 92
Hitler, Adolph 328
Hole to Hell 15, 53, 188
Holiday, Billie 172, 330
Hollander, David 318
Hollister, Northrup Sara 46
Homosexuality 130. See also Cameron, Marjorie "Candy": Lesbian leanings
Hoo, Dr. Marshall 286
Hoover, J. Edgar 47
Hope, Bob 116, 186
Hopper, Dennis 172, 202, 207, 208, 211, 240, 257, 268, 317, 336, 339
Hopper, Hedda 196
Hopps, Walter 170
Horn, Paul 203
Horus 44, 111
Horus, The Crowned and Conquering Child 44
Hubbard, L Ron 54, 48, 50, 51, 52, 56, 63, 78, 79, 95, 159, 258, 259, 281, 291, 292, 301, 315, 318, 335, 337
　Ruthless Adventure: The Lives of 291
Hughes, Howard 61, 73, 75, 317
Huncke, Herbert 173
Hunter, Meredith 271
Huxley, Aldous 114, 115
Hyland, Wendy 303

I
IATSE (International Alliance of Theatrical Stage 201
Inauguration of the Pleasure Dome. See Anger, Kenneth: Inauguration of the Pleasure Dome
International Order of the Rainbow Girls 20
Isherwood, Christopher 242
IT: International Times 269
Ivases, Nick 227

J
Jackson, Bobo 93, 101
Jacobi, Ed and Ted 154, 163
Janacek, Leos 134
Janiger, Dr. Oscar 211

JATO (Jet Assisted Take Off 40, 41
Jeffers, Robinson 82, 220
Jiddu Krishnamurti 45
Joan of Arc 86, 110, 115, 117, 150, 221, 295, 324
Johnson, George Clayton 189, 330
Johnson, Van 31, 147
Jones, Charles Stansfeld 46
JPL. *See* Jet Propulsion Laboratory
Jung, Carl 63

K

Kadell, Katy 135, 231
Kafka, Franz 175, 265
Kansa, Spencer 338
Kármán, Theodore von 74
Kaufman, Bob 329
Keats, John 176
Keeler, Christine 239
Kelinson, Bette 23
Kelinson, Sam 23, 117
Kelley, Edward 49
Kelly, Gene 31, 78
Kennedy, President John F. 239
Kennedy, Joe 239
Kerouac, Jack 173, 174, 177, 186, 218, 329, 344
Kesey, Faye 248
Kesey, Ken 247
Kibort, Mrs. Nadia 89
Kienholz, Ed 158, 170
Kimmel, Crystal Eve 157, 160, 176, 177, 244, 248, 256, 265, 266, 267, 273, 280, 288, 290, 315
Kimmel, Evie 147
Kimmel. Sheridan Abbot "Sherry," 147, 151, 153, 154, 157, 194, 216, 217, 218, 248
   Suicide attempt 216
King, Martin Luther 240, 270
Kinsey, Alfred 131
   Cefalu, Sicily, 155
Klacel, Frantisek Matous 11
Knowledge And Conversation Of The HGA 166
Knox, Ronnie 241
Krock, Arthur 57, 77
Ku Klux Klan 269
Kubla Khan 134, 169
Kynette, Earle 96

L

Lady Godiva 221
Lady Grey 14
Lady of the Lake 187
Lamantia, Phillip 172
Lambert, Gavin 242
Langlois, Henri 208
Larson, Jack 242, 317
Laurel Canyon 280
LaVey, Anton 260
Lawrence, D.H. 175
Lawson, Linda 202, 203, 207
Leadbeater, Charles Webster 323
Leary, Timothy 228, 246, 247, 270
Led Zeppelin 278
Leffingwell, Reea 223
Lennon, John 240, 269
Lessing, Edith Maida 45
Liber AL vel Legis 44, 107
Lilith 122
Lion Path 292
Liquid light shows 226
Lockheed Aircraft Company 128
Loomer, Dr. Harry Pincus 72
Loose Ends 284, 318
Losch, Tilly 18, 165
LSD 228, 229, 246, 247, 249, 260, 261, 326, 345
Lucifer 270
Lucitron 177

M

MacAlpine, Deirdre 58
Macdonald, Julie 71, 80, 82, 83, 84, 85, 90, 99, 111, 121, 324, 334
Macfarlane, Linda 297, 298
Madame Grey 121
Magic 272
Malaby, Dr. Zachary Taylor 94
Malcolm X 270
Malina, Frank 40, 74, 280
Manifesto of the Antichrist 61
Manifesto of the Antichrist, 92
Mann, Thomas 128
Manne, Shelly 203
Manson, Charles 271
Manson, Marilyn 318
Martin, Don 214, 215, 237
Martin, Joan 214, 215, 216, 229, 237, 245, 249, 259, 302
Mason, Fred 214, 215
Mathison, Paul 73, 85, 110, 134, 136, 139, 166, 203, 222, 231, 241, 303, 317

Matrix 277, 298
Maymudes, Victor 186
Mayan Factor 292
Maysles Brothers 271
McCartney, Paul 240, 269
Meltzer, David 150, 171, 173, 174, 175, 181, 256, 296, 332
Merry Pranksters 247
Mexican art 165
Midgette, Allen 242, 246, 248, 249, 258, 260, 266, 267, 273, 277
Midsummer Nights Dream 130
Mikita, Ruth Swalm 15
Millay, Edna St. Vincent 15
Miller, Dorothy 15, 16, 17, 18, 249
Miller, Jack 16
Mirror gazing 168
Modern Jazz Quartet 82
Mojave Desert 224
Monroe, Marilyn 64, 330
Montauk 301
Moon, Peter 300
Moonchild 95
Moore, Evelyn 111
Morand, Donald 146, 149, 153
Morante, Elsa 243
Morgan, Frank 81
Morgan, Robert 81, 110
Morrissey, Paul 266
Muir, Gavin 203, 204
Muir, John 154, 287, 328
Muldoon, Sylvan 97, 62
Muses, Charles 293, 343
Mysterions 283

N

Napoleon, Arthur 31, 34, 50, 51, 322
Nathanson, Andee 280, 281
Nathanson, Rick 129, 281
Nazimova, Alla 128
New Isis Lodge 141
Nicholson, Jack 278
Nietzsche, Friedrich 43, 165, 175, 277, 318
Night Tide 213, 260
Nin, Anais 127, 132, 136, 137, 250, 272, 327, 345
Nord, Eric BigDaddy 214
Norton, Rosaleen 167
Nurmi, Maila 196

O

O.T.O. 79, 108, 290
Oak Hill Cemetery 20
Odessky, Ira 191, 211
Odetta 186
OKeeffe, Georgia 343
One Flew Over the Cuckoos Nest 248
Oppenheimer, Robert 33
Order Of The Golden Dawn 43
Osiris 297
O'Sullivan, Paddy 329
Ouspensky, Peter 269

P

P-Orridge, Genesis 289
Page, Jimmy 337, 278
Paglia, Camille 343
Pan 167
Parfrey, Adam
  Feral House 313
Parker, Charlie Yardbird 80, 83, 84, 172, 324

Parsons, John Whiteside 39, 45, 49, 52, 53, 54, 60, 61, 72, 79, 99, 158, 232, 259, 279, 287
  black box 171
  Freedom is a Two Edged Sword, 271
  Laboratory was now a blown-out 88
  Manifesto of the Antichrist 230
  Songs for the Witch Woman 109, 277
Parsons, Louella 196
Parsons, Ruth 40, 87, 88, 89, 90, 91, 92, 105, 299
Pasolini, Pier Paolo 242
Patchen, Kenneth 82
Patriarchy 298
Patterson, Nancie and Bill 92, 111
Paull, Anita 212
Pauwels, Louis and Jaques Bergier, Morning of the Magicians 273
Pearl Harbor 29
Pendle, George 314
  Strange Angel 313
Percy, Margaret 291
Perkoff, Stuart Z. 215
Peyote Vision 115, 145, 150, 246
Peyrefitte, Roger 260
Piaf, Edith 58
Picasso, Pablo 41
Piscean Age 239
Poe, Edgar Allan 11, 131, 201, 208, 211, 314
  Fall of the House of Usher, 131
Powell, Michael and Emeric Pressburger

138
Power, Tyrone 147, 259
Presley, Elvis 64
Price, Jo Anne 85, 87, 88, 100, 111, 116
Price, Vincent 189, 212
Profumo 239

Q
Quigley, Joan 286
Quinn, Pat 265, 266, 277, 278, 280, 292, 305, 336

R
Rabelaisian 44
Rainbow Girl 20
Raleigh, A.S. 297, 342
Reagan, Ronald 286
Reflections of a New Aeon 315
Regardie, Israel 44
Rice-Davis, Mandy 239
Rico, Dianne 196
Rico, Don 196
Ridenour, Cyrus 13
Righter, Carroll 286
Rivera, Diego 72
Robert 91
Robeson, Paul 82
Rolling Stones 255, 261, 335
Romero, Elias 146, 226
Rose, Norman 145, 146, 150, 151, 153, 175, 273
Rosemarys Baby 316
Rosenfeld, Herbert T. 74
Ross, Katherine 250
Rotten, Johnny 284
Rowan, Helen 89
Rusk, Betty 14, 16, 249
Russell, Alexander 12, 146
Russell, James Cameron 14

S
Sad Eyed Lady of the Lowlands 277
Santa Monica 204
Sartre, Jean Paul 175
Scientology 79, 258, 281, 292, 334
Seal of Solomon 166
Seldis, Henry J. 212
Selby, Jean 31, 78
Semina 150, 161, 170, 171, 174, 223, 225, 240, 255, 316
Sennet, Mack 157
Shelley, Percy Bysshe 174, 176
Sherry 147, 148, 158, 185, 328. *See* Kimmel. Sheridan Abbot "Sherry,"
Shiva 134
Shonberg, Burt 199, 211, 257, 330
Death 282
Signoret, Simone 250
Silver Star 166
Sinatra, Frank 82, 239
Siqueiros, David 72
Smith, Harry 318
Smith, Helen 47, 55, 98
Smith, Helen Parsons 299
Smith, Jack 230
Smith, Wilfred Talbot 45, 54, 55, 95, 98
Songs For the Witch Woman 220
South Orange Grove 56
Spalding, Jeanne 20, 283
Spare, Austin Osman 318

Stalin 60, 342
Stevens, Matthew Levi 338
Stockwell, Dean 257, 171, 172, 336
Strand, Chick 283, 284, 318, 339
Street Fair San Francisco 177, 183, 329
Symonds, John 215, 139, 270

T
Tai Chi 294, 303
Tamblyn, Russ 7, 197, 254
Tane, George 77
Tarot 244, 253
Tate-Labianca murders 271
Taylor, Edward Silverstone 177, 329
Tchelitchew, Pavel 165
Temple of Thelema 195
Tennyson, Lord 187
Tesla, Nikola 194
Thatcher, Margaret 286
The Beast 178
The Book of the Law 44, 50, 55, 94, 113, 116, 119, 139, 269, 344
The Cauldron 338
The Children 110
The Great Beast 46, 278
The Great Beast 666 41
The Wormwood Star 165
Thoreau, Henry David 42
Thumbsuck 266, 267
Tom, Heather 316
Torres, Salvatore 111
Tree, Christopher 226
Trocchi, Alexander 172

Truffaut, Francois 230
Truman, President 82
Tutankhamen 293

U

UFO 92, 95, 190

V

Valentino, Rudolph 130, 135, 259
Van Gogh, Vincent 174
Van Johnson, Schuyler 147, 148
Van Tassel, George 194
Vaughan, Sarah 80
Vietnam 270
Vigne, Dion 178
Vigne, Loreon 178
Von Bingen, Hildegard 294, 295
Von Däniken, Erich 273
Von Sternberg, Josef 130
Voodoo 197

W

Walther, Rodolfo P. 324
War-engine 107
Warhol, Andy 266
WAVES (Women Accepted for Volunteer Emer-
gency Serv 29
Wavy Gravys Hog Farm 268
Weber, Carla 290
Webster, Lisa 219
Weegee 91
Welles, Orson 205, 208
Whitman, Walt 42
Whitney, Joan 85, 111, 112, 113, 116, 120, 135, 152, 176, 327
Whore of Babylon 49
Wieland, Ruth 45
Wilde, Constance 43
Wilde, Oscar 43, 127, 128, 303
Wilkinson, Louis 141
Williams, Tennessee 129, 131
Williamson, Jack 50
Wilson, Colin 174, 175
  The Outsider 174
Witchcraft 203, 228
Wolfe, Iris 288, 290, 294, 303, 304, 307
Wolfe, Jane 46, 108, 109, 115, 118, 121, 127, 139, 141, 151, 154, 156, 159, 220, 224
Wood, Leona 166
Woodstock 268, 337
Wordsworth, William 134
Wormwood Star. *See* Harrington, Curtis: The Wormwood Star
Worthington, Netta and Dorie 91, 98
Wrigley Jr, William 117
Wynn, Keenan 147
Wynn, Ned 148, 149, 216, 218, 225, 328

X

X 285

Y

Yeats, William Butler 43
Yorke, Gerald 118, 234

Z

Zimmer, Heinrich 63
Zorthian, Jirayr 84, 85

www.ingramcontent.com/pod-product-compliance
Lightning Source LLC
Chambersburg PA
CBHW070835160426
43192CB00012B/2202